sometimes surprising views on women's progress in the workplace.

The final chapter tackles "the answer." Dismissing the phony approaches such as "dress for success" that distract women from putting their energies into their jobs, the authors have a clear message: Don't get caught up in wasteful games; your knowledge and competence should be the key to success, and your confidence the key to personal power.

Authors Easton, Mills, and Winokur are highly successful businesswomen from San Francisco, with experience in government, corporate, and independent enterprises. SUSAN EASTON is currently involved in the formation of a new national television network. JOAN M. MILLS, owner of J. M. Mills Associates, an executive search firm, is also involved with brokerage in the communications industries. DIANE KRAMER WINOKUR has had twenty-five years' experience in management and administration and currently operates Winokur Associates, Inc., management and organizational consultants.

Equal to the Task

EQUAL TO THE TASK

How Workingwomen Are Managing in Corporate America

SUSAN EASTON

JOAN M. MILLS

DIANE KRAMER WINOKUR

Seaview Books / New York

Manufactured in the United States of America.
FIRST EDITION
Seaview Books/A Division of PEI Books, Inc.

Library of Congress Calaloging in Publication Data
Easton, Susan.
    Equal to the task.

    Bibliography: p.
    1. Women—Employment—United States. I. Mills,
Joan M. II. Winokur, Diane Kramer. III. Title.
HD6075.E18   331.4'0973   81-52073
ISBN 0-87223-752-4   AACR2

In memory of Lillian Dumont, Ph.D., and Kate Polacheck, two young women who were equal to the task. Let no talent, no contribution, be denied, for the promise can be ended far too soon. And to Terry for today and tomorrow.

—SUSAN EASTON

To my co-authors, Richard Dale Wilson, my father, my friends and associates who have helped make our book different and important.

—JOAN M. MILLS

To the men in my life:
My Father, who raised me to be the Anonymous Woman
My Husband, who has been the Ambivalent Man
My three Sons, who hopefully are part of the Answer.
—DIANE KRAMER WINOKUR

Thanks to:
Katinka Matson, our agent
Jeanne Murphy, our transcriber
All of the women and men that we interviewed
Julie La Perle Bradford, our researcher

Contents

Introduction

Women in the Work Force

The massive influx of women into the work force has been hailed as a major phenomenon of the twentieth century, yet a *Saturday Review* article on futurism noted that not one individual or forecasting institution had predicted this dramatic event. The worlds of women and business met each other unprepared—in a collision which rivaled the Big Bang. The force of this phenomenon sent shock waves reverberating through corporate America and millions of homes. Social systems which had served in the past became antiquated overnight. New precedents were set as basic cultural precepts and patterns were called into question. Few aspects of the social universe escaped untouched.

The past several decades have won, among other titles, the label "The Era of Self-consciousness." And it is said that our preoccupating with the search for meaning signals that meaning has, perhaps, been lost. Modern technology has added to the era's confusion through its tumultuous children—the information industry and the mass media. Ideas were suddenly being packaged like so many disposable soft-drink bottles. They often required no deposit of thought, nor did they return much in the way of in-depth understanding.

Turned upon the workingwomen of the nation, this analytical trend and state of information overload combined to create a complex set of myths, misconceptions, formulas, and fallacies surrounding every aspect of their lives. And the women at the center of the commotion became increasingly uncertain over how to distinguish between fact and fantasy, progress and propaganda.

Business and government, journalists, sociologists, and other scholars all joined in the marshaling of resources and data to answer one single question: How *were* workingwomen managing in corporate America? Yet no one answer seemed to satisfy. Indeed, how was one to measure or to judge?

As three among the forty-three million employed women in America, we decided to risk the search for meaning—to find our own answer—and we began the process of assessing what was happening to all workingwomen by looking first at ourselves. Armed with stacks of books and magazines, drawers full of brochures, and a myriad of personal and professional experiences, we formed our own think tank and set out to create a sorting system to account for the changes around us.

Preliminary discussions and a cursory survey of the literature on workingwomen quickly disclosed just how much of language and letter had already fallen into the categories of buzzword and cliché. Equally disconcerting was the tendency of these studies and articles to isolate the phenomenon of workingwomen from the greater confluence of history and cultural evolution. What seemed to be missing from the bounty of data and theory were the voices of those workingwomen in the front lines and trenches of change.

So we decided to go out and talk to our friends.

What we rapidly learned was that no event or situation was unique. On the contrary, all of us had a lot in common. We had all endured unsolicited advice on everything from how to dress to how to shelter our incomes. We had all been courted as students for dozens of self-improvement classes. The crisis and crunch points in our lives had begun to shift from struggling to strategizing as we moved up the ladder. Our energies, rather than being concentrated on the newness of our work roles, were now directed at integrating the many facets of our lives. We had all joined networks and sought out mentors. Our checkbook balances were growing, as were our concerns about inflation and control of our financial security. We had heard that women could have it all and wondered if we were really cut out to be superwomen. Sometimes our feelings got us down. The men in our lives seemed confused by us. They often made us angry. We had read about the corporate superstars and the fast track and had all dreamed of being the CEOs of tomorrow. We felt powerful. We felt isolated. We wanted recognition. And all the while, the corporate machinery, which had ground down so many organizational men, turned its wheels in our direction.

The women we interviewed in both the United States and Canada provided us with thirty-five individual perspectives on the world of workingwomen, yet through them all a sense of commonality prevailed. While we didn't start out to do a true statistical sampling, we managed to interview women across a fairly even distribution of generations, incomes, family patterns, and professional accomplishments. The bulk of the women worked in midmanagement, but some were at higher levels. Five were entrepreneurs. Some were just starting out, others were starting over. A few were near the close of their careers. Our interviews took us across a wide industrial spectrum as well—from food to cement, finance to high tech, government to international business, small firms to mega corporations.

We also decided that it was time someone interviewed the men who hired, worked with, and married the executive women we were writing about. Our group of male interviewees reflects a varied distribution across age and management ranks.

From the outset, we agreed to report our interviews anonymously. By protecting the identities of our sources, we hoped they would feel freer to express their ideas and experiences. As a result, there are many true confessions, honest appraisals, and searing commentaries amid the five hundred pages of transcripts we generated.

Our questions were designed to probe beneath the surface of current theories about women executives. We wanted to explore the state of change, not simply validate popularly held beliefs or scholarly findings. Our male interview questions were based on a similar format, with emphasis on monitoring personal and cultural attitude shifts.

Eventually our sorting system settled into nine distinct categories around which we built our chapters. The Assimilated Woman—redefinition and self-repair for the workingwoman. Finding one's individual par amid the sand traps of organizational culture. The Achieving Woman—the birth of ambition. Pioneers, stars, and tokens in new and uncharted lands. The system and some solutions for incorporating the talents and recognizing the achievements of women. The Ageist Woman—setting the cultural stage for understanding the workingwoman society. New directions and new decisions for a new set of choices and problems. The Associated Woman—networks, alliances, and mentors. Getting power and getting by with a little help from your friends. The Autocratic Woman—from the power behind the throne to the rule of the self. Mavericks and other rugged individuals. The age of the mass society meets the day of the female risk-taker. Definitions and redefinitions of power. The Anonymous Woman—taking credit and taking control. Personal styles, rewards, and recipes for conquering invisibility. Women's liberation meets the automated world. The Alienated Woman—Breakups, breakdowns, and breaking even in the age of uncertainty, challenge, and stress. The Affluent Woman—the American Dream and the workingwoman. Status symbols and images in transition. Consumerism versus feminism. The Affluence-Influence connection. The Ambivalent Man—identity and ego, threats and therapeutic change for today's man. Stories and comments from mates and the men who hire and work with workingwomen. This final category, we believe, has as much influence and effect on all aspects of a woman's personal and professional life as the choices and routes she decides to take on her own.

A Word About Culture Shock

Stories abound in anthropological circles of societies in which roles, traits, and cultural patterns shift within a single generation and, alternatively, of others which resist change entirely. Social and cultural patterns generally determine the needs and the mores of the day, but there are no reliable predictors of the rate of change a society will adopt. Culture, however, tends to flow in a stream of events between one generation and the next, so the question we posed was: "How has the flow of culture been altered by the steadily increasing number of women who work?"

In *The Science of Culture*, Leslie White writes:

> We are now approaching a point in modern thought where we are beginning to suspect that it is not man who controls culture, but the other way around.[1]

In our final chapter, ambitiously entitled The Answer, we speculate on what lies ahead based on our development and reading of certain cultural continuums. Predictions are, to some extent, an expression of our need to control the future, but predicting as an art form is far from foolproof. But in the end, we returned to several people we had interviewed to ask them what they thought the future held for workingwomen and the society as a whole. Through a little artistic dabbling, we suggest in The Answer which signs and symbols, if understood today, can minimize further cultural shocks.

Equal to the Task has, therefore, two goals: to report on how workingwomen are managing in corporate America, and to begin asking new questions which will help move women and the system to change, in an atmosphere of understanding, what needs to be changed.

Equal to the Task

How many cares one loses when one decides not to
be something, but to be someone.
                                    COCO CHANEL

1

The Assimilated
Woman

The dinosaur and the dodo bird are no more. They are biological
casualties. Their blunder was to adapt too successfully to the existing environment. When the environment shifted—ecosystems
have never been stable—they did not develop new survival strategies.

The modern-day assimilated woman has not learned from nature. She has adapted to or been channeled into so narrow a line of
development that her very existence is endangered.

Many women in corporate management have interpreted assimilation as requiring the abandonment of their own individuality.
They view the process as one-dimensional. They overadapt to
their surroundings, and in doing so, lose some of their personal
strength. The evolutionary process may be pushing them toward
the fate of the dodo bird. These women have become so focused on
fitting in that they have forgotten themselves. Personal style and
individuality have given way to a generation of business clones.
The machinery powered by the managerial-woman mentality
churns out growing numbers of M.B.A.s with Ralph Lauren
blazers. They have bought into the prefabricated, color-by-

the numbers, one-size-fits-all, clone-for-success propaganda barrage.

The messages to assimilate are often transmitted by the corporation itself. A corporate counsel described the situation in her company this way:

> It took the infusion of about nine women at all levels of the company, mostly in finance, to persuade the company that women were very, very capable of rapidly assimilating into the organization. It was not that they couldn't find talent in women, it was that they were afraid they couldn't assimilate women into a very diverse, but mostly production-oriented firm.

Most companies have a corporate "look," sometimes including a company necktie or lapel pin. No wonder women have succumbed to the gray-flannel suit. But the corporate look requires more than the superficial medium of dress, and it is here that women are receiving more complex messages than men. If there is one theme most organization observers agree on, it is the dependency nature of management. The higher up the corporate hierarchy you are, the more people you must depend on to get your job done. The uncertainty in this situation can be controlled only to the extent that the manager has some measures to evaluate expected behavior of those on whom he/she depends. The critical element in this equation is trust. Whom can you trust? How do you minimize the risks? In most cases, the answer is to pick people whose credentials are easy to read and who, by background, personality, and lifestyle, are similar to you. By this line of reasoning, if you could clone yourself, you would have the ultimate certainty of trust, and the further one gets from the self-clone, the greater the uncertainty.

When dealing with people who are "different" in such fundamental ways as race and gender, most male managers have little working experience on which to base trust, and a lifetime of exposure to stereotypes about "their" unreliability. This makes the uncertainty and anxiety levels escalate. The easiest way to handle this anxiety is to exclude such deviant people from your working group.

One Size Fits All

There is an assumption that women, because of their relative newness to managerial ranks, cannot possibly be as competent or as
committed as men. In the final showdown, the smart money is
saying a woman will revert to her natural role as wife or mother,
and will abandon the company. She cannot be counted on. In their
efforts to disassociate themselves from this group stereotype,
women may disavow their femininity, disassociate themselves
from other women, and pattern their dress and behavior after that
of the men with whom they work. It is these women who, if they
make it, are referred to by their male colleagues as "just like a
man." For the woman who sees assimilation as the only route to
success, that is the ultimate accolade. To the men who, by reason
of the circumstances, must accept her presence in their circle, this
accolade is face-saving and reassuring. "It isn't really that women
can do my job," the rationale goes, "it is that this one woman is so
different from her sisters that she is more like a man." But the status is tenuous. No matter how many times the assimilated woman
hears she is just like a man and no matter how effectively she
maintains that image, to her male colleagues she is still different,
still a woman—albeit an exceptional member of the group. The
only woman senior vice-president of a large bank was described as
exceptional, "one of us" by all the male officers at her level and
above. Several said, "We never think about her being a woman,
only how she does her job." But each of the men who were interviewed told a version of the following story: "One month, when
her child was ill, she canceled bank meetings several times and
went home to take care of her child."

This incident demonstrates that in spite of being "just like a
man," this woman was seen as having a lesser level of commitment
to the bank than a man, because of her "natural" female responsibility. Another woman explored the commitment issue:

> One of the other things that holds women back is a lack of total com-
> mitment. If a woman is not committed in the same way a man is, she is
> going to have problems. This tends to happen as women cling to the
> responsibilities of personal life at the expense of work life. They are not
> willing to make the decision to be work-directed. On the other hand,
> I'm not so sure that I'm personally willing to accept the model of the
> workaholic leader. If I want to be a president or a chairman of the For-

tune 500 Company, do I have to be a workaholic? Can I have a family too? What will I have to give up along the way? These are things that get in my way in political situations at work because I am a woman.

What is commitment? What is loyalty? Women, historically, have acted out high levels of commitment and loyalty within their traditional roles. It is only when women have entered "man's world" that their ability to display commitment and loyalty has been questioned. Commitment and loyalty seem to be values reserved for middle-aged men in corporations (with younger men being suspect, but not to the degree experienced by women and minorities).

A Harvard M.B.A. currently employed as a researcher and futurist drew a perspective on the evolving psychology of women in business:

> Women have gone through three steps in their development. These steps parallel those taken by the black community in their struggle for equality. The first step is waiting to be equal, in this case, like a man. Women rallied against being the underdog. The second step is questioning. Why do I want to be like a man? Getting heart attacks. Not having or doing a satisfactory job. Removed from his culture. Then came the realization that we didn't want to be the same . . . which led to the third step—integration. In this step, we are synthesizing. We are using our intuition. The pendulum is swinging away from the status quo.

But the assimilated woman has not climbed the steps; she has stopped somewhere between them. She has been persuaded that she must disown to excel. She has rejected or suppressed her individuality, and in doing so, set traps of deceit for herself and impossible snares for other women as well. She is a victim of self-depreciation, self-doubt, and self-defeat. She is unsure of her own abilities and is willing to substitute the form of corporate success for its substance.

THE SELF-REPAIR SNARE

There is a very real danger in the current plethora of self-repair courses for women. You know, the ones that tell how to talk like an executive, or how to dress like an Ivy League M.B.A., or how to order lunch in a French restaurant.

These courses are dangerous because they imply that there are prescriptions for success which men know intuitively and which, if women could only learn, would eradicate their deficiencies. The hidden message is that the road to success is fraught with stumbling blocks found within the female psychology!

At every turn, the aspiring female is assaulted by books and seminars which imply she has a lot to learn. Survival in the business jungle, they warn, is nearly impossible for the female of the species, unless she first learns the predatory ways of the executive male. Women are encouraged to abandon their individual attributes and to adopt some third-party perception of the organizational requirements. If a woman is at all receptive to self-doubt, these suggestions for adaptation can begin to intimidate. They dig in just deeply enough at the most sensitive pressure points to make many women flinch while they reach for their checkbooks, fill out the enrollment cards, or buy the books. This is a major flaw in women's reasoning. Once on the job, the most effective learning takes place in the work environment, not in books and seminars. In the world of business, women are too ready to believe that they have gender-related deficiencies and that they can overcome these by taking lessons.

Women fight hard to insist on their equality, but find it so easy to succumb to "patterning." It is as if women believe that they could take the results of a survey on the characteristics of the top one hundred corporate women in America, and by reading it, pattern their own lives. Nothing can be farther from the truth. Each life is separate and unique, and that fact is the only philosophical and moral cornerstone on which to lay grounds for equality.

The Managerial Woman, by Margaret Hennig and Ann Jardim, and *Games Mother Never Taught You*, by Betty Harragan, have become classics in their own time. These books are quoted by men as well as women to explain the problems of women in business. "Well, you know, you women never played team sports and that's why you can't . . ." followed by a litany of things women supposedly cannot do. One woman told us: "After I read *The Managerial Woman*, I thought I should give up. I'm the youngest child and only daughter. For the first half of my life I truly thought I was a princess. I have none of the childhood experiences of those women and I cannot do anything about that."

Another said:

We talked about the book *The Managerial Woman*, which I find to be a very confusing and, in many ways, damaging book. By my interpretation, the book is based on the notion that the reason women have difficulties in the corporate world is because of things that we didn't do when we were growing up. Like playing football or team sports, or not taking enough science classes. I think it has nothing to do with what we did. We did what we did. That's irrelevant. There are a whole other series of things going on that I think those authors make light of. Once again, they put the burden of proof in the woman's court. They say we must work harder to figure out how to overcome the handicap of not playing team sports. Or they imply that we must, somehow, overcome the psychological differences which we acquired by growing up female rather than male. Absolutely not true! The psychological difference in my experience is a net positive, not negative. I can interact and talk with a whole series of different people. I have learned an interviewing style that tends to be nonthreatening. I can go from being hard-nosed and analytical to being soft, approachable, and attentive. I have a much wider range of behaviors and skills than are acceptable with men. So to say that those qualities are a detriment to my success is just absolutely not true!

The rate at which women have latched on to these books as gospel is an indication of the fervent quest for prescriptions in society as a whole. The authors of *The Managerial Woman* made no claims about the generalizability of their findings. They were clearly describing a small sample. It is the readers who have used the profiles as models, seeking to measure their own potential for success by matching personal attributes with women in the book.

There are a large number of seminars that link success to dress. Take the seminar with the title "From Survival to Arrival," which promises to tell "what success really means." The afternoon session is almost entirely devoted to creating "the total look"—an update of the latest ways to dress for success. A well-known management consultant relates her continuing amusement at women who announce their intention to return to the work force, proudly describing the wardrobe they have assembled. When asked about their résumés, a blank look comes across their faces. The former president of a women's organization said that one of the toughest tasks during her term of office was facing the onslaught of wardrobe consultants who wanted to present programs to the membership.

There is a double message in the emphasis on external trappings. First, that you are what you wear, and second, if you want to make it, dress as though you already have. Underneath the stridency of these messages is some ordinary common sense. If being different is a handicap in the corporate setting, one is well advised to minimize the differences in whatever appropriate ways are available. Wearing jeans in a gray-flannel-suit environment adds a dimension of difference. You don't need a book or a seminar or a guru to tell you that. All you need is the ability to understand the specific organizational climate in which you work. The reliance on labels, certificates, and stamps of approval is related to the need for reassurance and to the yearning for an easy fix.

Some political reality around dress and image was contributed by one woman in the following anecdote:

> I had occasion to go to the White House during the early Carter years. Even though I was not a Carter fan, I have to admit that going to the White House was very exciting until I got there. I was wearing what I call my "sincere suit." It is navy-blue wool gabardine, well tailored, and exuding affluence, achievement, and accountability. As I waited for my appointment, I noticed the comings and goings of White House staff members and realized, with a shock, that everyone was in blue jeans. I was the only one in sight wearing a suit. I am old-fashioned enough to have been offended. I felt they should take their positions more seriously and reflect their location at the seat of power in what they wore to work. Two years later, as Carter's image was causing re-election anxiety, I returned to the White House. Again, I wore my "sincere suit," but so did everyone else. All the men and women I saw were dressed for success. The look had changed.

However, "dressing for success" was not enough to change the record of accomplishment. The lesson provided by the electorate was that, in the final analysis, it is performance that counts.

The how-to seminars are perhaps the most worrisome of the self-repair inventory. The brochures come in various shapes and sizes, but all impugn a woman's ability to think things through for herself and promise that a "quick fix" will be revealed in the advertised services.

How about the seminar called "Balls Up," a delightfully mixed sexual-success suggestion which proclaims, "To survive and lead a full life in today's complex society requires knowing how to juggle a lot of balls without dropping any."

Another recent offering took a serious bend and added a twist of guilt by asking the question, "Why is it that bright, educated, experienced, competent, dedicated, confident, and ambitious women are having so much difficulty getting ahead?" If *they* are having trouble, one might well ask, what hope is there for me?

A major university sponsored a program entitled "Special Problems for Women Managers." This two-day event outlined a long list of difficulties brought to the work place by women. Nowhere was there a single, positive quality mentioned that a woman could add to a company or to a job. Nowhere was there any acknowledgment that many of the problems of female managers are also problems for male managers.

But these and hundreds of other similar seminars are selling out. *The Wall Street Journal* has run major stories, indicating that the business of teaching women how to make it in business is a big business indeed. Women seem eager to hear someone tell them what is wrong with them as long as the session promises also to unveil the secrets of repair.

An international-law expert was describing his experience with Chinese manufacturers. He said:

> They have had no contact with Western business for so long that they lack understanding about how it operates. They assume that responding to Western requests is the way to success. If an American company tells a Chinese manufacturer to keep a large inventory, he will do so, even when other business indicators make this an unwise strategy. If, however, someone else urges that same manufacturer to ship his stock-on-hand immediately, the Chinese will change his inventory procedure to comply. It is as though they are ignoring their own historical success as merchants and entrepreneurs and are psyched out by operating in an environment that is new to them. They latch on to every suggestion as though it were gospel.

Women, new to the upper levels of corporations, are much like the Chinese as they enter the Western market.

Because the secrets and prescriptions presented in these seminars are often illusory, there is a high rate of recidivism. Again, women assume the fault is theirs. The brochure says the secret will be divulged, and if it wasn't, it must be because the participant missed it. Seminar speakers report seeing students return regularly. One frequent lecturer at business start-up programs is constantly amazed and increasingly depressed at seeing women in the audience whom she knows to have been in their own businesses for as many as three years. Her comment:

It is a shock to see them there with no embarrassment. I can't imagine that these courses have to offer what these women don't already know. How many times can you be briefed on the basics of a business plan, or listen to a banker tell you how to get a loan? I began to wonder if, when they were young, these same women willingly returned themselves to the first grade after being promoted to the fourth. It is such an admission of failure that I wonder how their egos survive.

When women try to carry their version of the seminars' magic tricks back to their daily routines, sometimes the results are funny. Take the story of the woman who confessed she had taken great pains to watch the last Ali fight so she would not be left out of the next day's office banter with the guys. Primed with every gory detail memorized, she waited at the coffee machine to impress them all. But to her surprise, not once did the topic come up. So she asked her male co-workers who among them had viewed the boxing match. None had.

These books and seminars have created the impression that by their very existence what they teach must be necessary and true. They offer themselves as replacement experiences for having been born a woman, as remedies for having been taught to care and feel, as Pygmalion panaceas for insufficient social skills in the corporate graces.

You are all Eliza Doolittles, they say, and we are Professor Higginses, who will teach you how to abandon the urchin and acquire the secret of captivating the revelers at the corporate ball. Women must dress, speak, and act in ways that deny their own individuality. It is only then that they can make others believe they were to the corporate manner born.

Sometimes the shock of seeing herself mirrored in the behavior of others can jolt a woman into a deeper awareness of her own life pattern. A strategic planner in the banking industry relates such an experience:

> After graduating from Pittsburgh with an M.B.A., I felt entitled to all the top jobs. I knew that I was bright and that translated across the board to those companies I spoke with. On my first job at an oil company, there were thirty of us, all M.B.A.s; two of us were women. I was warned as a new kid on the block that if I was to be part of the gang, I was not to be familiar with the secretaries, to have lunch only with my corporate peers, and not to act as if I were a "research assistant." I just wasn't snooty enough, I was cautioned. I would become, they said,

another female casualty, hard-working, but considered second-rate. One afternoon while walking down the hall, I overheard a woman, who I knew hated the oil business, tell the V.P. of Refineries that her goal was to reach Refinery Operations Management. I was shocked at this outright lie made to score points. It dawned on me that women were even more prone than men to react to the organization's pressures, to sway under evaluation and criticism. I decided that all I wanted was to be a pro, and to do whatever I did well.

The ultimate entrapment in the assimilate-for-success route is that the woman who has abandoned essential parts of herself as ransom for corporate acceptance may be like Cinderella's stepsisters. These miscreants cut off toes and heels to fit into the glass slipper when we all knew it wasn't intended for them anyway. It is at her peril that a woman gets so lulled by effective adaptation that she ignores the situational factors in the organization structure which may close gates to her.

The need for value clarification was noted in the following comment:

> The key is knowing yourself and following your own direction. Each person has to define success for herself and you can't always define it in terms of corporate titles or position. Sometimes that isn't true at all. Upper management is not a guarantee for success, or happiness. Just look at some of the people up there. I don't define success as going up the ladder. That's something I think it is important for women to understand because there are so many out there now taking courses which define success only in those terms.

Another underlying motivation in the search for self-repair tools is the fear of mistakes. Women want to be taught appropriate behavior because they do not have confidence in their own ability to figure it out. They take these courses based on the belief that being a woman makes error inevitable. In fact, being a woman in business may be the ultimate business error. So no other mistakes must be allowed, and these courses and books become insurance policies. Emily Post wrote the rules for social behavior sixty years ago. In her world there were a finite number of situations any of us could ever confront. For every situation there was an appropriate behavior. To read her books was to know what to do. Well, Emily Post is no longer appropriate; new situations have developed that Emily never anticipated. Figuring it out for yourself is certainly a more demanding way to learn the ropes than simply memorizing a litany of dos and don'ts. And it is riskier. But the bigger the risks women are prepared to take, the bigger the successes they are likely to achieve.

Hair Ribbons in the Races

There is a paradox in women's eagerness to affect the external trappings of their male colleagues. On the one hand they wish to be seen as "just like a man" on the job, while on the other hand they fear losing their femininity. The paradox exists because the idea that some traits are male and others female has gained such acceptance that it is hard to refute, even with statistical evidence. Ambitious, competitive, and aggressive characteristics are all "male." Therefore, the woman who has these traits has crossed the gender line and risks being described as unfeminine.

Dr. Suzanne Keller, professor at Princeton University, says:

> As long as women strive to hold on to the traditional feminine virtues, they will remain bound to all the other traditions that they are trying to leave behind. Stereotypical thinking about gender has hardly changed. Research has shown that the majority of men and women admire not competence, independence, or leadership in women, but the traditional qualities of gentleness, self-effacement, and dependency. Such stereotypes not only keep the old patterns in place, but act as a deterrent to women's ambitions in a subtle way.

Researchers have observed that the fear of a threat to femininity can cause a woman to modify her behavior. Some women, when accused of losing their femininity, pull back from their efforts. Other women react to having femininity tied to their efforts by attacking the source as sexist. The connecting link in both of these behaviors lies in the fact that women are so sensitive to criticism based on gender identification that they open themselves to easy manipulation.

Michael Korda, in *Male Chauvinism*, said:

> You may be as cheerful, presentable and polite as you like, but there is no substitute for shrewdness, judgment, a realistic appraisal of one's possibilities and a weather eye for the moment of opportunity. Men tend to undermine women's self-confidence by drawing them into a

network of masculine attitudes, a task which is easy enough, since in most cases, men have the power, and therefore form a ruling group.[1]

A successful woman entrepreneur responded:

I've worked very hard, but there was never a sacrifice. Except that I've always felt that I had to be very careful not to let my independence cost me my femininity. I don't believe that total independence is right for all women. If women want to be protected, have doors opened for them, and cigarettes lit, that's what they should have.

But are independence and femininity mutually exclusive?

A survey of women cadets at West Point showed that their particular work environment and career selection play a role in their value orientation. These women, when questioned about their own strengths, rated the typical male characteristics of physical prowess, roughness, competitiveness, and assertiveness far above the more traditional feminine values.

A long-distance runner was asked, in an article on women athletes, whether she has any "feminine hang-ups" about running:

Yes, I have lots of hang-ups. You wouldn't believe it. I always worry about looking nice in a race. I worry about my calf muscles getting big, but mostly I worry about my hair. . . . I suppose it's because so many people have said women athletes look masculine. So a lot of us try, subconsciously maybe, to look as feminine as possible in a race. There are always lots of hair ribbons in the race.

A male business-school professor told us:

Women who just learn males' games, who imitate the worst qualities of men in business, without developing a sense of their own worth, a feeling of personal competency, aren't helping themselves and, in fact, are seen as obsequious by men. The women I know who are making it are doing none of this.

The president of a marketing research firm offers her solution:

I think my greatest asset is my ability to think quickly. I play by my own rules, which are probably not that different from the rules that men play. Competence, professionalism, and performance are what count. I play by whatever the rules of my business are, more than by any male/female rules.

The lesson here is that women need to focus more on the arena in which they operate and concern themselves less with characteristics of gender style. Sure, there are special difficulties for women in business, but the key to avoiding the self-repair trap is in the kind and content of knowledge one chooses to pursue. The lop-sided effect of many self-repair courses is their concentration on personal factors, with little balance or attention given to the inesti-mable importance of learning the way a business works and mak-ing the business work for the individual.

A different kind of professional-development seminar helps women gain insight into the organizational culture and especially into their own work environment. They focus on such dynamics of the work situation as politics, power structure, and success fac-tors. They help women move from asking, "What did I do wrong?" to "What is really going on here?" Many of these sem-inars are conducted internally with participants drawn from com-pany personnel. However, company programs for women are running into criticism on two fronts. The first objection is that they run the danger of causing a backlash from men, many of whom feel they need to learn the same things. Second, many women are unwilling to be singled out for this training solely on the basis of being a woman. A systems analyst described the situa-tion in her company:

> We went to management three years ago and discussed the problems exempt women were having. We had conducted a study, prepared a report, and presented the statistics to back up what we were saying. As a result, they hired a woman consultant to conduct management-development seminars for women. The greatest thing about the sem-inars was that we got to know women in other parts of the company. I never had a way to get information efficiently before I connected with these women in my seminar. Also, many of us would never have dis-cussed our problems as openly if there had been men present. We would have been afraid of looking like whiners or being trivial. Now the company is no longer having the seminars. They say there is no reason for separate training for women. Some of the women are saying the same thing, but I think the seminars should continue for those who need them.

A seminar leader commented:

> Seminars are a way of presenting blocks of information in such a way as to increase your level of understanding. For women, many seminars offer a forum in which they learn they are not alone. They begin to share experiences and they realize that they are not the only one who has had a particular set of experiences, self-doubts, those kinds of

things. It has to do with feelings of isolation, which lead to a feeling of powerlessness.

The seminar brochures that fill the mails and the articles that crowd the shelves are responding to a market demand. The same rules apply in this market as in any other. Why does Baskin-Robbins make thirty-one flavors of ice cream? To serve a greater variety of consumer tastes. Before making a financial investment, you would study the background information on the investment, analyze the risk and potential for returns, and select a broker with experience and credibility. Today, women are recommending the same method be applied in choosing self-development programs.

> As a trainer, I will have to say that there is a lot of second- and third-rate stuff out there. One needs to be selective. Most of us have had very limited experiences in what a learning event is. We've all sat through long lectures in college or at business seminars where all we did was listen. But learning is an experiential process. People only remember about 10 percent of what they hear, so if you go to a seminar where all they do is talk, you're in a bad seminar. A good rule of thumb is that for every ten to fifteen minutes of their talking to you, there should be forty-five minutes to an hour of your processing information and interacting with other people . . . or even with yourself. So a good seminar is valuable—hard to find, but valuable.

A comment from a broadcast journalist:

> I think books and seminars have been very helpful, but I think we are overdoing it. You have to do the hard work yourself. If you're not prepared, if you haven't gotten to a certain point yourself, the books and seminars are only Band-Aid therapy.

The sum of all this advice appears to be *caveat emptor*—let the buyer beware. After they had time to synthesize and internalize the prescriptive seminar fashions, many women suddenly found the material had shrunk and faded in the light of corporate day. Erma Bombeck once quipped that the greatest lie of the twentieth century was "One size fits all." She certainly was on to something.

The Fantasy Trip

Out of the fairy tales of childhood are often created new fantasies of life—fantasies not set in castles and magic forests, but in corporate skyscrapers and executive suites. Since, in reality, few women are there, the greater number fantasize themselves in the roles. Others project fantasies about the lives of the women who have made it. The dearth of firsthand experience with other women as success models has led many women to weave illusions about the career of these models and to fantasize themselves in similar positions. This results in frustration, alienation, and disappointment. It is the fantasy trip.

Expectations have both a positive and negative polarity. With them come a built-in set of potholes—insecurities or uncertainties—which can trip up the runner anywhere along the course. In some cases expectations become confused, as it is difficult to sort out one's own goals and visions from those projected upon one from outside forces. Many a life is a quiet personal battle fought against the onslaught of others' expectations.

A particular phenomenon among businesswomen is the massive demand for role models—women who have achieved a position or career that is viewed as the goal of someone still in the building stage of a career. The role model, ideally, according to advocates, is a successful woman. She is approached by an admiring aspirant who seeks to become her apprentice. Should she accept the challenge, the apprentice then comes under the teacher's wing to "learn the ropes."

However, when women begin to develop fantasy visions of what it took for a role model to achieve her success and similar fantasies about what the apprentice would be like in that sought-after position, trouble can be in the offing.

Some women in this trap endow a role model with certain attributes, creating in fact an idol from an ideal. Once elevated to her pedestal, an idol is permitted no deviation, no normal human characteristics. Any display of ungoddesslike behavior pushes the apprentice to a feeling of betrayal. The snare is then set.

Some women who hold positions of power or prominence may resist expressing their humanness out of fear of that backlash and actually begin to deny that the more human characteristics exist.

They buy into the fantasy and place themselves under the very great strain of trying to live up to expectations of others, of becoming the idol. Other women, fearful that they will be found a paper saint, barricade themselves against any communicating with other women. Either way, the going is tough.

After a well-known woman lecturer had delivered a speech, she was surprised to later find a letter from a listener that simply read: "I envy you your career."

The courage to expose human traits was shown by San Francisco Mayor Dianne Feinstein. Addressing a group of women business owners, she made an indelible impression on many when she took the podium and admitted that after putting together the first post-Proposition 13 budget, she went home and asked herself if she really wanted to be mayor. She went on to comment that she was sure many of the women listening had similar days in their professional lives. That sort of admission is still a calculated risk, as much for a woman among women as for a woman among men.

If in your fantasy you are obsessed with the image of yourself in all the executive trappings—clothes, office, car, staff—you are on another fantasy trip. You are imagining away the distance between where you are now and where you want to be. Reality is what you need to do to reach your goals. Those whom you envy or admire or aspire to be like have put in their time and paid their dues. A teenager we know fancies himself a rock-music star. He has bought an electric guitar, wears the appropriate clothes, and can effectively imitate the moves of the TV stars. He spends hour after hour playing his tapes and accompanying them while strumming his guitar and singing into a standing lamp (microphone). The problem is, he hasn't learned to play. He can act as though he plays and he can use someone else's music to enhance the impression. In his fantasy he is the star, but he will never make it in reality unless he learns to play the music. That learning process is slow and demanding. It will be a long time before he sounds as good as the tapes, but there is no substitute and no quick fix.

The new glorification of work and achievement for women, which has replaced the old glorification of marriage and family, is one part reality and nine parts romantic fiction. So-called glamour people in glamour jobs account for an imperceptible fraction of the population. A woman who manages pension funds and who travels a great deal captioned a speech she made recently to a group of new managers in her company, "I Never Saw New Orleans." She went on to describe the realities of her business travels—from airport to hotel to meetings to evenings alone in her room, watching TV, and eating a room-service dinner. So much for the glamour of business travel.

Not until women can deal honestly with the realities of their position can they individually do something about it. Creating idols of other people or clinging to future dream scenarios diminishes the ability to deal effectively with the present.

The Impostor Caper

There has been an interesting study, based on a sample of academic women, called "The Impostor Phenomenon in the High Achieving Woman." The theory the study examines is that some women are convinced that they have reached their current level of achievement by "fooling people" along the way. That they are, in reality, impostors.

A woman Ph.D. candidate feels she will never pass her oral exams, even though she has been able to fool her professors until now. A successful writer fears she will not be able to produce the manuscript that she has been able to sell. The woman who has been promoted to vice-president is scared stiff. Somehow, she has gotten away with her inadequacies up to now, but in the new job she will surely be found out.

In *Sexual Politics*, Kate Millet notes that "the growing suspicion which plagues any minority member, that the myths about his/her inferiority might after all be true, reaches remarkable proportions in the insecurities of women."[2]

Some women, believing they couldn't possibly have gotten this far on their ability, use their sexuality to distract male superiors from recognizing their imagined deficiencies on the job. This is a negative reinforcement of the impostor syndrome. In effect, it permits the woman to support her spot in the trap by saying, "See, I knew I couldn't do it on my own. I have to resort to my feminine wiles to get that promotion." And everyone around her will agree. "You know why she got the promotion," they say with a wink and a knowing look.

Another manifestation of the pathology of the impostor syndrome is an unintended outcome of many corporate affirmative-action programs. For some women corporate EEO (Equal Employment Opportunity) is proof that the stereotypes about their inferiority are true. That is why there is resistance to these programs by some women who have been in companies for a long time. They feel their accomplishments are being devalued by newer women who are coming on board as part of a special company hiring program. This in turn creates a rift among women in these companies and alienates the two groups who need each other the most. The impostor trap, played out in programs to improve women's opportunity, thus only reinforces women's powerless positions. Impostor women (as reported in the study) were subject to early-childhood expectations which seriously deterred their functioning in life. One type of impostor has always been expected to do well—told, in fact, that she could do anything. When she found something she couldn't do, she felt as though her previous accomplishments were a fluke. She had been an impostor all along. A second type of impostor was told she was a "loser," and tried desperately to achieve as a method of disproving the title. But internally she is still bound by the label and discounts her achievements as "not good enough." She continues believing, despite a quest for validation which sometimes takes on obsessive proportions, that her family was right about her.

Some women have driven themselves to tragic extremes. A recent example is that of a highly successful woman—author, lecturer, teacher—who began to suffer self-doubts. In her case, she believed that it was because she had an incredibly supportive husband that her success was great. Though she loved him and appreciated his loyalty and encouragement, she separated from him. She told friends that she had to know if she could make it on her own without him.

The central issue is that impostors are trapped into fulfilling external expectations on their lives. Waiting for that outside voice to provide validation, they lose all personal insight into their accomplishments and become unable to judge what constitutes happiness for themselves.

Marie Bowen, a practicing psychologist in California, was quoted in *Working Woman* magazine as saying:

The concept of serving is a central theme for most women. We are conditioned to put others first. When a woman begins struggling for her own rights and her own needs, conflict and guilt can surface.

This conflict is double for the impostor, who has such a fragile sense of her own worth.

Listen to self-doubts of a woman who was the youngest officer in her organization:

> I think one thing that works against me is that I grapple with a very negative self-image; I too frequently compare myself to other people and the comparison is negative. I was reading something yesterday that said: "If we only wanted to be perfect, that could be attainable, but we always want to be more perfect than somebody else and the reason that's unattainable is because other people aren't ever as well off as we think they are." So, I have to think about that a lot. I have a problem of a negative self-image, of feeling that I'm not as good as . . . , not as intelligent as . . . , not as capable as . . . , not as . . .

The fantasy trap and the impostor syndrome are linked. To play out the fantasy of corporate success, women are impersonating their interpretation of the corporate success figure. Because one must mask out the reality of oneself to take on the characteristics of the role, one becomes, to one's own inner knowledge, an impostor.

At a seminar for women M.B.A. students, the discussion turned to the topic of job satisfaction as it related to freedom of expression. Before the floor was a suggestion by the seminar leader on taking the liberty of being one's self on the job. One woman in the group took extreme exception to this advice: "You are suggesting that I just be myself on the job! Do you want me to get fired? I have two children to support. Do you know how upset I would be if I were fired?" In response, another member of the audience rose with her answer:

> I was just like you once . . . very unhappy in my job, but afraid to speak my mind for fear I'd be fired. I was tense and began to find myself snapping at my husband and children. I thought that the salary I pulled in was for them until I saw that the price of the strain I was under couldn't begin to be paid for by my weekly check. I quit, took two weeks off, and thought, perhaps for the first time, about what I really wanted. When I found an answer for myself, I went out and got a job where I can really be me. I took a risk, but living with fear and bottling up my feelings was no way to live at all.

The Play's the Thing

The kernel of fear that haunts the impostor is not only the dread of being unmasked by someone else, but the internal fear of self-discovery. There was a Dennis the Menace cartoon that pictured Dennis' mother helping him pull off layer after layer of heavy winter clothing. About halfway through the process, a worried Dennis asked, "Are you sure it's really me under all this stuff?"

Often the behavior of the impostor is so defensive as to invite revelation. While the fear of revelation runs high, the liberation from having to play a role forevermore holds certain appeal. The tragedy of the impostor is not unlike the curse of the Method actor who can no longer differentiate between her true identity and the character being portrayed. To lose the self so successfully in any single role is to risk being typecast and constrained for the rest of one's career.

Individualism

"Historically," says Bertrand Russell, "some societies have been centralized, some diffuse. Some have encouraged individual initiative, others have placed a premium on obedience. In modern times," laments Russell, "giant bureaucracies are ever decreasing the chances for exceptional individual achievement."

In the past decade women have attained new heights and are beginning to feel entitled to ever-widening options. The trap of assimilation, however, stalls the upward spiral. Women are losing the vision of their beginnings, their position, and their ultimate goals. Through the denial of self-expression and through the suppression of individuality, these women rob themselves of a positive experience—living and achieving as they are, being recognized and recognizing themselves as unique. By acting out someone else's role or script, such women often lose the prize they seek.

A woman executive explained it this way:

Women have to stop looking for the game plan, because it doesn't exist. A game plan purports that there is a single pattern to follow. Better perhaps to strive for seasoning—to experience politics as they are rather than being buffeted by them or holding them at arm's length by assuming a rigid pose.

As women reach for handholds higher up the mountain, it is clear that the major barrier they face is the inability of men in power to differentiate and evaluate individual women's potential and achievement. Therefore, in place of homogenization we propose the process of adaptive individualism. Rather than channeling the self into a how-to program, which teaches regimental rules, why not a process that relies on your own unique qualities as a person? Rather than being slave to a staged routine, how much better to acquire an understanding of the business environment from the vantage point of your own perceptions. Adaptive individualism implies that one can assert one's uniqueness in the context of adapting one's behavior to fit the situation. It builds on a belief that people can move in creatively advantageous directions without altering the core of the true self.

A corporate training officer summed it up very well:

> Have the courage of your convictions. Stand up and out on the job. But be a consistent human being. Don't go for the schizophrenic method of trying to be one person at home and another in the office. Have a variety of behaviors in your bag, and use them to fit the situation. But only use behaviors that are appropriate for you.

Adaptive individualism is very different from prescriptive assimilation. The how-to programs assume that women need to hear the canons of success from someone else, that they then will accept them as gospel, and that the steps, rules, and regimens will work in any situation, for any woman, under any conditions, until death do us part. Adaptive individualism, on the other hand, is a process. It assumes that you can acquire the skill to understand your organizational system, to read the directions of change, to move creatively in advantageous directions, and to choose from a repertory of behaviors the actions most likely to achieve your goal. This may seem at times more difficult and even painful, but the bottom line is that you'll never go the way of the dodo.

If I succeed I will make it easier for the women
who follow me. If I fail they will say that a woman
can't make it.

CLARE BOOTHE LUCE

2

The Achieving Woman

It has been said that life in today's world differs more from conditions in 1830 than did 1830 from the days of Noah's Ark, and that two of the elements responsible for these extraordinary changes are the emergence of mass culture and mass media. Attitudes and values are no longer measured solely on an individual basis, but by popular perceptions of social need, by cultural fashion, and eventually by the press, television, and the editors of the nightly news.

The definition of what constitutes achievement for women has shifted dramatically over the twentieth century. Confusion and frustration are running high. When women decided to go to work, to seek something beyond the lives they had previously led, the traditional guidelines along which those lives had been drawn were rendered obsolete. Or so it seemed. The blueprint which emerged as women attempted to integrate multiple and often conflicting roles became known as "Having It All," and its adherents often found themselves exhausted from having to keep up the superwoman image. It is clear that these multiple commitments and the conflicts they generate are being resolved in as many ways as there are women trying to resolve them. For this reason alone, there can be no definitive how-to manual for today's woman.

Like the westward pioneers before them, women heading out into new corporate territories soon learned that success is not equally distributed, nor are rewards equally reaped. Many workingwomen go unrecognized for their small, but significant contributions. Others bask in the limelight, legends in their own time.

The achievements of the firsts, the stars, stoked the engines of the media machinery. Their stories were written as if these corporate women were movie stars, the only precedent the press had to follow in covering women in the spotlight. But the effect of this star treatment was to distort both the meaning and measure of all women's achievements and to disregard those trends which made the eruption of women's ambitions such a cultural shock to corporate America.

At Odds with the Times

The year was 1940. America had lived through an economic disaster. The Horatio Alger myth had been sorely tested and had lost much of its luster. Like a volatile commodity in a panicked market, the value of ambition had suffered a terrible collapse. A government report issued early that year sounded the warning that, for some, the American Dream might be ending.

> Industrial workers . . . face in their occupational lives, a pattern of culpable disparity between the exhortations of tradition and the realities of their own experience. On one hand, they are encouraged to pursue ambitious goals by the assurance that anyone with ability and determination can, by his own efforts, get ahead in the world. On the other hand, only limited opportunities are open to them.

This report had little meaning for workingwomen of the day. The majority in the labor force at this time were either single, middle-class women in white-collar work, biding their time until marriage, or poor women, both single and married, who toiled in factories or in domestic service for sheer economic survival. Only a handful of women, second-generation suffragettes and other aberrants within the ranks, pursued ambitions or cried out for equality of opportunity. In 1941, all of this was altered overnight.

In *The American Woman*, William Chafe noted:

> The eruption of hostilities generated an unprecedented demand for new workers and, in response, over 6 million women took jobs, increasing the size of the female labor force by over 50 percent. The war marked a watershed in the history of women at work, and, temporarily at least, caused a greater change in women's economic status that half a century of feminist rhetoric and agitation had been unable to achieve.[1]

By the start of the 1950s, government statistics revealed that 22 percent of the nation's couples were already established as two-career families. The number of middle-class married women at work was steadily climbing, as was the national number of female-headed households. On the surface, America seemed to have settled down to enjoy victory and unprecedented prosperity. But the fortunes of ambition did not appear to be keeping pace with the rising standard of living. What had afflicted the 1940s industrial workers, a sense of limited opportunity, had found its way into the drives of white-collar men of the day. William Whyte observed them:

> They do not lack ambition. They seem to, but that is only because the nature of it has changed. It has become passive ambition. Not so many years ago it was permissible for the ambitious young man to talk of setting his cap for a specific goal—like becoming president of a corporation. Today, it is a very rare young man who will allow himself to talk that way.[2]

Just a few years after Whyte's identification of this passive ambition in men, Vance Packard embarked on his study of *The Status Seekers* to find that "aggressive ambition, long assumed to be peculiarly American, just doesn't show up on any substantial scale anymore."[3]

In 1963, Betty Friedan touched off the explosion of women's ambitions with *The Feminine Mystique*. A paradox had come full circle. Just when men believed, and acted on the belief, that their opportunities were lessening, women were experiencing a new passion for the American Dream. Small wonder that their ambitions sounded so dissonant to the organizational ear. Like a contemporary wave of immigrants, women suddenly found themselves standing on the edge of a continent that they saw brimming with opportunities, after having spent generations watching the dream come true for men.

From the outset during our interviews it became apparent that if Horatio Alger had met an untimely end, his sister was alive and well and flourishing:

> Success can't be predetermined or I wouldn't exist. I came from a very poor family. My father was a wonderful inventor who made many technological breakthroughs for a major airline, but all he ever got was fifty dollars and a certificate. He was afraid to go out on his own. My family tree is full of nonachievers. I'm the only one who has ever gone to college. My family severed their relationship with me when I was seventeen years old. Everything seemed to be going against me, but I somehow made it work.

> My friend Penny came from a poor area of Boston. Her father died when she was just a teenager. She had two sisters and three brothers, but nothing to help her in her background. She has come a long way and it was purely on her own motivation.

> Men used to say I had balls and I really used to resent that, but now I don't because it was those balls which got me from the cotton fields of Alabama to the twenty-fifth floor of this office building.

And finally the story of a true latter-day immigrant who now works for a major American oil company:

> America was always my dream country, my ideal. It was the place I felt where it paid to work and to be ambitious. In Sweden, from the cradle to the grave, those who work take care of those who cannot. But the price of this system is the curbing of private initiative. There is no motivation to work because taxes take virtually 90 percent of one's earnings. My friends from school began to say, "Why work hard when they take it all?" That climate was not for me. It held no inspiration. There are things about America that I disagree with, but overall this is the ideal country for a person who has dreams and goals.

Yet the spirit of ambition which had infused the ranks of workingwomen did not escape the cultural quandary over ambition's value, nor were women free from doubts raised by their socialization as women. The expression of ambition and the willingness to risk have been bugaboos for many a workingwoman. In exploring

"What Keeps Women Out of the Executive Suite," Cynthia Fuchs Epstein commented:

> What is unique about the situation of women today is that almost ev-
> eryone is to blame, including women themselves, who have joined the
> conspiracy by accepting the idea that they must monitor their ambi-
> tions and goals in terms of what everybody else expects of them. . . .
> Our culture expects and encourages women to hold back, not to "go for
> broke."[4]

Part of the philosophy of Having It All is based on that sensitive nerve in women that triggers the abandonment response—the feeling that their decision to go to work sounds the death knell of the nuclear family. Having It All emerges, then, as the social bargain women strike to ensure that neither career nor family rewards need be sacrificed or risked. But to the extent that women succeed in levering themselves out in two directions, they subject their goals, both personal and professional, to being lowered or diminished. Men, on the other hand, can be single-mindedly ambitious, even if they have a wife and children.

In their eagerness to get their new lives under way, few women stopped to develop a changed blueprint. Instead, they adopted for themselves what they believed was the blueprint for the lives of workingmen. If men could have wives, kids, and jobs, women reasoned, then why couldn't they have husbands, kids, and careers? But this line of reasoning failed because the roles of husband and wife were not interchangeable in the prevailing standards of society. And it was, and is, this difference that lies at the heart of the dilemmas and conflicts women face in balancing their personal and professional lives.

During our interviews we asked two questions of every woman: "Can you have it all? Do you want it all?" We did not specify what we meant by the word "all," but every single woman interpreted the question to mean the combining of a career and a family. Here are some of their answers:

> I think it is possible and desirable. I haven't done it because I have
> conflicts. My job is too demanding. I don't get enough time to spend in
> developing personal relationships. Therefore, whatever I start tends to
> disintegrate in a few months.

There is a new definition to the word "all." I think you can perform all the roles and be relatively satisfied, but if your goal is to be a corporate CEO, and that requires moving all over the country or heavy job involvement, then you are going to have to compromise.

What would worry me is the guilt over leaving my child. I couldn't turn over that job to someone else. I couldn't live with having his or her emotional and intellectual growth established by someone else. Even though I would climb the walls having no one but a little baby to relate to.

As for a family, I like other people's children. I like to play with them, then leave and go home.

My husband wants to have a child, so we are going to adopt an older child. That is my compromise. Someone we can drop off at school in the morning and pick up after work at night.

I think you can have all the roles. You can have a career, parenting, and marriage, but you have to have some balance. You have to decide that something is not going to be 100 percent as far as you're concerned. What I mean is, someone else's view of what a mother must be—not and have a career at the same time. And you're not going to be able to do all those things a housewife is supposed to do either. You may have to learn to live without waxed floors and clean windows. You can't have a career and do all the things your mother told you must be done to a house.

I read somewhere recently . . . that you can have it all, but have it differently. For instance, a professional woman who must leave her child in a day-care center told me that one night her daughter asked if she could ride her friend's two-wheeler. The mother said no, but only because she believed her daughter did not know how to ride one. The child proceeded to go outside, get on the bike, and ride it. At that point the woman was struck by the thought of how many other steps in her daughter's life she had missed. I know how she feels. I have a wonderful relationship with my daughter, but I can never forget that it would be a very different kind of relationship if I didn't work.

I am concerned about how much time I'd personally be able to spend with my children. I have to ask myself, why have them at all if you have no time to spend with them? Am I just trying to populate the world or doing something because others think that's what I should do?

I have a fantasy that I could get married and live in the country and have four children and nurse one after the other and wear long dresses.

But I realize that this is a fantasy and that in reality I'd go nuts. I can take the glamour of motherhood, but I don't think I could handle the peaks and valleys. I'm already thirty-two years old and am set in my ways. If I couldn't have a housekeeper, just getting the food together at the same time for all those people would make me neurotic. Even the idea of a husband is unsettling. I can barely stand to spend the night with someone now. I don't know if that's because I'm getting inflexible or that I can't tolerate having my privacy invaded. At the same time I believe that an unshared life is empty.

No, it's not possible to have it all. If you have a commitment to your job and career, your home life and personal commitments are bound to suffer. It's a conscious trade-off. And I personally feel guilty about not being able to maintain a relationship because I was married once and the reason we split up was because I was so career-oriented. Much more than he was. There wasn't much compromise between us. We ended up being two people who lived together out of convenience. And that is ridiculous.

Among the women we interviewed, whether they were planning a pregnancy or already had children, there was much confusion about the best time to interrupt a career. Each of the women felt caught between the professional and biological time clocks, and behind all their suggested strategies was the haunting impression that there must be some one way to do it best. We have no answer for that. But if there was anything we felt could be said with certainty about having it all—combining a career, a relationship, and children—it is that neither a career nor family life will be the same as if there were one without the other.

Another disquieting trend we noted was that many career women who had taken just a little time off when their babies were born, were now giving up their jobs to raise their child or children full time. The overwhelming sense that they were missing something could no longer be denied. Perhaps this is all part of the same cultural change noted in a study conducted at Brown University. College women polled in a survey indicated a preference for a far more traditional kind of life than did the group immediately preceding them. A majority of the women also responded to the questions asked by challenging the values implied—those of their immediate predecessors—and questioned whether pursuing a career *was* more important than having and caring for children.

What is suggested by study findings such as these is that women have begun to realize that the grass in corporate America is not

greener than the grass in their own backyards. And the apparent
indifference of the society in providing adequate day care does not
put a woman's mind at rest, nor make the decision about a career
less troubling. The support systems that allow women to give vent
to their ambitions, to strive for achievement, still function under
dual standards. Society expects, rewards, and even praises the ambitions and achievements of men under a different set of measures
and models than those applied against workingwomen.

Clearing the Passage

Women have to travel through two stages on the road to achievement. In stage one, women have to gain access to a new sphere or
occupation, acting as trailblazers, gaining presence in new roles.
Yet the crossing of the first barrier, of gaining presence, by an individual woman is regarded not solely as a measure of her own ability to perform but also as an indicator of whether the women who
follow her will be able to duplicate her success. In other words, the
presence of a trailblazer casts a shadow over the potential of all her
successors. This is the essence of the Clare Boothe Luce quote we
use to introduce this chapter. One woman's achievement or failure
weighs heavily upon her and becomes the precedent by which corporate America opens or closes its mind and doors.

A second shadow cast on the achievements of women in the
business world is that their accomplishments are eclipsed by the
mere fact that they are women. The poignancy of this filtered recognition is made clear in this excerpt, from a *Savvy* interview, with
architect Denise Scott Brown.

> . . . the conversation gravitates—as a compass does to north—to issues
> of her conflicting role as wife, partner, and collaborator, her disap-
> pointment at not getting the recognition she feels she deserves and the
> pain of constantly seeing her work attributed to others. Then, after a
> monologue worthy of a George Bernard Shaw character, she insists the
> interviewer not dwell on them. "Talk about what I *do*," she admon-
> ishes.[5]

The literature on workingwomen is filled with the novelty of the
"firsts" and with a pervasive propaganda message which asserts

that all women *can* make it. But this propaganda denies that there
is such a thing as institutionalized sexism which acts to discredit
and fails to discern women's achievements, that each woman is an
individual who carries her own level of ambition. In addition to
these oversights and distortions is the practice of overkilling the
achievements of women with empty superlatives. No matter how
many men have accomplished a task or filled the same job before
she did, the workingwoman finds that her achievement is somehow altered by her gender. Hence, the first woman stockbroker in
a firm, who performs as countless men have in the same position,
finds herself labeled "incredible." This is the syntax of achievement for women. More insidious than damning with faint praise,

Range of Subtopics Under the General Listing of Women

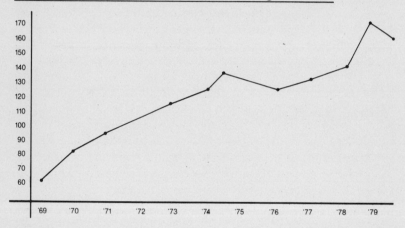

Employment

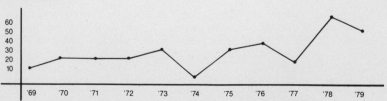

sense that something big was happening and every-
to garner a share of the scoop. A simple reflection of
minine push can be found in the following charts,
ted by counting the numbers of articles listed, under
ading "Women," from the past ten years' issues of
Guide to Periodic Literature.

sting to us was the complete disappearance of the
nen's Liberation," after 1976, for it suggests that this
in which the propaganda surrounding women's
had been accepted by the majority of the population.
a fad had passed through its trendiest phase and
en had been out in corporate America long enough to
ey were fighting for something far less philosophical.
ement was recognized as being one of sheer survival.
y the insidious effects of this media blitz had already
a workingwoman believe everything the media said
nd their lives.

Home and the Corporate Range

cle in a respected business magazine profiled a house-
financial executive. Early on, the woman is quoted as
re is nothing a man can do that a woman can't, at least
ss world." But this aggressive statement of equal po-
ickly dissipated. The copy goes on to describe the
ot your normal money man." The accounting of her
success is interspersed with depictions of her role as
ther. She caps her twelve-year ascent to the top by
still the same housewife I always was."
an, like so many others, did not intentionally mean
er own achievements. She was simply responding to
s learned, unconsciously or otherwise, society wants
a successful woman: that her traditional side is still

no clearer example of the fate that awaits the truly
al woman than Mary Cunningham. At a luncheon
onor in early 1981, Ms. Cunningham assessed her ex-

Occupations ("Women as...")

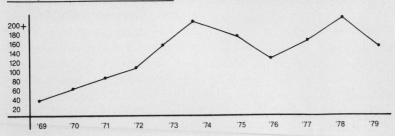

Equal Rights

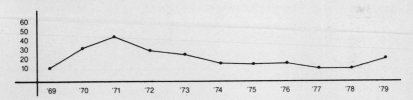

Women's Liberation Movement

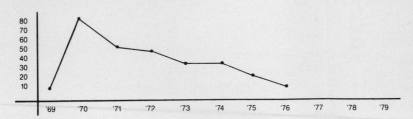

such conditional measures of achievement serve only to perpetuate stereotypes.

Media Darlings, Media Dupes

In the 1970s the attention focused on women (much if not all of it coming out of the coverage accorded to women's lib) sent hundreds of reporters scurrying to find the nearest achieving woman.

There was a sense that something big was happening and everybody was out to garner a share of the scoop. A simple reflection of the media's feminine push can be found in the following charts, which we created by counting the numbers of articles listed, under the general heading "Women," from the past ten years' issues of *The Reader's Guide to Periodic Literature.*

Most interesting to us was the complete disappearance of the heading "Women's Liberation," after 1976, for it suggests that this was the year in which the propaganda surrounding women's achievements had been accepted by the majority of the population. Liberation as a fad had passed through its trendiest phase and workingwomen had been out in corporate America long enough to know that they were fighting for something far less philosophical. The real movement was recognized as being one of sheer survival. Unfortunately the insidious effects of this media blitz had already made many a workingwoman believe everything the media said about them and their lives.

Home and the Corporate Range

A recent article in a respected business magazine profiled a housewife turned financial executive. Early on, the woman is quoted as saying, "There is nothing a man can do that a woman can't, at least in the business world." But this aggressive statement of equal potential is quickly dissipated. The copy goes on to describe the woman as "not your normal money man." The accounting of her professional success is interspersed with depictions of her role as wife and mother. She caps her twelve-year ascent to the top by saying, "I'm still the same housewife I always was."

This woman, like so many others, did not intentionally mean to devalue her own achievements. She was simply responding to what she has learned, unconsciously or otherwise, society wants to hear from a successful woman: that her traditional side is still intact.

There is no clearer example of the fate that awaits the truly nontraditional woman than Mary Cunningham. At a luncheon held in her honor in early 1981, Ms. Cunningham assessed her experience and denounced the media for "constantly focusing on the biologically female side of a woman's success by sensationalizing events." She said that reporters faced by a successful young woman "feel obliged to describe the color of her hair, her shape, and assign an overall 10 point rating." It is also difficult to overlook the "we told you so" attitude which many of the press adopted when rumors of a Cunningham-Agee marriage began circulating.[6]

And if Mary Cunningham was a symbol of what can happen to a woman on the corporate fast track, Sandra Brown stands as the symbol of what awaits the empire builder who falls under the double-edged sword of achievement. A November 1980 *Savvy* article on Brown's indictment for questionable financial dealings honestly appraised the role played by the press in heightening Brown's achievement image and, hence, the length of her fall. The author of the article admitted "our zeal to herald the heroic attainments of an attractive woman in an especially male-dominated part of the business world. We had too unquestioningly accepted, and even inflated, Brown's claim of wealth and empire and lucrative corporate rescues. Now it seems her business career has been little more than a dreary succession of failures."[7]

Yet the fault for this distortion of women's achievements and the fervent zeal for heralding heroines cannot totally be blamed on the press. Much of the problem is the direct result of the rush by so many women to become media darlings. If the language of the reports served to undermine feminism, so did the verbiage and naiveté provided by the women themselves. In fact, when we began to collect and review articles written about successful working-women, no matter the source, a certain unsettling pattern began to emerge. If a journalist asked slanted questions, it was also obvious that women fed the system with predictable "new woman" answers. In such unfamiliar territory, it seemed, no one—not the media, not the readers, not workingwomen—was able to discern the difference between information, propaganda, self-interest, and pure entertainment.

Rather than quote endless examples of this circuitous problem, we devised a do-it-yourself exercise in analytical journalism. From the mountains of clippings on successful women, we extracted the most frequently recurring patterns in which both the interviewer and subject indulged. We call the result "Fill in the Blanks for Success!"

With her appointment as the new vice-president of marketing for Consolidated Peaches, Sandy Silver becomes the first woman in the company's forty-five-year history to hold such a high-level post. A perky thirty-two years old, Sandy also becomes one of the youngest executives to fill such an impressive management slot at Consolidated. One senses that this is just the beginning of the precedents this honors M.B.A. student and former homecoming queen will set. There is nothing wrong with Sandy that a few flaws wouldn't cure.

She wears a genial grin and her stride is brisk as she circles from behind her impeccably organized desk to greet me. Her handshake seems a bit tentative, perhaps because this is the first interview she's given since her appointment was made public.

The daughter of a Midwestern engineer, Sandy's earliest ambition was to become a teacher, but she headed in a new direction when that job market constricted. When asked how she managed to come so far so fast, Sandy replies that she was "lucky. I couldn't have done it without the support of my family and friends," she admits candidly. "I worked hard during grad school at a time when women M.B.A.s were not yet fashionable. And I was fortunate in finding a mentor who taught me everything he knew."

Up at 5:30 A.M. every morning, Sandy jogs for half an hour before coming to work. "It increases my energy level and helps me to focus on the day's upcoming events."

When asked how the men in her firm had responded to her appointment, she confesses that there were some problems at first, but adds, "I guess it is like this for all new people, especially those who are hired from outside the company. But we're learning to work as a team."

Client reactions, she says, were varied. "Some were supportive from our first meeting, others took a while to warm up to me. I credit my ability to get along with everyone in making the adjustment a smooth one."

Sandy tries to leave her office by 6:00 P.M. every day in order to spend time with her husband, a financial analyst for a major oil company. "We eat out a lot so that neither of us has to be bogged down with domestic concerns right after work." Children are a definite part of their future plans. "I think that I will be a part of the trend toward motherhood after thirty," she muses.

Is the job everything she thought it would be? "Sure," she says. "It's tough and challenging. Many women are afraid of this type of job because they think that such ambition is unfeminine. But nothing could be further from the truth. What I do has no connection at all to my sex."

Would Sandy recommend her life-style to other aspiring career women? "It depends," Sandy says thoughtfully. "I feel a high level of satisfaction and fulfillment in my work. And I made sure that this company was deserving of my talents and could offer me a future. The hours are long and there are sacrifices, but for me it is worth it. If I found that I was no longer fulfilled by my job, I'd move on. If this kind of life is what a woman is looking for, I'd say go ahead and try it."

Where Sandy Went Wrong

It seems politic to restate that every quote from Sandy's story was paraphrased from actual interviews with real career women. The questions and descriptive remarks came from the body of articles in our files. A review of Sandy's story makes it easy to see where she went wrong and allowed herself, and by extension all other women, to be isolated, discredited, and undercut.

Isolation. It may be assumed that the company set up this interview to benefit its own public image, but Sandy's comments do not indicate that she made an attempt to control the situation. She acquiesces in being identified as a "first woman," isolating her from her male peers and from all other women in the company. More tragic is that Sandy perpetuates the gap many first stars have created between women and their own working history by isolating herself from all the workingwomen who preceded her in the company. She is adrift in time. She makes no comment on why she is a first, on the significance of the timing of her appointment, on the status of other women in the company. She states that she was the one who chose the job, but it can be suspected that the job was out looking for a woman. She lays out the history of her isolation by implying that she was surrounded by men in grad school, which she surely was. But in doing so she only reinforces the image of an achieving woman as an oddity. Her descriptions of interactions with clients and co-workers feed the "me against them" position, however gently, and heighten the picture of Sandy as a woman who spends a lot of time and energy explaining that she belongs. We think the lady doth protest too much.

Discrediting. Sandy takes little credit for her own success on the basis of natural abilities, but showers praise on her family, friends, and her mentor. She works hard and sacrifices (translation—grunt and martyr). She identifies herself as "lucky," the kiss-of-death word for any woman who wants to be taken seriously. A divine providence capable of giving Sandy her break is surely capable of throwing a lightning bolt across her career path with the same whimsy. Sandy's lack of political savvy is evident in her description of how she came to the firm and the responses she was met with, and note of this weakness has almost certainly been made in the appropriate quarters for future use. Sandy will probably be equally naive about motives when latent hostilities and plots begin to surface later. And last, but not least, she allows herself to be called Sandy.

Undercutting. Sandy gets along with everyone, including the reporter, who labels her demeanor as "perky." She has freely given of background material of a stereotypical nature, such as her girlhood ambition to be a teacher and her homecoming-queen title. And why tell him she was an honors student when everyone knows that girls do better in school? She talks about her work in terms of "satisfaction and fulfillment"—words that can be alternatively used to describe the quality of one's sex life. Her plans for motherhood are a red flag in the face of anyone who is after her job. By describing herself as someone who will become part of a trend, she raises questions as to whether her career is a similarly trendy act. Her comment that many women fear that ambition is unfeminine gives credence to the trait-gender stereotype. She speaks of the company as if it were a suitor for her hand. And in her parting shot, Sandy gives fainthearted encouragement to women considering a career in a phrase that echoes the ad copy for a dishwashing liquid ("If you are looking for softer hands, go ahead and try ...").

The composite Sandy and Mary Cunningham and Sandra Brown are all stage-one achieving-woman casualties, with uncertain hope of ever gaining recognition for what they do. Under her picture in the September 14, 1981, *Newsweek* article on "Women and the Executive Suite," Cunningham is said to be "battling against gossip and preparing for the worst." The treatment these women received from the press and, to a significant degree, their own lack of sophistication and exposure to the manipulating power of mass media have placed them among the sacrificial lambs of women achievers. But successful women executives are not about to fade as media heroines when the story mix is right, nor can they give interviews from behind screens or with bags over their heads to prevent biological identification and the application of the Bo Derek rating system.

The women we interviewed, who had been the subjects of media exposure, were well on the way to developing new insights and skills about handling the media and its effect on their personal and professional lives. Some had decided to limit future articles because the fallout within their firms (such as male resentment) and calls from outside sources (such as requests to be speakers or mentors) had become more prevalent than any benefits accrued from publicity. Some said they had also received mail from disturbing sources, including mail from convicts, and one woman found several marriage proposals amid her correspondence. Like many a politician before them, these women had learned the chagrin of being misquoted or misinterpreted. It is here that Sandra Brown's case must be recalled, for some of our interviewees had also experienced having their achievements overblown and were constantly paying the price of being looked upon as superwomen. Some women had been in the news long enough to feel that their early exposure placed them in the position of being yesterday's story. They wondered about the impression of readers who knew only of their beginnings, but not what they had made of their opportunities. And how many stories does one ever see about the *second* woman to hold some position in management?

Many of the women spoke of having taken stands within their companies on how much time they would agree to spend in external activities, while others risked disfavor by making it clear they would not be used as public-relations icons. This was particularly true for two women from a major consumer-products company in the Midwest. The company, which has only one woman in management, and that position being out of the power mainstream, is now involved in a push to sell their products to the emerging woman's market. To exhibit the company's interest in women, the single management woman and another woman who holds a lower-level job were sent to a national woman's meeting as representatives from the firm. The presence of these two women, the firm hoped, would be prima facie evidence of the affirmative action of the company. In reality, the futures of these two women were virtually nil within the organizational structure. But apart from the motives of their employer, these two women felt the crunch of being used. Not to go to the meeting would obviously result in a confrontation which could cost them their jobs. On the other hand, participation in this ruse, they believed, made them accomplices to a misrepresentation.

There are other signs that women are becoming more aware of the pitfalls of fame and of the statements they can make in the public eye to change the awareness of others. In 1979, Rosalyn Yalow, winner of the Nobel Prize for Science, refused a *Ladies'*

Home Journal Woman of the Year Award by saying that it was "inconsistent and unwise to have rewards restricted to women or men in fields where excellence is not inherently sex-related." She urged all women to shun awards which fail to "distinguish between women of achievement and the wives of men of achievement."[8]

Sexism in Reruns—Some Thoughts About TV

No assessment of the media impact on the image of workingwomen would be complete without some commentary on the contributions to confusion made by television. Despite the fact that the number of workingwomen in America now exceeds the number which stay at home, television continues to present programming which operates under outdated statistics. Amy Orrick, in her article "The Success and Failure of Working Women in Television," monitored a composite week on prime-time television, recording occupational information for 279 television characters. She found 72 percent of the men characters versus 44 percent of the women were employed. Sixty percent of the women versus 36 percent of the men worked under supervision. "Believe it or not," Orrick concludes, "in ten years this ratio has not changed."[9]

A parable, of sorts, can be found in the long-running *Mary Tyler Moore Show,* for Mary's career rise (if it can be so labeled) took place within the 1970s, when the issues of workingwomen were enjoying their greatest media attention. Mary and the women around her reflected much of the reality gap in the presentation of the achieving woman.

Mary Richards was the princess but never the queen of the newsroom. The situations she confronted in various episodes included: lying on her résumé about having a college degree, fighting for the same pay as her male predecessor, fixing up her boss with dates, and becoming the fantasy wife of the three major male characters. Though Mary occasionally rose to mild anger and once even came close to slugging a chauvinist, on the whole she was sweet and forgiving. She put herself last, and because she did, she appeared to be nice. The audience liked that niceness in her.

Mary always reacted and responded. She was not an innovator.

Her only moment of professional glory came when she was jailed for refusing to identify a source, but she diffused this distinction by deciding to rescue and reform the prostitute with whom she had shared a cell.

Mary always called her boss Mr. Grant, eliciting from him a sweet, if strained, fatherly response. He never acted in mentorial fashion and on those occasions when Mary asked for more responsibility, he handed her tasks that were singularly unpleasant. When Mary took charge of a project, she produced, by her own admission, "the dullest documentary ever made."

Rhoda worked, but primarily at finding a husband and battling fat. She was assertive, in a New York sort of way, and eventually moved back to the Big Apple, where this trait would be less obvious. But when Rhoda found love and then lost it, she lost a great portion of her audience as well. She was scripted into being a divorced career woman whose weekly efforts centered on dumping the latest drippy date. The mix was too nontraditional to garner viewer loyalty and support. Social changes always have to wait awhile for their constituencies to catch up.

Phyllis was a prig and a phony who found herself a reentry woman by virtue of her husband's death. Once in her own show, she became another character whose situation could not sustain audience identification and interest. Even reentry women must have found it hard to relate to a woman who moved in with her in-laws in a comfy San Francisco town house.

And, of course, there was Georgette, the fluffy Kewpie doll whose love for the hapless Ted offered the model of the woman who stood behind her man. As dumb and as dull as he was, she worshiped him. As subservient and empty-headed as she often appeared to be, there was always a hint that she was the brains of the duo.

Mary's true alter ego, however, was Sue-Ann, the viper chef and TV hostess whose appetites for both sex and food were voracious. On the surface, Sue-Ann was a traditional woman. She cooked. She sewed. She knitted and gave household advice. She always smiled, even when she was at her viper best or worst. She was not the least bit hesitant about asking for raises, top billing, and creative control of her show. She used up directors like Handi-Wipes and chewed out the crew without a thought for her feminine image. Sue-Ann was portrayed as a misfit; she was the butt of ridicule and sometimes was begrudged sympathy by her colleagues, and by extension the audience. The value judgment transmitted across the screen was that Mary was good, whereas Sue-Ann was bad.

An annual episode in this series revolved around the local television awards dinner and it is here that the attitudes toward women's achievements were communicated with the intensity of a morality play. Mary can never seem to make it through these events. She sabotages herself in front of her peers. Her hairdo falls down, her ankle gets sprained, her eyelashes disappear. At the moment when her contributions are about to be recognized, Mary is made to look a fool. This may be fine comedy, but underneath the laughter is the implication that Mary is afraid or incapable of real success.

The Achieving Woman—Traits and Situations

"Women have been ambitious ever since Eve," a management consultant told us. "It was Eve who wanted to risk for the sake of knowledge and bite the apple. Adam was content to sit back and do nothing but follow the rules. Of course, they lost everything, but Eve ought to be acknowledged as the consummate risk-taker she really was." This comment brings us to another part of the problem women have in getting their achievements recognized.

There is the impression from all that one sees, hears, and reads in the media that women have made it; and there is the quantitative reality of women's growing presence in the work force. But there is also increasing evidence that women remain grossly underrepresented at the higher levels of virtually every occupation. Since American society tends to operate on the premise that opportunities are now greater for women, there is a swelling chorus within corporate America which attributes women's relative lack of progress to their lesser ambitions and lack of managerial traits. Women, so this faction says, are either genetically incapable of high-level managerial activity, or as a result of their socialization process, have developed behavior patterns which are incongruous with those demanded in an executive position.

Studies and articles abound that analyze the traits vital for those who aspire to upper-management positions. Other research work has examined the qualities that make up the managerial style. Most of these studies agree that what is needed is a blend of people and task-focus. Identified as a key element of style is the ability of a manager to motivate other employees. There is universal agreement that management is a dependency activity—that is, a manager must depend on other people to get the job done. Throughout all of the research that has been done, there is, as yet, no evidence which makes a case for sex differences in either leadership aptitude or leadership style. In fact, the findings indicate that men and women vary in ability over the same range and that there are no conclusive sex-related advantages. Given all the data on traits, skills, and styles, it seems logical and obvious to conclude that women are at least as well-suited to management as are men. So why aren't they there?

The answer has three distinct components.

The skills and traits required for management are perceived to be male characteristics. This perception exemplifies the very tricky cultural tendency to give gender labels to things which do not inherently have gender. Once something like a characteristic has a gender, the societal inclination is to assume that all members of that gender possess the characteristic. This exercise in nondifferentiation, when it occurs on a national or ethnic scale, produces things like racial discrimination and Polish jokes. So even though the research verdict finds women in possession of managerial traits, in the same proportion as men, the truth has not set women free in the marketplace because the marketplace lacks a genuine point of reference. Until recently, women have displayed their managerial abilities in a different arena. Being a successful motivator of people in the office and getting the kids to do their homework are not seen as the same thing, though both require a considerable motivating skill. Men have been credited with motivating people in the work environment for such a long time that this particular skill has been assigned as a male-gender trait.

Research data also show that when an incongruence exists between someone's sex and job role, the disparity can be tolerated only when that individual is significantly overqualified. The end result of gender-trait assignments leaves men and women operating under the impression that managerial jobs require typically male characteristics, hence, women are inappropriate for those jobs unless they are overqualified.

The circuitous nature of trait assignments is also highlighted in studies which seek to identify "ability trait models." The premise of developing such models is that one way to identify the people who may have potential is to compare them with people of proven high ability. High achievers are assumed to be those in the corporation who are moving up and making it. Since women are not well-represented among the ranks of the upwardly mobile, the assumption is that they lack the ability to make it.

The second root of the problem is attribution. The expectations which revolve around the success of women are historically negative and are based on the assumption that women are missing certain traits. When confronted by a successful woman, the tendency of many is to attribute that success to factors other than her abilities—things like hard work, the ease of the job, or the ever-whimsical element, luck. In all of our interviews with both men and women, these three reasons were constantly given as explanations of women's achievements. Some of the women we interviewed, in fact, bragged about how hard they worked. Several invoked the observations of the first woman mayor of Ottawa, Canada: "Women have to work twice as hard to be thought half as good as a man, but luckily that is not too difficult." Yet working twice as hard and being twice as good *is* difficult when one has no clear idea of what hard work means in the organizational context or what constitutes the baseline definition of good.

A by-product of differential attribution is that a woman's performance tends to be praised disproportionately. Some minor achievement is viewed as "incredible" because the expectation of what a woman can do is so low. The same grade of performance in a man goes unremarked because it is taken for granted that men can accomplish so much more.

Attributing women's performance in a job to hard work, ease of the job, or luck relegates them into a lesser organizational reward system. A performance review will recognize diligence and high production through some sort of merit pay increase. On the other hand, promotion is a more common reward when success is attributed to ability and its sister quality, potential. "Them that has

gets," as the saying goes, and therein lies the closing arc in the circle of attribution.

Within industry, there is a pattern of promotion for women
which differs noticeably from the pattern for men. Women generally have to somehow prove they can do a new job before they
are even considered for it, while men are promoted on the basis of
their perceived potential. This staging quality of achievement for
women means that by the time they are promoted to a new job,
they are usually ready and qualified for the job above it. The promotion of women also carries, in the minds of those who operate
under gender-trait assumptions, a higher element of risk. The
"cover my ass" nature of midmanagement organizational behavior
is to delay or diffuse risky decisions. However, promoting or hiring someone for an executive position is a risk not easily delayed
and one nearly impossible to diffuse. It is too important and public
a decision to be hidden under a bushel. The underrepresentation
of women in mid- and upper-management levels is nothing less
than a commentary on the dearth of organizational gamblers. Few
are willing to wager in favor of a woman—an unknown quan-
tity—the long-standing fiction that a man is more likely to have
what it takes to do the job.

The third clue in the mystery of the missing managerial woman
lies in the composition of the jury deciding her fate. Common law
calls for a person to be tried by his or her peers, but women, and
their behavior in the corporate setting, are judged on the peerage
of male standards. Positive proof of women's ability to perform is
always subject to this skewed criterion and to the two-tiered measure of all of women's achievements. As stated before, what a
woman does is not yet separable from the fact that a woman is
doing it. And if she succeeds, her achievements will thrust her
away from other women. She will be anointed a star or superwoman. This gender-trait assignment system renders virtually
every woman in management an exception to the stereotyped view
that women have lesser ambitions and abilities.

For women, this standard creates a double bind. When a woman
is employed at lower levels within a company, she is part of an
anonymous and powerless group. When she reaches the top, the
executive woman stands out from the group—she is different from
other women; she is different from her male peers. Frequently

these top women are lulled into believing that they are judged only on the basis of how they perform as managers. This is not so. Women can never escape being judged, at least in part, on the basis of their behavior as women.

However, a new body of data asserts that it is the characteristics of the organizational situation, rather than individual traits and skills, which define individual behavior on the job. Rosabeth Kanter and others have shown that the factors of being an organizational oddity, in a job with no power and little likelihood of leading anywhere, has more to do with influencing behavior and performance than any real or assumed gender or personal traits.

As one of our male interviewees commented:

> In many large organizations, and mine would have to be included, the brightest women, when they are given top-management positions, are being put on display. The ulterior motive of the company is to say to women—"Look, here is a woman V.P. of Marketing or whatever. If you do as well as she did, you can attain the same." That is tokenism.

A consultant we interviewed described a client experience she had had with division managers in a marketing firm. Her findings substantiate the effects of the environment on individual behavior—both male and female.

> There was only one woman manager in the group. The interviews I conducted focused on each person's present job, past job history, and perceptions of future mobility. The attitudes of the managers toward themselves, the organization, the management of the organization, and toward their job options directly reflected the power and opportunity they perceived for themselves. The woman echoed the classic symptoms and attitudes of a token, but most striking to me was the similarity between her responses and that of one other male. His job was in an area peripheral to the company's main business. It was an important job, but its importance was linked to maintenance and ongoing satisfactory performance. The quality of this job means that this man would be noticed within the company only if something went wrong. The woman manager's job could be described in much the same way. Both of these individuals were bored, demotivated, angry at management, and thinking of leaving, but for the moment they were stuck. It was clear to me that the situations which they were in had far more to do with determining their behavior than did their individual levels of competence and characteristics. The structural determinants, in this case, were truly gender-free.

Many of the early books aimed at the workingwoman audience approached the concerns and issues these women faced (or would face) in the context of traits and characteristics. But in time, as women accrued more work experience, many became aware that their problems were, at once, more simple and more complex than these early theories foresaw. Beyond the black-and-white pronouncements on which skills to acquire and which to divest, beyond the cut-and-dried dicta and game strategies, was the growing realization that the mobility of women in management was subject to a matrix, not a laundry list, of factors.

A matrix is a crosshatch of columns created by listing one set of items down the Y axis and another set across the top of the X axis. Each of the squares in a column is called a cell, and it is within these cells, where any two elements converge, that the origins of a problem can be identified with precision and clarity. The matrix allows cause and effect to be lifted from the one-dimensional frame. Each cell is a window which offers a far better view of what is happening than do lists, which isolate one factor from another. The value of the matrix approach for women is twofold. First, it supports the valid theory that hierarchical barriers, not missing traits, are frequently responsible for women's lack of mobility. This knowledge should serve to assuage the self-doubt which has put women in the second-class, catch-up mode. Second, for whatever consolation it brings, the matrix shows that these barriers can and do exist for men, although men as a group will not suffer the generalized negative assumptions as to performance and ability that are applied to women. In the example provided by the consultant, the male manager who was stuck did not disprove the ability of all men to make it in the company. The woman manager was not only individually in a hopeless situation, but carried with her reinforcing evidence that few women could succeed in the company.

The System Is the Solution

In large measure, the problem for women in corporations is no longer one of entry. Across a wide spectrum of industries today, women tend to be fairly well represented at entry-level positions. Many of these women have recently been promoted from secretarial or technical positions, and have often been with their companies for several years. *The reality is that these women will not progress much farther in the hierarchy.* The basis for this prediction is the rarity of women currently in top management who started at the bottom and worked their way up. This is in sharp contrast to the Horatio Alger quotient for men. A full 25 percent of the men interviewed in one marketing firm by a woman consultant had begun their careers as office boys or at other equivalent low-level jobs. Despite Affirmative Action and changes in social roles for women, the chances are slim that any woman could duplicate the rise of a John deButts. He retired in 1979 as the chairman of the board of American Telephone and Telegraph, the world's largest company, having begun his career with the firm as a telephone installer.

On the other hand, many women now at midmanagement levels of companies have been hired from outside their firms and come to their jobs with experience and/or credentials. A significant portion of this group hold M.B.A. degrees. It may well be too early to predict the future for these women, but there are a few trends we noted in our interviews and research.

Women remain clustered in a limited number of areas within a company, areas usually designated as "soft." In addition, women's corporate exposure to varied experiences is constricted. They do not move freely from one area to another. Down the line this limited experience and peripheral work history are bound to affect their organizational mobility.

Another trend has grown out of the legislative mandate for corporations to hire women officers and the subsequent creation of a new, but meaningless set of titles. Until the infusion of women into management, the bestowing of corporate titles represented rewards for long service or high performance. They also signaled future upward mobility within the hierarchy. The titles held by many women today sound impressive, but win no greater honor or respect than dime-store trophies. Arm in arm with the bestowing of devalued titles has been the discounting of women's competence. The effect that these titles have had on organizations is, in some ways, amusing. The lists of officers in many firms read like the roster in a Keystone Cop army! If gold braid were appropriately applied, as suggested by title, few managers would be able to wear their uniforms sitting up.

A woman in accounting told us of her interview for a job in which the hiring partner explained how the company was looking for "a female vice-president in the next few years." She turned the job down out of fear that if another woman got to be the female vice-president before she did, she would have little future with the firm. They would already have had their one, first, woman.

Being on the receiving end of these titles has had, for more than one ambitious woman, a very seductive appeal. But since these titles represent no change in the division of the company's power pie, the women who bear them are subjects to imagistic duplicity. Outside the company, they are not the superwomen achievers they appear to be. Inside the company, they are seen as part of a facade and are credited with neither power nor credibility.

When a traffic jam occurs and cars are not rerouted, a tremendous backup is created; this is essentially the situation for women in corporate America today. Unless the barriers to mobility are removed or other changes made to reroute the flow of women into corporate hierarchies, American business, already faced with a severe productivity and market-share decline, will be further frustrated by a human-resources crisis.

The Unambitious Female—
Getting Rid of a Bad Statistical Reputation

While society's fickle values make a concrete definition of success hard to come by, social scientists have never shied away from their belief that one can measure an individual's potential for succeeding. The massive influx of women into the work force sent countless sociologists into the field, armed with good intentions, to monitor this seismic event. The goal of most of these early studies was to detect any differences that might exist between the ambition levels of men and women. The problem was that the preponderant number of these surveys was necessarily constructed on rather shaky foundations.

By reasoning that the achievements of men (and only some men at that) could be used as a measuring standard, researchers had placed somewhat narrow boundaries around what were considered appropriate levels of ambition. The ambitions of women were then measured on the basis of whether or not they fell within those boundaries. Predictably, women always fell short of the mark. For what most of these studies failed to take into account was that the external rewards for men and women were different, even if the amount of energy expended in the pursuit of a goal had been the same. By insisting that ambitions could be measured by filling out questionnaires, researchers ignored the basic premise of their behavioral modification fellows: that rewards must be consistent to guarantee the desired effect. By further ignoring the variable of social attitudes, which were out to sabotage the ambitions of women before they even put the key in their Drive ignitions, these studies were doomed. Unfortunately, since they carried the imprimatur of science, the findings became accepted as fact.

Most of these studies reported only that women exhibited lesser aspirations than did men, but this verbiage gave rise to a problem of syntax. Aspirations are not necessarily ambitions, nor is being credited with the potential for success an accurate indicator. What kept getting measured were the fragmentary parts of male and female energies—portions of external actions, but not necessarily the passions behind them.

So how do you tell if someone is ambitious?

President Reagan is seen as ambitious because you don't get elected to that office without having a lot of ambition. Society measures ambition, then, by the outward symbols of achievement. A person's title or position or level of power is accepted as a behavioral clue that ambition is present in that individual. The studies which purported to measure aspirations were operating on the psychological plane, but society measures ambition by looking at achievements. So when women were denied the rewards of achievement, when discrimination and cultural lag kept them out of the executive suite, the formal measures used by researchers clashed with the informal measures applied by society to gauge success. As a participant in the study of *Achievement Among Minority Americans* noted: "Achievement may too often be defined by the person who has the power as what you have to do to rise up to where he is."[10]

The reputation which women have acquired of being less ambitious than men does seem to rest on the question of whose criteria are being used to make such an accounting. Perseverance, patience, stick-to-itiveness, and determination certainly appear to qualify as measures of ambition. And if anyone has had to exhibit these qualities, it is the women who have made it even as far as the middle-management ranks.

Change in our time can only be a step toward preparing our daughters and our daughter's daughters
to think and act in new ways.

MARGARET MEAD
Aspects of the Present

3

The Ageist Woman

To call someone ageist is to imply that his or her attitudes about
people reflect a chronological or generational prejudice. But to the
extent that each of us carries around a set of age-linked concepts
and beliefs, we can conclude that ours is an ageist society.

In her book *Culture and Commitment* Margaret Mead developed the concept of three levels of culture. A society in which
elders carried the total imprint for future generations, she termed
Postfigurative. In a Configurative culture, each generation learns
from both its parents and its peers. Mead asserted that our society
had moved into a third and more revolutionary stage of culture,
which she named Prefigurative. In this type of society, the links to
the past are broken. Every generation learns from its children. "In
this sense," Mead admonished, "we must recognize that we have
no descendants, as our children have no forebears."[1]

As a subset of the society as a whole, workingwomen find their
attitudes defined, and both their personal and professional lives
affected, by the emergence of a Prefigurative culture. Alliances between the generations of workingwomen, which would seem natural and effective, have fallen apart in a recreation of the cliché
"generation gap." The imprints of the past do not serve as models

for the future, while the fallout from present-day choices has yet to be felt. Every woman we interviewed, no matter her age, expressed the opinion that she was somewhat trapped in time. In older women there was a wistful musing and envy of the young, mixed with a longing for things that might have been. In the young, there was both anticipation and a feeling of isolation. No one denied that change was all around, but none was deluded that utopia was at hand.

Crisis and Crunch Points

An instructor of young women students at a metropolitan business college begins every semester with a special assignment. Each of her students is asked to select a woman whose life or career serves as a model for the student's own dreams and goals. A time line or continuum, based on the achievements of the model, is drawn. The student must choose, from her own perceptions, the turning points in the life of her subject. The instructor devised this exercise based on her belief that women need to have a heightened sensitivity to such points in their own lives.

Until recently, the life continuums of men and women have been drawn along two sets of milestones. For men, the continuum was marked chronologically. The passage of each decade was supposed to connote certain expected achievements. Chapter Three of Herb Goldberg's book *The New Male* is entitled, "Alive at 20, A Machine at 30, Burned out by 40." The model for women has been quite different. It was charted by events such as marriage, the birth of children, graduations, grandchildren, menopause, and the like. What the women's movement has succeeded in doing is to combine the male and female continuums, and to present women with the challenge of doing it all. But the combination of the traditional and the new has served to double the prospects for gains and losses. Women are finding that there are as many chances to make mistakes as there are real opportunities. Consider the "New Model Continuum."

The New Model Continuum is the flow chart for the popular theory among women that they can have it all. It must be remembered, however, that this new model has emerged only in the last ten years. It has not been lived out to its conclusion by those who are a part of this revolution in the culture. Even those relatively few women pioneers, now in their fifties and sixties, who chose to live out the combined continuum, are not realistic models for women in their twenties. Each step forward has offered new challenges, but it has also tended to grind under its heels the answers which served in the past.

This is the price of a Prefigurative culture: the loss of guidelines and guideposts, the uncertainty of change. Each succeeding generation has redrawn the major points of emphasis and thereby shifted all the outcomes along the continuum. The woman of forty looks not to the woman of fifty, but to the thirty-year-old. And thirty-year-olds find themselves in the front lines of change without historical reference points. Women of all ages experience fear and anger. The older woman may feel her entire life experience has been devalued. The younger woman feels she has no one to turn to who has been there before her.

Dickens' *A Christmas Carol* is famous for the passages which describe the visitation upon Scrooge of ghosts from the past. Some of the older women we interviewed had already experienced these types of visitations; younger women had a hint that they might soon arrive. For all the women, the ghosts had three distinct faces: The Ghost of Careers Past, The Ghost of Relationships Past, and The Ghost of Children Past.

The Ghosts of Careers Past

The classic philosophical question posed by those who advocate equal opportunities for women is, "Do you know what benefits society might have had if women had been encouraged to work and contribute?" There is, of course, no definite answer, but it is reasonable to assume at least one unclaimed Nobel prize. On a lesser scale, there have been untold numbers of smaller successes lost to the machinery of free enterprise. For the women we interviewed, all of whom had jobs, if not careers, the measure of benefit was not one of all or nothing, but of degrees. Many comments indicated that the fault lay in garbled messages about a woman's place in the scheme of things, her role as opposed to her dreams. A message delivered to University of Minnesota graduates in 1959 (women who would now be in their forties) struck the tone for those who preceded the Feminine Mystique of the early 1960s and its aftermath. Advertising woman Sally Gibson told the graduating class:

> I'm not a career woman, I am a woman. It is because I am a woman that I have a career. You are hired because you are a woman. If they wanted a man they would have hired one. Don't slip out of your high heels and clobber around in a pair of brogues too big and too tough to fill. Stay in your I. Miller's, kids. Be sure they are pretty and fill them well and you will do better than you ever dreamed.[2]

Sally told it like it used to be. For women in her day, every career message had a second edge which cut to the essence of being a woman—above all, be a lady. From our interviews with women between forty and sixty years of age, it was easy to identify examples of mixed messages and the havoc they caused. A sixty-year-old retail-store manager provided a litany of confusion:

> Any woman can do and get out of any man in any situation. She doesn't have to put a man down. Deballing is not necessary. There is always more than one way to skin a cat. Let him be what he is. Without him life is going to be pretty dull. One area where I do believe women should be on an equal basis with men in business is in salary. If a woman produces and performs the same job as well as a man, she should get the same money he does. But this ERA and Ms. business repels me because I'm a woman and I want to remain a woman. I want to be known as a woman. And if I'm a married woman, I want to be called Mrs., not Ms. I want my designation. Why be neuter gender inside your own sex?

A woman with four children (now in their late teens and early twenties) began the process several years back of going for a Ph.D. She has since become vice-president of a major high-technology firm. "The problem I had goes back to the early days when I decided to return to school. I lived in a typically Midwestern Ohio suburban neighborhood where everyone said, 'It's okay to get an education, but for God's sakes don't use it.'"

Another woman, now in her late forties, talked about a ghost imprint which causes her to flinch at large social business functions:

I am very shy and I think that goes back to what I was taught about being a woman. I absolutely dread going to cocktail parties for the company where I may know three people out of a hundred. I was taught that women do not go to parties alone, let alone as businesswomen. And when you get there, if you speak before you are spoken to, you are probably looking for something that a good girl should not be looking for.

Then there were strong and exclusionary messages centered around the choice of a career:

About twenty-five years ago, I used to read the want ads. I would jump from one job to another because I needed to make more money. I saw that draftsmen made a lot more money than secretaries, so I went to a drafting school and made an application, only to be told that women were not accepted into drafting school. I never became a draftsman, nor did I go on to become an engineer, though I know I would have been good at it.

Old hat, you say? Everyone knows that women were discriminated against, not encouraged to work in a man's world? On the surface this seems to be so, but there is danger in believing that our culture is over that hump entirely. One woman we interviewed commented: "The difference between the generations of yesterday and today is that the messages are getting clearer." This led us to wonder if she was correct, or if one set of garbled messages had risen up to take the place of the old. One method of testing for an answer was to analyze the remarks of our interviewees by age to see when, if, and how the messages had changed.

We started by looking for clues about education, since many women believe that there are no longer any holds barred or obstacles remaining for women there. But take these two comments, from women now in their thirties, as a hint of lingering ghosts.

I was the only woman who ever graduated from my school without an education course. Every year the guidance counselor called me in and said that there must be some mistake in my transcript. I kept telling him that there was no mistake and he would counter with "But what will you fall back on?" I told him that it never entered my mind that I would fall.

Another woman, representative of those in school during the turbulent 1960s, only a few years after Friedan's *Feminine Mystique*, said:

The worst piece of advice I ever got was at college. My guidance counselor told me to go on in liberal arts and forget business. This was
pretty easy advice to take given the social consciousness of the day. I
was married the week after I received my B.A. and went to work in the
city jail system.

And where parents, guidance counselors, and cultural taboos
failed to penetrate, there were always peer pressures to direct
career goals. A woman now thirty-five and an executive in banking
remarked: "In the late sixties, business was considered revolting. I
couldn't have held my head up in my sorority if I had admitted I
was interested in business. I went to school for six years and still
came out as a bank teller."
Recent studies of intended majors of college women indicate
that, in spite of widely publicized gluts in certain occupations,
massive unemployment in teaching and social services and increasing opportunities in scientific, business, and technical areas,
women are still overwhelmingly seeking degrees in the traditional
"helping" professions. A group of women college seniors who appeared in early 1981 on *The Today Show* evidenced no better understanding of the life choices they faced than did their mothers or
grandmothers. One young woman assured Jane Pauley that if she
left the show to have a child, NBC executives would be sure to
hold Pauley's job for as long as three years. Jane did not appear
persuaded.
But if attention to an issue is based on percentages, women at
midlife, who comprise the largest segment of the adult female population, represent the most prevalent group experiencing the
career-versus-family decision crunch. The anguish of finding oneself at the end of what was thought to be a lifetime contract can be
felt as much by a woman who married her job as a woman facing
divorce or widowhood. For the career woman facing eventual retirement, as well as the woman facing the end of her wife/mother
role, the crunch is loss of identity and loss of security.

The Ghosts of Relationships Past

It was not so long ago that an unmarried woman was a social out-
cast. Those who had become divorced or widowed were somewhat

less marked, but they were still relegated to a misplaced step in time. For these women, there was less choice about work because there was economic necessity. The cultural efficacy of the institution of marriage has been under considerable attack in the past few decades. Many young women are choosing to delay marriage in favor of a career, or not to marry at all. At one level there is a superficial social acceptance of the validity of their choice. But at another level it is clear that the ghosts of relationships past haunt those women who have entered midlife as singles. It is not only the trappings of tradition which haunt, it is a special kind of loneliness that appears more shattering to them the farther into the future they look. A woman in her early forties, executive vice-president of a major corporation, expressed her feelings by saying:

> When I am involved in something exciting in the company, I have no one to go home to with my feelings. I fear this loneliness. I fear I will never have anyone in my life. This is the fall social season. I am invited to all of the fancy parties, the opera, the symphony, because of my position, but I will not go without an appropriate escort and my options are increasingly limited.

On the other hand, women who continue through midlife as homemakers find themselves having to defend their choice. As one woman said: "Everyone thinks I'm dumb and couldn't do anything else. Many of my contemporaries are all swimming around trying to find themselves. I found myself and they make me feel guilty about what I found."

For the mature woman who chose to attempt both marriage and a career, the messages of society made it clear that any additional responsibilities assumed outside the home were solely her own and were not to affect the workload of duties to husband and children. And yet there must be extremists on the end of every issue who set the outer limits and define the common ground. One woman told us that she was currently married to her third husband because he was more suitable as a mate for someone in her position and with her goals. About the previous marriages she commented:

> When I was about twenty-seven, I decided that my life was going nowhere. I had been married to Roger for four years and all he wanted from me was to join the country club and have babies. It was at that point I decided a career was more important to me. So, even though I liked him a lot, I told him it wasn't going to work out long term and divorced him. The first time I married was when I was right out of

high school and really didn't know what I was doing, so that one really doesn't count. We were divorced after seven months. I've learned that for me it is easier to get a husband than it is to get a good job.

Compare this attitude with that of a woman some thirty years older: "There is nothing I want. I never wanted to be tops in my field. My husband was *número uno* and my job was second. Women should remain women. Men should be masculine."

For some older women, it has become fashionable to reverse the pairing of older men and younger women. The older woman/ younger man syndrome has warranted an entire book on the subject. *People* magazine ran an interview with a woman in her sixties who has become an outspoken advocate of such pairings.[3] The article came complete with photos of famous women who had dated or married men many years their junior. The primary genesis of these couples lies in the fact that older career women cannot find men of their own generation who accept them as successful working peers. One woman banker who has dated younger men since her divorce told us: "I laugh at myself that I am having a harder time accepting the age difference than they are. Someday, I hope to be able to stop feeling this way and learn to sit back and enjoy."

The pairing of older women with younger men is related to another trend we heard about: the pairing of successful, well-educated women with less-educated men in lower-level jobs. A marketing consultant in her early thirties said that she dated a young construction worker because "What I did was so alien to him that I was never a threat to his ego." The common thread in both these trends is the complete break with traditional patterns. Such a break makes it possible for these women to change the traditional power relationships they found destructive.

The Ghosts of Children Past

These are, perhaps, the most amorphous of all the visiting spirits because those women who are now choosing not to have children have yet to reach the age of reflection. Of the middle-aged women we talked to, those who made such decisions seemed to feel that they had missed something in life, but they were uncertain about the origins of this feeling. The consensus was that a sense of loss was generated as much from a conflict with cultural values as from the price paid in loneliness for their choice.

A woman of forty-six said: "I'm not so sure that I made a mistake in not marrying, but last year it hit me that I would never have a child of my own and I find that painful."

A recent best-seller for workingwomen in the 20–35 age range was *Up Against the Clock.*[4] The book examined the biological pressures which women face at a certain chronological point when the decision to have or not to have a child must be made. Our system of child care certainly gives no solace or aid in this decision, and the reordering of male parenting responsibilities is in its infancy. Accompanying the biological pressures are the realities of corporate life, which dictate the cost of interrupting a career climb. Less obvious are the generational conflicts which arise in the work place. As one woman noted:

> A woman who is fifty years old and at a senior management level doesn't worry about pregnancy. Many have lost touch with the urgency and anguish over this problem. Their indifference cuts them off from communications in several areas with younger women in the company, who are really concerned about what will happen when and if they take maternity leave. Since men in corporations do not face this problem at all, younger women find themselves with virtually no support or sympathy.

Several of the younger women we talked to had chosen to fill their lives with "alternative motherhood experiences." These included the "mothering" of nieces, nephews, and children of friends, volunteer teaching, participation in Big Sister programs, and lavishing attention on household pets. It remains to be seen if such substitutions will suffice for those women in later years. The question is a poignant one.

No one has really explored the link between parenting and a career woman's ability to enjoy her success. One middle-aged woman mused that society gives more leeway to men in turning out bad apples than it does women, since parenting is still considered the primary responsibility of the mother. Reflecting on her decision, some twenty-five years ago, to combine children and a career, she told us:

> I have enjoyed my own success, but if I am to be honest, I must admit that the ultimate satisfaction that I have with where I am in life is

directly related to my relationship with my husband and kids. A real high at the office can be ruined if one of the kids has a problem or if my husband and I fight. Conversely, nothing sets me up as much as a good interaction with my children. It is as though, in spite of everything I am and know and have achieved, I still judge myself on how well my kids turned out.

It is not difficult to see the origins of this link between the success of mothers and their children. Middle-aged women can recall the speculation of neighbors and friends that the children of a working mother would somehow be deprived and neglected. But tides do turn. That same woman who faced gossip and innuendo twenty-five years ago has lived through sufficient cultural change to find herself inundated by the onetime gossips with requests to "make me a career woman in two easy lessons."

The issue of children provides an excellent barometer of overall cultural mobility and of changing values. The Department of Labor has predicted that the number of working mothers in the labor force in the next decade and a half will be directly proportional to that number who can find appropriate child care. This issue will simply not go away. As the mother of a ten-year-old asserted: "Without having found a solution to the day-care problem, the only option left to us is to stop having children, at which point society comes to a screeching halt." Her words made the ghost of children past seem an ominous specter, indeed.

Arsenic and Old Lace

The most widely acknowledged and regrettable result of age ghettoization among workingwomen is the failure to create natural alliances between experienced and emerging women in corporations. Nowhere did our research reveal a better example of the unsettling nature of a Prefigurative culture than in this particular generation gap. It is as though the generations of women were running a marathon. The older women are out in front because they started the race first. By all the rules, they should be the winners. But at some point along the way, they find themselves being passed, first by one generation, then another, even though each succeeding group had a later starting time. Finally, what we observe is a cultural field that has been totally reversed. The late starters are leading the pack. The problem is, they are unaware of where the milestones are on the course. The culture did not tell them because it was assumed that each generation would follow the trail of those ahead of them. For younger women, this reversed field has forced them to create their own milestones. But the finish line is obscure and feelings are running high. As Elizabeth Cady Stanton once said of midlife women:

> We, who like the children of Israel have been wandering in the wilderness of prejudice and ridicule for 40 years, are being made to feel we should hold a certain tenderness for the young women on whose shoulders we are about to leave our burden.[5]

Images of "the queen bee" and "the impatient young" colored many of the responses in our interviews. "The queen bee" is the usual designation given the rare woman who made it in management long before the woman's movement arrived. She generally believes her position is the result of luck or personal characteristics, or a combination of both. In any case, she feels, justifiably, that her success was a struggle for which she paid a high personal price. She tends to view younger women as having different or lesser values and often resents the advantages they seem to have had. The younger women feel the rejection of older women acutely and, despite attempts to be sympathetic, cannot seem to rid themselves of negative judgments, born out of their sense of loss. These comments were typical:

> The portfolio manager here is in her forties and she will have nothing to do with the rest of us. You do have a generation gap. It would be unrealistic to think otherwise. You have younger women being so optimistic and thinking that the world is out there for them to take. This naturally brings resentment on the part of older women.

> I'm very sensitive to the needs of older women because when I was first starting out in women's organizations, I went to older women first, women whom I considered to have status in the community. I said, "Look, we need your leadership and support." Nine times out of ten, I was told, "No. Why should I help you? I did it on my own." I guess they looked at me as a young upstart, getting a lot of rewards for doing much less than they thought they had done. Maybe that is true.

Back in Chicago, I met a few women who had worked their way up through the ranks and they were bitter about the young women moving up. I had a hard time understanding them. But they are probably still there and still feeling the same.

The comments from older women were typified by these remarks:

The opportunities here are for women in their twenties and thirties, but for women in their forties and older, it's another question. This is a youth-oriented business. Because I am older, I feel I have to be better than men and younger women as well. Young women have opportunities coming out of their ears today that I never had when I was twenty.

If I knew today what young people do, I could be the general manager of my company. If I had read a book like *Games Mother Never Taught You* when I was twenty, I'd be at the top of the heap. You know, I've never told anybody that.

There have been mixed messages for women of my age. We were told our place was in the home. Young women know, because of things like Affirmative Action and advertising campaigns, exactly what their choices are. They know they have the options of either working or staying at home, or any combination thereof. They have it a whole lot easier than me, or even the generation behind me.

On the surface, these comments reflect the dismal possibility that the difference between generations will always be so opposite as to cause a predictable breakdown of communications. In the wider cultural perspective, especially if a society is operating under Prefigurative conditions, such a possibility does seem inevitable. But workingwomen can bridge some of these cultural gaps by replacing ageist attitudinal barriers with support and understanding.

The major ageist fallacy which appears as a recurrent theme is the perception by older women that succeeding generations of women have more opportunities and fewer problems. This belief is shortsighted at best, destructive at worst. Take economics. The question of being able to afford a home in today's inflationary economy, let alone providing food and clothing and education for one's family, certainly qualifies as a significant problem facing young career women. To argue that these women receive far higher salaries is to deny the reality that even two-income families find their power to provide severely limited.

The perception of older women that the young career woman holds a greased ticket to success, through affirmative action, if not through changes in female role definitions, belies the statistical realities at hand. In 1979, the Dartnell Institute of Business Research surveyed 19,000 people in managerial, supervisory, professional, and clerical positions and found 48 percent of that total were women. The number of women in managerial positions was no more than 3 percent; the same was true of supervisory positions. Affirmative Action consultant Barbara Boyle Sullivan has stated that her experience suggests only 20 percent of all corporations pay more than lip service to regulatory employment reform.

Two of the older women we interviewed commented, in almost identical words, on the resentment they felt about the lowering of standards and the lack of commitment to quality evidenced in younger women. "When I look at some of today's young people," one said, "I am not even sure that they know what standards are." The second observed: "You can always do a little bit more and that's the thing they have to learn. Now, quality alone will not take you to the top. You have to keep on taking more responsibility and show that you can perform. If you can't do it, at least you'll know you can't. You have to push yourself toward quality and I don't see that push in the generations behind me."

Only preventive action will keep these remarks from being repeated by the twenty- to thirty-year-olds when they reach midlife. There can be no more convoluted logic than that which makes older women resent the achievements of younger members of their own sex. It denies them the chance to take credit for breaking down the first doors. It keeps them trapped in time not to see that affirmative action came out of their own contributions.

If, as it appears, older women do not credit younger generations with the ability to maintain standards, then the young must begin to examine their culpability in the charge. But to link the production of bread which tastes like paste to the fallen virtue of the young is to evade the issue of where such standards were learned. It seems that declining values have more to do with overall trends of American culture than with any one generation or gender.

The Arsenic and Old Lace Syndrome is a cycle which can be broken and must be broken if women are to make the most of their skills and the time they have to implement them. The continuing

polarization between younger and older women in the work place
is a division of strength the society cannot afford.

Relics and Remnants

Libby has worked for the Atlas Construction Company for thirty
years. She began as a secretary, went overseas when her boss was
promoted to head of European operations, and became multilin-
gual as well as skilled in selling the company to foreign nationals.
When she returned to the United States, she was promoted to a
management position in the public-relations department and was
one of half a dozen exempt women in the firm. Eventually she was
given a job with international responsibilities because of her
foreign-language capabilities, but she was not moved up in grade.
She has become a "fixture" at Atlas. Everyone likes and respects
her. Young men, as well as young women, feel comfortable talking
to her. Libby feels this is because she is viewed as being "safe."
"After all," she says, "they know I'm too old to be going anywhere
in the company. They know I'm not in competition with them."
She enjoys a friendly rapport with senior management because, as
she say, "They know I'm loyal and won't create waves." But
Libby is angry because she knows she is stuck.

Frequently Libby calls attention to being old, but she dresses,
moves, and thinks like a much younger woman. She is carrying as
much responsibility as men who are in higher positions and who
turn to her for direction. But men in her age group with the same
length of service are considered "in their prime." Libby is regarded, and regards herself, as "over the hill."

Libby's situation points to a corporate and cultural double standard about aging—less traumatizing to the traditional woman than
to the woman who works. The traditional woman, the homemaker,
ages with her peers. Intergroup competition is not age-related. But
women like Libby interact with a range of age groups. Moreover,
because she tends to be older in "grade" than younger men, she is
viewed as "less able" or "finished" at a point when she still has
more to contribute.

The older corporate woman has often been work-focused all of her adult life. She usually exhibits the kind of loyalty for the company that is in increasingly short supply. Such a woman may find herself closer in outlook to women in their twenties or thirties, but with values that are drawn along the lines of Whyte's Organizational Man of the 1950s. The problems that this kind of generational straddle produces can be seen in the story of "Ida," told to us by a younger woman.

The older generation are much more identified with the corporation. They are corporate people. They are loyal to a fault. A perfect example is Ida, an older woman here at the company, who has a broken arm and leg. She's walking around here in her casts and presenting quite a picture. I think the average twenty-year-old would not do what Ida is doing. Two broken limbs would be sufficient cause for them to stay at home. I'm in my thirties and I sure wouldn't walk around here in plaster. Maybe it's because I don't have the same personal identification with the corporation that Ida does. The corporation does not define me. I'm a separate person outside my company role. I was out for an operation for nine weeks. I felt better after seven weeks, and maybe if I was Ida, I would have come in. Instead, I took nine weeks because the doctor said that's what I should take. I suppose those two weeks are the difference between Ida's value system and mine. Ida, by the way, has been called by insurance poeple asking her if she is going to sue. I guess she figures a lawsuit would take her away from her job, because she is not suing. I don't think a lawsuit would have even occurred to her if she hadn't been asked.

For the reentry woman, who is set to embark on a redefinition of her role in life, the relics and remnants of age-related attitudes fire old synapses in new environments. She may have lived her life believing that her role as wife and mother was ordained to last forever. At midlife, she finds herself, not only jobless, but as naive about work as any twenty-year-old. Her only advantage is that she has built up many layers of life experience. The reentry woman, then, becomes another victim of the generational straddle. She belongs neither to the peership of corporate women of her age, nor to the generation whose lack of experience most closely resembles her own entry-level status. She will never attain the management rank of her male age peers, nor will she run on the fast track along with the young who are just starting out.

In *Women of a Certain Age*, Lillian Rubin addresses the problem faced by these women. They must find something to do, some way of making each day worth living; in short, they must answer

the question of what to do with the rest of their lives. Our interviews with reentry women offered no simple solution to bridging
this particular culture gap. Any hope these women felt was based
on their individual ability to adjust their goals to coincide with reality, and on their personal senses of adventure. But the possibility
exists that the generations of workingwomen can reach across age
barriers to form alliances which will benefit one and all. It keeps
coming back to being aware enough to understand each other's
place in time. As a woman in her mid-thirties said:

> As for older women, I'm very sympathetic. I feel very supportive of
> them, even though I'm not sure what can be done to help them. Theirs
> was the generation which got caught in the middle of it. They had all
> the skills, but they weren't always able to use them. They are probably
> more frustrated than I'll ever know. But I'm frustrated too because I'm
> a few years ahead of my time. Now I have enough perspective to look
> at a woman in her mid to late twenties, who doesn't know what it was
> like ten or twenty years ago, who doesn't sympathize with the prob-
> lems of a forty-year-old woman, and to realize that she has no sense of
> her own history. And I've come to feel that it is important for me to tell
> her that.

Sleeping Beauties and Rip Van Winkles

In *Atlantic Magazine*, John Brooks wrote: "Generations are a
passing thing." It is true, he said, that every age group moves
through what a recent best-seller has labeled "passages," but in
understanding the nature of an ageist society, it must be remembered that these transitions do not happen simultaneously to an
entire generation. Some people succeed early, some late, some
never at all. "Quite independently of this individual parabola,"
Brooks observed, "its rise, its plateau, its decline—each person also
moves through another kind of 'passage,' the constantly shifting
context of one's times."[6]
One of the older women we interviewed expressed it in this
way:

> We are in future shock and for us to assimilate mentally the speed with
> which things are moving and changing is difficult and frustrating. Our
> generation was used to doing things a certain way and it was a good

way. This place was built on a certain reputation and it is hard for me to accept new things because I don't see that they are any better.

Change in an ageist society centers around an integration of youth and age in each individual. There will never be a stopgap against the passage of time, but there is some comfort and command in understanding that "young" and "old" are symbols which the culture has the power to redefine.

A Future-age Scenario

In the past decade the work force has been growing at an annual rate of 2.3 percent, but in the 1980s, this figure is expected to drop to 1.1 percent annually. The population bulge created by the baby boom is moving down the age spectrum. Within fifty years nearly 20 percent of the U.S. population will be sixty-five years or older. Coupled with the declining birthrate of the past few years, the demographics of tomorrow's work force will be dramatically different from that which is the norm today.

When the baby-boom generation approaches middle age, there will be continued competition within the bulge, but a shortage of entry-level people. This change will create a greater need for those with experience. Retirement will be forestalled as corporations find they need the services of accomplished workers to maintain productivity levels. Age discrimination will become a major issue, as will hiring, promotion, and wage-system changes. Older workers will become more militant and corporations less able to disregard their needs and demands.

Two recent developments presage this future-age scenario. In one court case, the jury found a retail chain store guilty of discrimination against older employees. A critical point in the case was the belief of management that marketing efforts to attract young customers could only, effectively, be implemented by young employees. The announcement of the jury's verdict was followed, in only a few days, by a demonstration at a major engineering firm to protest allegedly discriminatory treatment of older women employees.

Margaret Mead's three-level cultural system may have been

more correct in style than in substance. The demographics of the future seem to indicate a resurgence of the Postfigurative, or at least, Cofigurative model of society. The statistical ascent of the workingwoman will continue, with Department of Labor projections reflecting an expected sixty million women at work by 1990. It appears that there will definitely be an upcoming course adjustment in the flight of the Prefigurative society which will force creation of new alliances across the ageist grids of American life. For the workingwomen of this country, an understanding today of this future-age scenario, and of their own life continuums, offers the prospect of landing a lead role in the drama of cultural change.

New links must be forged as old ones rust.

JANE HOWARD
A Different Woman

4

The Associated Woman

Sociologist and author Lionel Tiger traces the lineage of the old boys' club back to genetic transmissions among male primates. He suggests that with the dawn of "the hunt," women were marked for exclusion from all male groups. But whether or not one subscribes to this evolutionary explanation, the impenetrable old boys' network became the bugaboo of the modern executive woman. The "Old Boys' Network," in fact, became a code phrase for the denial to women of success through denial of access to the centers of information and power.[1]

The associated woman, however, knows all about networks, alliances, and mentors, three forms of bonding that have become part and parcel of the workingwoman's culture. The associated woman learned quickly that in the corporate world commerce is not conducted in a vacuum; she, in fact, managed to cope with the idea of the old boys' club.

The old boys' network in reality is many networks that overlap and complement each other. First, there are the informal systems that exist in all business organizations. As Peter Drucker observed, the term "informal" is a misnomer, because this parallel organization is very formal indeed. Its power is tremendous. Among its formal aspects are the rites of inclusion. These informal networks protect their collective self-interest by selectively including or excluding individual members. Not all men are accepted into membership and those who are excluded usually are destined for limited futures. Very few women have been included. A man is excluded on the basis of some characteristic or action directly attributed to him as an individual. But a woman is excluded on the presumption of characteristics attributed to all women as a monolithic group.

Exclusion deprives women of support, influence, and the acquisition of information and resources. Inclusion in these networks is an anointing action. The difference it makes in a person's career is incalculable. The energy it takes to make it without this seal of approval is awesome.

Then there are men's clubs. These are formal organizations which bring together men from a variety of professions, industries, and companies. Membership rules here are formal and restrictive. Relatively few, even in 1980, admit women—or even men from racial or ethnic minorities. (It is interesting that when ethnic groups who were denied membership in these clubs formed their own copies of the clubs, often they too barred women.) Although the stated purposes of these clubs are usually social or philanthropic, the real business of the clubs is business.

Business takes place at the lunch table, in the swimming pool, and on the golf course. The circles grow and intersect and overlap. Contracts are wired, promotions are greased, and corporate plays are telegraphed. Beyond this, however, is the less obvious business: the subliminal reinforcing of man's place in the scheme of important things and the complacency that all is still right with the world of male entitlement.

By about 1970, the women who in small numbers had moved into the managerial ranks of companies were experiencing the trauma and brutality of the formal corporate environment and suffering the pain of isolation from the informal system. Attempts at creating a cushion through parallel women's networks within corporations often won them the image of troublemakers or simply served to reinforce their separateness. The need for cohesion, support, and information exchange made external networking an idea whose time had come. Like a scientific discovery made at the same time in disparate parts of the world, women's networks were established in cities across the country simultaneously and without reference to one another. For the woman who had felt the alienation of the disenfranchised in her place of work, these forums with other women in similar positions, with similar goals, were heady stuff indeed. The Utopian vision emerged that these networks could serve as hothouses for the cultivation of women leaders who would lead the assault on the sleeping dogs of the establishment and snap them into awareness. Necessity had mothered yet another great social experiment. The vision of networking's potential was perhaps best captured in this story:

> When I first became involved in a network, I was describing the networking concept to a French-speaking friend. I used the word *"filet,"* which means "net." She was confused until I elaborated on our purposes and activities. "Oh, you mean a *réseau,"* she said. "You see, a *filet* is a fisherman's net, a number of fragile loops, some of which are attached to others, but none of which is overlapping. A *réseau* is a railroad center where numbers of tracks cross each other, then continue on in new directions. A *filet* is merely string. A *réseau* is mighty iron."

There was much to be righted in the business world and the early networkers braced to take it all on. This was the *reaction* phase of networking. The motivation to act, and act quickly, seared the members' spirits, but implementation was somewhat diffuse. Network organizers were faced with a multiplicity of bottom lines. Frustrations grew as the elements of democracy, bureaucracy, ego, and eagerness were unleashed during this formative stage of development.

Mixed Models

The idea seemed so simple in concept. The founder of one of the early networks described how it had started for her:

> In my work as a consultant, I had been inside a variety of companies all over the country. Everywhere I went, the women in the companies sought me out, and we talked about women in their positions in other places and about the common problems. It was clear that all these women were experiencing a new kind of alienation and that they were

desperately lonely. I put together a list of twenty-five corporate women
I had met in my own city and invited them to lunch. At lunch, I presented my idea for organizing our own network. It was enthusiastically
received, and the network is now four years old.

Another network founder described her experience:

This is a very lunch-oriented city. There must be fifteen or twenty
men's luncheon clubs. They are open only during the two- or three-
hour luncheon "window." When I first began my job at the bank, I had
no problem being accepted by my colleagues in the morning or afternoon, but at lunchtime they all disappeared. It occurred to me fairly
quickly that there must be other women in the city in the same position
as myself. So I went to the president of the bank and told him I wanted
to form a professional women's luncheon group . . . and why. I told
him that I would need to do it during business hours and asked him
how much time he would allow me to spend on this project. He
thought it was a great idea and suggested some women he thought I
should call. He added that as long as I did my job, it didn't make any
difference how long I spent forming the group. There were soon 150
women in the group, but we didn't have a regular place to meet. By this
time it had become illegal for those all-male luncheon clubs to exclude
women, so I joined one. I told them that the reason I was joining was so
that I could bring my group in on a regular basis and asked how many
tables they could reserve on any given day. They agreed to take as
many as twenty of us at one time. So we have arranged our schedules
and we meet in groups of six or eight, depending on the mix. But the
beauty of it is that we never have the same mix of women at any two
luncheons. I soon got to know many women very well and we found
new ways to create support systems. There have been big job changes
which have come out of those lunches. We have occasionally asked
younger women into our discussions. We have helped women who are
moving to other towns and helped women moving here to find places to
live and necessary services. Other women across the country have
heard about us as well, so we have had out-of-town visitors join us.

Pumping Mighty Iron

But like many ideas which seem simple on the surface, the concept
of women's networks had many hidden problems. The first signals
of trouble usually flashed during the organizational phase of development. Should the network be a formal organization with
bylaws, articles of incorporation, election of officers, and rules of

operation? Or should it be an informal relationship? The dilemma was disturbing and disruptive because there were no answers to these questions. There were no answers because no such creature as an organized informal network existed. Men had informal networks and formal clubs. Women had formal clubs and, to a lesser extent, informal social networks. A totally new organization concept was needed. But, at the time, few recognized this, and networks were continually forced into one or another of the historical organization molds.

Another part of the organization crisis was the leadership conflict. Weight lifting is not a sport in which many women have participated. Women's networks had their own brand of reservations about pumping iron and exercised great care in preventing members from flexing too much muscle. The leaderless group, unfortunately, is also the powerless group, as many women soon learned. While stating, in principle, that networks had been formed to grow and groom leaders, women suffered from confused and conflicting ideas on the nature and desirability of authority. Women envied the grid of influence held by the old boys' networks, but balked at the notion of vesting command in the hands of a leader. Feeling that they had been repressed by authority all of their lives, women disdained anything that hinted at further domination. The dilemma of dominance became a swamp which sucked in the energies of many a fledgling group.

A founder and activist who survived those anti-authoritarian days told us that the tendency of network members to want a leaderless group resulted in endless reinventions of the wheel. She said:

> We were afraid that if we had a president or chairwoman, it would be interpreted as a cop-out. And that was very unfortunate because what it did during that time was to say that women couldn't get their act together. It made us look ridiculous. Some recently formed organizations still bear the residue from that philosophy. One group's membership committee just submitted a very tight package which was rejected as being undemocratic. What it implied was that no one should be in charge. But organizations just don't work that way.

Another veteran of women's groups commented:

> The first year that I was on the board it was an incredible experience, mainly because of the people I worked with. We did a lot of leaping,

thinking, conceptualizing, and planning for growth, but we made one mistake. We thought that everybody was as interested in the issues as we were. Lo and behold, that wasn't true. This is my second year on the board and I find myself dealing with a lot of negativity. The current group would rather be in control than do what is right for the organization. The authoritarian-controlling thing is still a big problem.

The Multiplicity of Bottom Lines

A second organizational impasse often occurred around definition of purpose. Historically women's organizations were founded and supported on the basis of their devotion to some greater good. As it became apparent that the prime purpose of the networks was to enhance each member's individual personal goals, there was much soul-searching and discomfort. These organizations were not capable of serving a wide range of individual purposes. Every member looked to the network for fulfillment of her own needs, and priorities of self often took precedence over focus on urgent issues and matters of a pragmatic administrative nature. Women mingled, women talked. Cards were exchanged. Many complained about the price of dinner, the price of drinks, the price of membership. M.B.A.s balked at managing organizational paperwork. Superwomen couldn't find the time to attend committee meetings. Programming became the great ideological debate. No program suited everyone. Perspectives were distorted. Programs were only the means to bring women together. They were not intended to be the end also. The objective was to develop a network. The program debate obscured the issues that were really causing change and disaffection.

The most wrenching self-appraisal occurred, however, in the matter of membership criteria. Women who had themselves been excluded from membership in men's groups were unwilling to discriminate against other women. Yet many recognized that their own purpose in joining the organization could best be served if most members were at comparable professional levels. The battle lines were drawn on the fronts of elitism versus sisterhood. Subtly entwined in the membership issue were the strands of the feminist movement. Factions were often set against each other according to the nature of their special interests. The fanaticism and posturing of radical women, who declared themselves feminists, caused other women to disassociate themselves from such a reactionary image. This was especially true of women in corporate management, whose already tenuous positions would be even more fragile if they were seen as "radical libbers."

The "bigger is better" mentality added to the fray. Runaway membership growth in some groups strained management capabilities. Meeting organizers were forced to find new locations almost monthly. Duplicate groups within the same city often found themselves competing for market shares, claiming vested rights to territories based both on size and on the power positions of their most successful members.

The driving need for role models in those early days forced many a corporate star to hide her light under the nearest bushel. Younger managers clung to the more seasoned performers as though they were life rafts. Experienced women found role-modeling, in this frantic atmosphere, a drain on their energies.

The Network Revolution

By the end of the reaction phase, there was a clear dichotomy in philosophy. On the one hand, there were the true progeny of the women's movement who believed women were all in the battle together. This group favored networks open to all comers, with no distinctions based on career objectives or achievements. The message was that those who had moved up had a sisterhood obligation to pull others along. There was an assumption that unless they were bonded together, achieving women would abandon the younger, less experienced women who needed their support. The second group of networks was selective. These established membership criteria usually based on level of positions held. Most of these groups included women from middle management on up. A few took their slice off the very top and required that a prospective member be the highest-ranking woman in her company and have distinguished herself professionally and personally. The second group looked to each other for support and for access. Their assumption was that through their collective power they could

push one, then another of the group into higher-level corporate
positions, boards of directors, and significant appointments. In this
way, they would open new frontiers and broaden the opportunity
for all women. Although there was some interaction between the
two types of networks, more frequently there was antagonism.
The open-membership group viewed the other as elitist. The reality is they were both parts of the same animal. In his fanciful Dr.
Dolittle stories, Hugh Lofting invented a creature called a
Pushmi-Pullyou. This animal had two heads and two sets of feet.
One part pushed forward, the other pulled from behind. If both
worked together, the animal could progress. However, the two
parts of the animal seldom did this and so it stayed still.

In spite of the problems of multiple purposes, information and
communication overloads, and continued reliance on volunteer ad-
ministrations, networks did not become extinct; they matured.
The reaction phase of networking, born out of alienation, gave way
to the second, *revolution* stage. Darwin's evolution theory prevailed. Successful strategies begot survival. The open-membership
policies, which had fostered homogenization, underwent subtle re-
finements through application of more discriminating criteria.
Attitudes on the business of running a network grew more sophisticated as successful career women found that paid administrators
were a salvation. Individual recollections of this transitional period
document the evolutionary state of events.

I joined a women's network but stopped going to the meetings because
I thought that the programs were getting redundant and by then I
knew enough people so I didn't need the group to serve me in that way.

I developed a theory that some of those early networks would self-
destruct. In 1975, I joined a group of women in public affairs. By 1980,
the founders of the group had been absorbed into the citywide Public
Affairs Council; that is the next step for networks.

I was very much pro-networking, but found myself becoming much
more elitist than I ever was before. I started off thinking that all women
were marvelous. I had this kind of universal attitude that I must help
all women. I now believe that to be a myth perpetuated by the medio-
cre. Suddenly I realized that I only had an obligation to help those
women who helped me. It became a case of tit for tat.

When I belonged to a general corporate women's network I stopped
going to meetings because I was only partly interested in some of the

issues they discussed. The other deterrent was that I became amazed at the competition for my time and the increasing demands the group began to make on me. I had to become more focused. I abandoned the shotgun approach and turned my rifle squarely at a specific target.

I joined a new group which refers to itself as a roundtable. The membership comprises very successful women, each of whom takes the responsibility for coordinating a program once a year. But on the whole it is an informal group. It's just that the quality is higher. I only have to meet with women who are senior V.P.s or other top brass.

I have developed relationships with other women which are solely based on economics. We have become so blunt that we now say over lunch exactly what it is that you can do for me.

I now belong to a women's organization where I can interact with others who are at my stage of development and with whom I share common interests.

Before extending ourselves into visions of the future, there are lessons from networking's past that bear restating.

Lesson number one is that, for all its faults and problems, the infancy of women's professional networks was incredibly short. The entire history of this social experiment is contained in a single decade. Women should take comfort, if not pride, in the steepness of their learning curve.

The second lesson of networking is that experience does teach best. Once the initial network programs on dressing for success subsided, women reached beyond the externals to sharpen executive skills and contacts. Rather than invest all their time and efforts in a single entity, businesswomen now find that the wagon-wheel approach to membership affiliation offers an expanded base for professional operations. This development was hastened along by mergers between mature women's networks and the creation of umbrella alliances, some on a national level. And perhaps most important, by rejecting the elitist epithets on selective-membership standards, the women at or near the top have found greater freedom to develop their own careers and as a result have cut a wider, faster track for the women waiting to succeed them. There is a vital flow of people between networks. As one network observer put it:

You can chart women's progress on the corporate ladder by watching the membership of key networks. Women join groups where they feel a commonality with other members and move on when their personal needs can best be met elsewhere. This keeps the networks vital and gives women a new arena of choice. Corporations have only begun to recognize the assets provided them by the support and resource services of sophisticated national women's networks, in such areas as relocation and recruitment.

Lesson three can be summed in a single word: timing. Women's networks happened when and how they did, and are changing now, in response to the times. The old boys' clubs were, and many continue to be, closed to women. Today, however, as an article in *Savvy* pointed out, an all-male club in the city of Chicago would have to deny membership to the mayor, the president of the University of Chicago, the former president of the Chicago Bar Association, and the city editor of the *Chicago Tribune*, to name a few.[2] The movement toward integration may be slow, but it is inevitable as significant links in the old boys' grasp on influence continue to be chipped away.

The first, or reaction, phase of networking saw the structuring of an interim hybrid, a cross between the formal organizations and clubs women had known and the kind of informal male networks they needed access to. As women individually enhanced their networking skills, they moved closer to the revolution phase, which allowed for introduction and interaction. There were increasing numbers of joint programming efforts, collaborative planning sessions, and more crossover memberships. Mergers created larger, more powerful networks.

The Staging Process

The comments of the women we queried on the value of and prognosis for networking, along with our reading of other social indicators, incline us to believe that we are on our way to the third and final evolutionary stage of networking. The hallmark of the third, or *resolution*, phase of networking will be total integration. Over one-third of the women we interviewed were already members of network-type groups with male and female members; others expressed a desire to find and join such groups. Several women predicted the eventual merging of all but a few member-ship-by-gender associations.

The key to achieving total network integration is leveraging. An example is the creation of Women's Councils within the formerly all-male Chambers of Commerce. Although these chambers began with the concept of a women's council along the traditional lines of a women's auxiliary, the net effect has been a springboarding of women into the mainstream of the chamber's activities. This is not to say that there is an absence of some of the old boys' behavior, but women have resisted the temptation to return to the reactionary, separatist position. A woman involved in the formation of one Women's Council describes her experiences:

> The goal of the Chamber of Commerce was to create a sort of women's auxiliary, but the men in the chamber had absolutely no idea of the power and authority of the women they invited to form the council. Our first brush with disaster came during the planning sessions for a citywide trade fair, when it was suggested that the members of the women's council pour wine for visitors and guests. A hue and cry went up that was heard all over town. But rather than react and pull out, we stayed in and made our point. We reached the decision that we had created a toehold in this male bastion and we weren't going to give it up. We feel that we are slowly gaining acceptance as individuals and this will give us the opportunity to bring other women into the chamber's power centers. I think of the process as a laying on of hands. The merger may be moving only gradually, but it *is* moving.

The Phoenix Period

As with every other social phenomenon, opinions are divided on the state of the art and future of networking. Several of our interviews elicited personal evaluations and very candid predictions.

On the issue of whether total integration of male and female networks would come to pass, one woman said:

> I don't know if women will ever achieve power in male circles. I don't think I'm advocating separatism, but I think it is a pretty established fact that, as much as men may like me, they may never let me into their inner circles. Then again, I probably wouldn't let them into mine, if the truth were known.

A similarly cautious view of mergers and mainstreaming came from an activist in several women's associations.

I think networks are necessary, but I see them as a step on the way to something else, where women and men will be in professional groups together. But I think that women need more time to learn to value their own resources, intuitive thinking, and perceptions of situations. I believe that women's sensitivities to the world are far different than men's. My qualm is that these collective groups will find men putting women in the backseat again. There are a lot of old prejudices around. I'd sure like to be around in three or four generations to see what's happening.

Another woman had a somewhat pessimistic view of women's networks, but offered clear directions on what needed to be done.

About the middle of the 1970s, I started to see the first women's organizations coming forward. The groups were involved in very heavy issues, but were centered on getting access to certain things. Women's organizations slowly began to be built on the basis of mutual support, but I think these groups have stagnated somewhat in the past three years. Now is the time for us to pick up the ball. Some of the organizations I've been taking an interest in lately are those in which women get together to discuss subjects of common interest . . . such as what is happening to the country, the culture, the nuclear family, and marriage. Once women begin talking to each other on topics like this, they will learn more about the issues which affect them mutually. Then we can get to a meaningful level of trying to help each other and to support issues and programs that will help everyone in society, without having to be constantly aware that we are women.

But perhaps the most important value to emerge from the networking experience has a more individual focus. One woman gave us this lesson in a nutshell.

"Feminist" may still have a negative connotation, like money or power, to some women. I call myself a feminist, but I don't think about labels much anymore. There is something that now comes above women's issues for me and that is the overriding sense of purpose in what I am doing, in making sure that I do it right, that I do my best; that, above all, the quality is there. I don't want to get by just being a woman. It bothers me that so much of the women's movement found itself caught up in the sticky issue of retribution. I am part of the women's movement, but it is not just something that goes on inside of me. It goes on around the world. I see that being a workingwoman in America today is just part of a larger role that reaches around the globe.

These are hopeful words. They hint that women's networks may have fostered a strong *réseau*, a place where professionals come together and part in new directions, changed by the interaction and picking up speed as they go.

The Phases of Networking

PERIOD:	Reactionary Phase	Revolution Phase	Resolution Phase
AGE:	Alienation	Interaction	Integration
MEMBERS:	Homogenization	Diversification	Specialization

The Reactionary Phase: Women find the informal and formal corporate networks closed to them. They *react* by forming their own networks. They are alienated from the mainstream. Early membership is homogenized across all levels of management.

The Revolution Phase: The beginning of interaction and merger between women's networks. Distillation of membership occurs as groups diversify along lines of position and rank peerage. The gradual process of "the laying on of hands" begins as male and female networks exchange members. The establishment *revolution* is under way.

The Resolution Phase: Total integration of professional organizations, formal and informal corporate networks and *resolution* of gender-role issues. Membership by gender associations remains only in cases of highly specialized interest or by rank. Alliances and mergers will have created centralized power structures with direct input into the mainstream.

Alliances—Friends in the Right Places

While networking focuses on the development of external resources, the formation of alliances involves working relationships within an organization. An American Council of Life Insurance survey reported that one out of ten Americans subscribes to the opinion that knowing someone contributes more to success than hard work. Responses to our questions about alliances indicated a higher level of sophistication or perhaps a lower level of cynicism. Women we interviewed placed a high value on alliances, but recognized that their ability to forge effective alliances depended on their credibility or work performance.

WHO?

Who are your allies? "Everybody" "The janitor" "Secretaries" "My staff" "My boss" "Men" "My network" "Eccentrics" "Myself" were among the varieties of answers we received in response to that question. On the surface these answers run the entire gamut of the company payroll. However, the answers can be grouped into categories reflecting style and situation. Most people have a personal grid based on their own characteristics and the needs of their job and the nature of their work environment. None of these categories precludes any of the others. In fact, any number may operate at the same time.

THE PRAGMATIC APPROACH

The pragmatic view of alliance holds to a functional definition. Allies are tied to job functions. Thus, all people performing similar tasks in the company are a source of support and information to each other.

THE DEVELOPMENTAL APPROACH

Alternatively described as the ROI (return on investment) theory, the developmental approach centers on the belief that a good manager creates her own ally constituency. The underlying assumption here is that people you develop will feel a loyalty to you. An effective manager coaches and counsels her subordinates not only because they will perform better and experience personal growth, but also because they may become part of the manager's cheering section and radar system wherever they go.

THE PHILOSOPHICAL APPROACH

The combination golden-rule and serendipity techniques apply here. Philosophical adherents are prone to describe their sources of information in such phrases as "Anyone can be a potential next life," or "There is something good in everybody." The most serendipitous women we queried said that they were constantly changing the mix of their alliances to keep themselves from going stale. In this context it is important to avoid the pitfalls of subtle prejudice. Women and men, old and young, vice-president or secretary, are just as possible as allies.

THE NATURAL APPROACH

The natural approach begins with the self and radiates outward. The theory here is that one's best allies are drawn from a combination of chemistry and commonality. Allies in this approach are cultivated among one's closest peers and most frequently contacted co-workers. Naturalists presume that strong alliances will be centered around meeting common goals or on a project-related basis. The Three Musketeers' motto, "All for one, one for all," is echoed here.

THE SELECTIVE APPROACH

The selectivists hold back making alliance commitments until they get the lay of the land. Their motto is, "To choose, but not to be chosen." Political in nature, selectivists try to identify the powerful people within a corporation and make alliances accordingly. Relatively task-oriented, those who operate in this approach identify their job needs and fill them with key sources. Selectivists often seek out eccentrics as allies on the theory that rugged individualists are more likely to gain recognition.

THE SITUATIONAL APPROACH

This approach is reactive rather than active. Situationalists are frequently forced into alliances based on availability, because choices have been reduced significantly. The first stars or tokens become situationalists by virtue of isolation. Frequently they have no natural peers. Their co-workers are made distant by the mystique of the new. Situationalists are therefore very vulnerable to making poor alliances; many experience alienation. A common error resulting from this approach is to limit alliances among those people who are or appear to be "in." The danger here is that the situation often changes without warning and the situationist may be left hanging off a cliff.

What and Why

In one of the many books telling male executives how to succeed, the author employs a card-game analogy. The first rule for winning, he says, is to make sure that the deck is not stacked against you. This is the *why* of alliances. They furnish the knowledge of which cards are held in which hands, allowing informed action. Alliances, if properly constructed, are like intelligence networks. *What* they provide is seasoning, a blending of realism and timing by which women can master situations rather than being buffeted by them. Strategy development requires a solid constituency based on trust, inside tips, and feedback. The allies one chooses within the corporation become one's political machine.

Less clear to many executive women were the *where* and the *when* aspects of alliances. The quagmire here was a confusion between professional and emotional support. Whether an extension of the therapy qualities of a network or simply of women's romantic visions of the world, the alliances women tried to establish within their corporation suffered from something very much like unrequited love.

"I don't have what I would consider to be a series of close personal friends here at work," lamented one midmanagement woman.

> I couldn't have gotten as far as I have without some support and positive regard for my contributions to the organization. But I had experienced a time, in another job, when I worked with people who were my close personal friends. The personal connections made my job feel more comfortable. Perhaps when I question the amount of support I get on this job, what I'm really feeling is the loss of those previous friendships. I miss having someone who will listen to what my husband and I did over the weekend.

These days referring to a woman as a romantic can elicit the same response as if you had called her a "girl," but we heard countless examples like the ones above which suggest that corporate women don't know how to have a buddy system that isn't based on intimacy. The problem is that authority and vulnerability mix like oil and water.

The buddy system is something that men transplanted from summer camp to corporate America. Paired off with a near or total stranger to swim laps across the lake, men learned early that you can put your very life in someone else's hands without knowing his favorite flavor of ice cream or secret desires. It is not difficult to see how this kind of training can and did lead to emotional isolationism at work. The fraternal order often found its members working side by side for years with only the tips of their icebergs showing.

Women eschewed this system as being untenable and unhealthy without understanding that some division of the head and heart is necessary for personal health and efficient operations within the corporate camps. In looking for friends instead of buddies, many a corporate woman found her career caught up in an emotional undertow.

> I consciously develop allies at work because when the chips are down and I need help, I can go to them and say: "I've just had the shit kicked out of me," and they give me some encouragement. Everyone needs to have somebody whom they can go to and say, "Wrap up my arm, it is broken."

But women who try to set up personal first-aid stations at work run the risk of alienating potential allies and of presenting a one-dimensional, negative view of themselves. There is precious little privacy within the corporation. Running off for frequent emergency emotional treatment, no matter how discreetly it is done, will inevitably become grist for the gossip mills. This is not to say that women should give up friends for a career. What we are advocating is a sage distinction between positive professional support and negative, often crippling tendencies toward indiscriminate emotional catharsis. The key here is a balance. In rejecting what they perceived as the insensitivity of the organizational men, women often tipped the pendulum too far in the other direction. Wiser because of her experience, one enormously successful woman summarized her credo this way. "Emotional support is a whole different bag. I find that I don't look for that within the corporation. It is very had to find, but more important, I've learned that there are parts of me that are not the corporation's to share."

A Warning About Grapevines

While we are examining the downside of alliances, a word or two needs to be said about the perils of turning an alliance into a grapevine. Grapevines within a corporate garden suggest some serious management problems, especially if the fruits they bear are decidedly sour. One woman who felt she had been lied to about the promise and scope of her job openly expressed her frustration among the other women in her department and eventually the entire firm. This prompted other disgruntled women employees to turn to her as a conduit for expressing their anger, hostility, and petty grievances. If her future was in doubt before she created the tangle of vines, imagine what it must be like now. She was unable to move out of the firm, and her vision of the working environment around her is one of rampant espionage. While she may be an ally to the women of her company, this woman has clearly marked herself as an enemy of her male employer. She is most certainly thought, by management, guilty of a treasonable offense.

Three Models of the Balanced Alliance

From the descriptions given in interviews, we have selected three brief examples of executive women who have achieved a positive support channel, one that operates on a professional plane.

> I would either go to my boss or to the chairman of the company to get support, although the support I receive from my boss is more tangible. The chairman's support takes the form of letting the organization know that he has a high regard for me and that he has plans for me which go beyond my current position. This allows me to maintain an effective position within the organization. My boss's support is more direct. If I have a specific problem, we can sit down and talk about it. But both of these kinds of support are important to my ability to evolve solutions to

problems and to resolve them by working in concert with the other employees.

I feel that if, at any given time, I have a problem or concern, if I am really unsure of how I should handle something, I can talk to my boss. He has always been very supportive, and while he never solves the problem for me, he certainly helps me to look at the pros and cons of any given decision. I have made it my policy, however, to go to him only as a last resort. Since I know that I am supported and have somewhere to go, I find I can act with more confidence.

Professional support right now comes from my boss and from a new senior vice-president we've just hired in distribution whom I will be reporting to in a few months. These two people are supportive professionally. They will allow me to make decisions and to make my own mistakes.

The common thread running through our three balanced-alliance stories is an approach to managerial tasks as professional, not personal, proving grounds. The axiom which says that one cannot help others without first being able to help oneself applies to the formation of balanced alliances. One of the male executives we interviewed described the effect of bringing emotionalism to a management problem as "rubbishing the issues." Professionalism is nearly always recognized, if not rewarded, and is certainly preferable to rubbishing behavior.

Credibility is frequently identified as the most crucial issue for workingwomen. Alliances which provide the ability to act in an informed, seasoned manner can add immeasurably to a woman's credibility. The ultimate power of such alliances and their potential contribution to the ongoing rise of women in the corporate world was captured best by one woman who told us:

It doesn't make any difference whether or not you have a degree from the University of Timbuktu or Stanford. What is important more often is that someone opens the right door for you. Part of the sales potential of the major educational institutions are the links to alumni who can open doors. And that is a network. If women could establish these kinds of links, the kinds of traditional alliances men have had, we could give other women the opportunity to get in the door and start talking.

Political Alliances

Perhaps the greatest obstacle for women, next to overcoming sex bias, is overcoming their own misunderstanding and aversion to "politics." Politics as a word joins the growing lexicon of gender-rated words like power, ambition, and aggression. Invariably, when women are asked what it takes to get ahead in their companies, they will include politics and often add something like "I don't want any part of it," with the implication that it's dirty. Politics is the handmaiden of ambition, for politics, in the final analysis, is an individual's internal public-relations system. It's how word is sent out about accomplishments; it is how alliances are formed; it's the measure of an ability to deal effectively with people. Politics is also an important social-influence dynamic with potential for positive and negative effect on the organization and on individuals. From a woman who is a superachieving, highly ambitious bank vice-president:

> Probably the most important ability I have is to read political situations in a company and know how to react to them and what actions to take.

From a woman politician:

> In the work I have done politically, I have learned that it is inevitable that I will get into conflict situations in which somebody is going to win. If you're the person who wins, you don't step on the person who lost because you may have to deal with him/her another day.

Other women commented:

> What works against me is not understanding the true dynamics of a situation.

> It isn't necessarily what you do, but how you present it—I've learned that.

> In a corporation you must achieve your objectives within the established procedures and guidelines and ethics of the company.

There is a relationship between the patterns of women's role in governmental politics and their view of corporate politics. Many women have been politically involved behind the scenes. They have organized, supported, and done the lackey work on campaigns. They've seldom directed the campaigns. In general, they carved out a place where they felt insulated from the heat of the game. Now women are in the mainstream—running and winning political office. In the corporate setting they are moving beyond the anonymous roles and vying for recognition and reward. In many ways, moving up in a company is a continuing process of running for office. The same rules apply. For beyond a certain grade or level, an employee is more nearly elected than selected for promotion. And the best men haven't always won. Much has been written about "playing the game" and there are some gamelike aspects in political strategizing. The caveat here is that using a strictly games approach leaves the impression that playing the game is the end in itself. It leaves out the substance and performance aspects of political success. It implies that there is an established pattern out there somewhere; all one needs is to find it. There is no such easy way. Game strategy views each situation as an independent event. One analyzes objectively all the possible outcomes, understands the interests and positions of the other players, and chooses strategies that will ensure favorable outcomes in the context of current organizational realities. It is then time to invest energies to implement the strategies, as the bottom line is ultimately performance.

> The people whom I work with, the governmental types, are all game players . . . or they wouldn't be in that area. On at least one occasion I've had to come in and say, "Hey, I know what game you're playing on me and I'm willing to go along with it as long as you know I know." Then it's not a game. After that episode, the person never tried games with me again.

A male manager reported:

> I'm not a game player. I'm really honest. I don't play politics well because I make decisions on fact, not on people. The reason I got blown out of my last job was because I told them I didn't agree with what was happening.

A woman planner said:

> I am good at selling things. I see what I do as selling a product, and selling myself. Everything in life is sales.

A woman vice-president reflected on women in corporate politics:

A real area of weakness that I see in women in comparable positions and even higher is a lack of political awareness and lack of awareness in the sense that they don't know how to play the game as well as the men do. And it's a rude fact of life that competence, ability, is maybe 60 or 65 percent of who gets what and who ends up on the top of the heap, and the rest of it is politics. As dirty, as unpalatable as it may be to a lot of people, and as compromising as it may seem to be to have to play those politics, it's very important.

A recent study of managerial perceptions of organizational politics identified organizational political tactics and personal characteristics of effective politicians. The people who participated in the study represented four levels of managers—CEOs, executives, middle, first line. There was general agreement across the levels on tactics and characteristics, but there was a difference in attitude. Politics became increasingly important as the position level rose; political effectiveness was viewed more favorably the higher up the position was and most disfavorably at the lower levels of supervision and management.

Most women are in the second group, have less power in their organizations, and therefore are less able to practice politics as successfully. As a result, they are less generous in attributing favorable characteristics to those in power who do practice politics.

One tactic of politicians identified in the study was blaming or attacking others in order to get off the hook. This is a tactic to minimize an association with a project that is failing. It may get played out in putting someone else down or maneuvering someone else into the hot spot. However, it may be simply keeping oneself out of the wrong place at the wrong time. Two women viewed it in this way:

There is one person here you do not knock, even though he is often to blame. He's the president. You don't ever blame him. I know it and everyone else knows it too.

In a corporation, you're a little ant and you can get stepped on. But a smart ant knows to walk in the little grooves where you don't get stepped on.

Another political tool is the use of information. Information is withheld, distorted, or used to overwhelm someone. Here are examples from our interviews:

The grapevine here is incredible. You have to be careful whom you talk to. There are two or three people I can trust, but I've learned that people here are very territorial. No one wants to share information.

One of my boss's most effective techniques is to arrive at a wholly subjective decision and then have me collect "objective" data to support it.

Often it's not having all the information in our heads to do a job, but knowing where to get the information that we need to do a job—that begins to open doors, and it takes some of the pressure off. I think that's the way men have traditionally done the job. I know a number of guys that I don't think are any smarter than me; they are certainly farther along than I am. They know where to get the information. All you have to do is try one of them and say you need a certain piece of information and you watch them get on the phone or call someone else or redirect you and it doesn't make them any less powerful. But for us, we have tended to believe that we've had to know it all and that will cause you to burn out quicker than anything else.

The ultimate negative display of creating and maintaining a favorable image was portrayed in the film *Nine to Five*. The boss was groomed and dressed to look like senior management; he curried favor; he called attention to his achievements; and he blithely took credit for other people's work and ideas. Fortunately success based on these strategies is usually tenuous.

Most successful corporate politicians achieve the same goals, with more likelihood of permanence, by developing a reputation for people orientation, thoughtfulness and honesty, competence and enthusiasm. The reputation is the strategy, even though in some cases it is not the reality.

"Put your ducks in a row before shooting" is good advice. Higher-level managers were more sensitive to the importance of the tactic of developing a base of support than lower-level managers.

Ingratiation was described by higher-level managers as praising others and establishing good rapport. Supervisors used more colorful epithets such as "ass-kissing" and "buttering up the boss."

Establishing allies and associating with the influential as well as performing services or favors to create obligations was used more at the lower levels—"You scratch my back and I'll scratch yours." At higher levels there was greater use of rewards, promises, and threats.

A successful politician, according to CEOs in the study, is sensitive to people, situations, and opportunities; is highly articulate, intelligent, ambitious, and success-oriented; but always considers the well-being of the organization.

Many of the women we interviewed talked about "seasoning" as an important process. What these women are viewing as seasoning may well be a realistic approach to experiencing and participating in political strategies, or what Adele Scheele calls "self-presentation, positioning, and connecting."[3] It implies personal control of the situation so that there is minimal danger of losing the values brought to the work environment. It helps reduce the sense of urgency which in turn often gets translated into impatience, frustration, disappointment, and dysfunctional action.

> I wonder if we haven't let down our qualifications and standards. I worry about women not understanding that you have put in your time and pay your dues. I don't believe that you can just move along as fast as some of the young people think they can. It took me five and a half years to get this job and four years to get on the air. That's plugging along.

> You have to learn to get to the top. It's not just as easy as it looks, saying you want to be general manager, let alone president of the company. It's a tough job and it's a lonely job. And I'm not sure how many women out there are prepared to be lonely.

The women in our interviews, all of whom have moved beyond the early career years, now seem to be more comfortable in politicking themselves.

> My belief is that in the competitive world, peers or superiors or people who are underneath you would do you as much harm as they would do you good. They'll either support you or attack you. And it's my belief that one has to be prepared at all times for support or attack, from whatever circle it comes, or whatever point of the circle. For me, it's not having expectations that I'm going to be supported or helped by anyone. And I see that people will act from their own selfishness, their own needs, or their own ignorance. I see it because I see it within myself. I've developed this model for when I'm attacked in a competitive environment. I don't feel as though it's anything personal. I learn all I can about the situation and then I plan how to counter the attack: Do I want to maim? Do I want to harm? Do I simply want to throw somebody out of the room, but leave them fully intact? How do I counter that? So I view it as a battleground where there are people who are out to get me unwittingly, like I'd step on an ant, or on the other hand, people who are after my best interests. There are many styles

among individuals, whose motivations and actions I could never hope to understand. I have to behave, given the signals I get from them. If I get from them a quick knife that comes slipping out of a sleeve faster than a bolt of lightning, I have to be either ready to protect myself or hurt. And if I'm hurt it's because I wasn't there, I wasn't ready.

Another woman put it very bluntly: "If you know they're after your ass, you'd better keep it covered."

Several women talked about self-presentation and job myopia: "It isn't necessarily what you do, but how you present it. . . . I've learned that. Working hard isn't enough. You have to work smart." Some comments by James Reston on Jimmy Carter's "odd selection" of priorities puts into perspective the androgynous nature of job myopia:

> It may seem an odd selection of priorities, but this is the way Carter is and it's the way he does his job. He gets to his work in the White House before anybody else. He goes over more newspapers and documents—has mastered speed-reading for the purpose—presides over more meetings, sees more officials, members of Congress and foreign visitors and holds more press conferences and private interviews than any president in memory.
>
> You have to admire his determination, but question his judgment, and yet remember that these were precisely the qualities that got him to the White House in the first place. He simply worked harder than anybody else. He didn't convince the Democratic party in the election of 1976; he captured it. And having captured it, didn't unify it or make it an instrument of his policies because he had been thinking about other things.[4]

This would seem to be the ultimate in political naiveté at the ultimate in political power positions. An examination of successful careers in most companies will reveal that hard workers will be recognized with merit raises, in salary, but promotions go to those whose personal public-relations system has advertised their potential.

The difficulty most women have in establishing alliances is rooted in a failure to separate the means from the ends. When asked if they have allies at work, many women answer that they "get along with everybody." This response does not guarantee that they have established true alliances. Women give this answer because they have been taught that getting along with people is a commendable trait and an end in itself. Moreover, women have been brought up to believe that manipulative behavior is necessarily negative. In reality, negotiation based in mutual self-interest moves manipulation into the positive spectrum. Identifying one's self-interests and matching them with the interests of others is the first step in establishing alliances. If women in corporations can stop shying away from the concept of acting in a concert of self-interests, if they can accept that "using people" is not negative if based in reciprocity, then the foundations of effective alliances can be laid. The essence of the buddy system is creating a network of positive usage among one's corporate constituents. Brokering is not manipulating. Getting along with everyone is spreading oneself too thin. Managers can't expect to make everyone happy. Alliances should provide a means of getting things done; the end result is accomplishment, not popularity.

Mentors

"Prince Charming in corporate drag" is how one woman lampooned the fashionable picture of the mentor held by the bulk of her peers. "In the past few years," she continued, "the pursuit of a mentor has replaced the search for a husband. Women were told they had grown up to be the men they were supposed to marry. A mentor relationship seemed like the only game in town left that hinted at a little romance."

Many women have indeed translated traditional courtship patterns to the search for a mentor. If no traditional woman could face life without a husband, no corporate woman could make it without a mentor. And just as women believed that a husband was till death do us part, many now believe that a mentor relationship, once established, is a career-life contract. But beyond the romantic nonsense, the mentor experience remains a form of association which can be invaluable to boosting a woman's career. Part of making the most of the experience comes from an understanding of the parameters and developmental aspects of mentoring.

The son of the wandering Ulysses, Telemachus, had the very first mentor. Mentor, in fact, was the man's name, and that is where both the word and the concept originate. Since his father was off to parts unknown, Telemachus' mother, Penelope, ar-

mentor has since left the broadcasting business for a job in the print media but we do keep in touch.

The two final examples of positive mentoring associations offer living proof that keeping a developmental attitude lends the best leg-up.

I would have to say that there were three significant people in my professional life, three primary mentors who have had a lot to do with my process of growth. The first mentor was the confidence builder, the one who said, "Yes, you can do it." He entered my life at the age of nineteen and took the image of a surrogate corporate father. He pushed me along. The middle mentor was a woman who helped me sort out the myths of the corporate female and also helped me reach my own female corporate identity. That process helped me get down to some serious career planning. The third mentor was a male who allowed me to progress, in his presence, from a subordinate to a peer. In fact, I moved him out of his job. But I did so because we had chosen or agreed to this move.

When I first started that relationship I told him I had a desire to live out a definite learning cycle. "I want you to teach me everything you know, and according to my time frame." He sort of chuckled and said, "I'll do my best." So I went from understudy to working partner to a peer relationship in one job. Then it became a question of one of us having to leave the organization because I had completed my two-to-five-year cycle in only two years. He had been with the company for ten years and felt it was time for him to move on, so he left to give me the chance to practice what I'd learned from him in his old job. It was a voluntary thing. I gave him the impetus he needed to move on in his career, so I think this relationship worked very well for both of us.

Linda's story, as stated earlier, is a sad tale of overdependence on the part of a protégée. Other irreconcilable differences in the mentor relationship are overcontrolling behavior on the part of the mentor; rejection of the protégée, in bitter fashion, once career parity is reached; and a fall from grace of the mentor which drags the protégée down in the undertow. Constant reinforcement of a developmental approach to mentoring offers the only true survival technique through transitional periods.

LINDA'S STORY

"Linda" had a mentor on her first job and became very attached to him. She said to us,

I know that he shares more business and personal plans with me than with others on his staff. It is odd to me that he feels comfortable sharing his ideas with me prior to implementation. I feel like a psychiatrist on both a personal and professional level. He trusts me with his private thoughts. I can't help but think that I am the wife and the confidante which he never had.

Linda eventually left her job and mentor to take a better-paying position with another firm, but found that she could not function without the support of her mentor. She returned to her former employer and asked to be taken back, even accepting a pay reduction into the bargain. She had what she thought she wanted: she and her mentor were reunited. Unfortunately, the mentor felt no such bond. When he was offered a better job, he quickly accepted and left Linda poorer and, one hopes, wiser. She continues trying to rebuild her career with the same kind of anguish suffered by a deserted wife.

MARY'S STORY

My mentor turned on me when I got to be really successful. I worked for a phenomenal company where there were four principals and a lot of part-time people. This man was the classic and marvelous mentor. He never held me back and always pushed me one more step. It wasn't the kind of thing where there would be a hard challenge. It was just the kind of support climate where he would say over and over, "You can do it." I grew by leaps and bounds in a very short time. I worked there for three or four years. Eventually clients began to come directly to me and at that point my mentor became devastatingly critical overnight. He began trying to take away work from me, instead of giving me more to do. I guess he was threatened, but to this day I do not understand why. By the time I left the company we were barely speaking to each other, and we had been extremely close, although not lovers.

LAURA'S STORY

When I came to my job I had a mentor who was terrific. With his influence I made significant strides, until at some point I passed him by. I call this "The Death of a Mentor." I had pulled everything from him like a sponge. For a while I felt this incredible void. Then I realized the positive things—that I had incorporated everything I had learned into my own style. Now we are peers and have a very good relationship. But I can see that if you aren't prepared to acknowledge when the mentor phase is over, you can't go on. The important thing is to keep your own style so you can go on to the next stage of development.

There is a separate kind of negative mentor relationship which is unique to women, and that is the forced pairing of token women within a company. One woman described this situation as "the mentor trap." Having made her entrance into the previously all-male sales group at a major food-products corporation, "Joanne" soon found herself labeled as "the woman in sales," and was immediately saddled with training the next woman hired. The problem she explained was:

> The men in my department had serious reservations about how well I was going to do and compounded the problem by holding back on giving me access to their inside tips and contacts until they thought I could handle the job. I was glad to have a second female in the department, but having to take on training was an unfair burden on me. The men were not assigned responsibility for new male sales help. I felt that we women were both being trapped in a Siamese-twin double bind. They expected me to shine like a star, while at the same time they did nothing short of creating a near total cloud cover.

The Man as Mentor

When we asked our male interviewees whether they had ever helped promote a woman in business, their answers were particularly enlightening. On the whole, they bore out Levinson's developmental theory, although several men who had acted as mentors were slightly under the forty-year-old age bracket. Only one man, the division president of a foods company, felt apologetic about his lack of efforts to enhance the careers of women. Every other man we spoke with offered one or more examples of his mentoring activities, though motives and levels of intensity varied. And while most men apparently do take pains to close off the avenues to intimacy, one man freely admitted that his mentor relationships consistently veered into the sexual arena.

> Fifty percent of my job is spent in training subordinates, the other 50 percent in administering my particular functions as a brand manager for this company. One of the key determining factors of success for me is how well I train my people and in getting them promoted as fast as possible. Whether they are men or women, I tell them from day one that I expect all of them to be superstars. I have not been too disap-

pointed to date. Setting examples for people to follow is the best way to manage people.

As a trainer I was at an obvious place to assist women who came into my firm. Since I left that job, I have tried to follow the career path of the women I trained. I felt sort of responsible for how they did within that organization. One woman who stands out in my mind was at the key store level, the cashiering position. This is the point where thousands of dollars flow on a daily basis. I noticed that this woman, the head cashier, was more astute than most of the managers in the company. I told her to get out of that position because the opportunities were limited, in terms of both salary and advancement. I told her to try to get into management. I explained to her that working for three or four dollars an hour was ludicrous when she was one of the people who held the store together.

I think people who are in positions where they are underutilized or underpaid appreciate having someone go out of their way to recognize them and encourage them. When you asked if you could help them to better themselves professionally, most women were receptive. There were a few, however, who were quite content to be where they were.

I'm helping a woman in our organization right now. She was basically doing clerical work, even though she had a graduate degree. I got her working in a marketing sales function. I got her trained for saleswork and in how to put together promotional programs. She is doing great.

I don't think of what I do when I hire a woman as helping. I hire women when they are the best candidates for a job. I hired a thirty-year-old V.P. of finance. I've had to take some crap from people who weren't quite up to it. After some foot dragging, the momentum carries them along and they get used to it. Finally most of them volunteer, "Hey, she is pretty good." But there are still a few holdouts.

It is clear from the preceding stories that these men anticipated the eventual termination of the mentoring phase. Each one took an active role in promoting a woman at a specific point in her career, with the goal of helping her reach a higher level. When that goal had been accomplished, the relationship was usually concluded. Emotional ties, if they existed at all, were kept to an absolute minimum.

A level of mentoring with greater commitment and more personal interaction was evident in the following examples. But again, the mentoring relationship was limited by time or circumstance. There also seemed to be an awareness among the men that a male protégé who didn't pan out could be overlooked, but that a woman protégée was more difficult to disown should she fail to measure up.

I've been a mentor to quite a few women. The most outstanding example is a black woman who was hindered by the fact that she is very beautiful. She fits a stereotype that many men have a hard time overcoming, and she felt that she was discriminated against because she was a woman and a black. She and I had many long discussions. I defended her within the company to the point where she was able to get the job assignment that she was anxious to obtain. But now it is up to her to prove that she can do the job, and while I think she can, I'm not absolutely sure. I do think she was denied the right to perform, so at least now she has that chance. There are six women in my department, all of whom I counsel on a regular basis, just as I do the men. They all have a wide variety of personalities. Some of them come to me with problems ranging from personal to personality and business-related conflicts. I treat the women no differently than I treat the men, but I think that women are having a hard time overcoming the same underlying prejudices that men have. They seem to try and fit themselves into a mold. I tell them they are only going to be capable of succeeding when they are ready to step out of the mold. I try to encourage them to do that in every way that I can.

I was promoted to another position which left my old job up for grabs. There was a great deal of inquiry and responsibility placed on me as to who should have that position. The woman who worked for me was having a difficult time stepping up to that level of responsibility. We spent considerable time talking about how there were certain things she was going to have to take control of to be able to deal with the environment. I felt she had to toss off some of the insecurities she had, maybe shedding some of her aloofness—which is something I detect in many female professionals today. Many women have gotten where they are in the organization in a fairly easy progression, but when they reach a certain level, it seems difficult for them to make the next jump. I think this is because women don't have the kind of training it takes to make the jump. So for them, the going gets tough. It may involve such seemingly simple things as being able to make an unpopular decision. These are the sorts of things a manager will have to do and it requires that women quit trying to be a friend to folks. The jump may also require substantially increased time commitments that cause new imbalances in her family life. She may lose out on family vacations and other such events. This situation was one of those.

I went to the Treasury Department under very difficult circumstances and took over a number of offices, one of which was directed by a sixty-year-old man who had been there forever. He had an assistant who was a very competent young woman about thirty years old. It was obvious that I was going to get the job done only through that woman.

First I made her deputy director of the office, which shunted him to the side, and eventually made her office director. This was a very fast series of promotions. We jumped her from grade 15 to 17, a critical move since grade 18 is the highest rank in the civil service. She was, at that time, the first woman office director appointed in the Treasury. She continued to be competent in every sense of the word and she worked her tail off. I would really rely on her to get the job done. I could say to her, "Here is the job," and she would say, "I'll do it," and I knew that she would, and that it would be done well.

A secondary feature of these examples of one-to-one mentoring seems to be a new sensitivity, on the part of today's corporate men, to the unique development problems faced by women on their way up the corporate ladder. These stories reflect a genuine commitment to the advancement of women based on a strong belief in their qualifications to serve as managers. If the stories we heard are indicative of future man-woman mentoring trends, there is considerable reason for optimism.

As a final warning about the potential for sexual innuendo rearing its head in the mentoring relationship, we offer this candid description of one man's brand of mentoring. We know only his side of these relationships and hesitate to levy moral judgments, but the problems of the dalliance/alliance are clear.

I've had affairs with a number of women who are happy working as secretaries or some other menial job that is not really up to their potential. I have tried to say to them, "Look, take a chance and make a move." One woman got something published in a significant journal and is now determined to become a writer. I was also involved with the daughter of an associate. The daughter was well-known for sleeping with everybody. She was illegitimate and had low self-esteem. Word got around that I was to be her next conquest, but when we finally met at a party, I surprised her by telling her to see a good psychologist and helped her get a job as a clerk. I helped her buy clothes which didn't provoke an unconventional image. She was promoted at her job after just three months. When I had to leave the university town where we both lived, I informally turned her over to a mutual acquaintance we both agreed upon as my successor. I don't intentionally look for women who are wasting their time, but when I find them . . . these relationships usually end with the woman becoming a friend in her own orbit.

The Woman as Mentor

Levinson's description of factors conducive to mentoring raises some interesting questions about the future of the woman-woman mentor association. If the onset of mentoring occurs at a certain stage in a man's life, is there evidence that the careers of women will reach the same point in the same chronology? The emergence of women in management has certainly been subject to a different timetable. They commonly achieve significant corporate rank later, if at all. It may be that younger women will mentor older women as frequently as the other way around. Women who have temporarily dropped out of their careers or who enter business later in life may become protégées of women who are younger chronologically, but more mature professionally. There is also no way of determining how the decision to have a family, and that decision's accompanying effect on both a career track and personal time priorities, will affect a woman's mentoring phase. Such matters will doubtless form the basis of many sociological studies to come.

What is certain from the evidence at hand is that the scarcity of women mentors may be directly linked to their own lack of such an experience. If mentoring is learned behavior, few women have had an opportunity to learn it. Many women have won themselves the label of "queen bee" by their refusal to act as mentors to younger women. The most frequent justification for refusing a protégée is "I did it myself; therefore, you should too." While they cannot be faulted for telling the truth (in all likelihood, they did not have a mentor, nor much other help either), the specter of the domino effect is clearly on the horizon. The chain cannot be broken unless some women reach out to end the circle. It will not be easy. There may be no way to ovecome the void of never having had a mentor. But women, as they rise in the ranks, must give it a try. Levinson warns men that to deny this stage in their development may be a risk to satisfaction in later years. We cannot imagine but this warning will apply doubly to women. We heard two bright recollections of woman-to-woman mentoring experiences which are the best advertisements available for the decision to act as a mentor.

I was very lucky because when I was going to college in New Jersey I had to work. I got a job with a large Catholic charity hospital as a diet clerk. I reported to the chief dietician, who had a staff of 150 people. She was twenty-nine years old and black. Can you think of a better role model? She was, and long before that term was ever created. This was in the late 1950s. She was the most remarkable woman I've ever known. I know this will sound like a strong statement, but I think that whatever degree of success I have today, I owe to her. She said to me, "The sky's the limit. You can do anything you feel you have the ability to do. But you have to be persistent. You have to go after it. Don't ever let yourself be fooled into thinking that just because you're a woman, you can't do it." And she was right.

When asked about her greatest achievement, one highly successful woman said:

. . . elevating and promoting two women who work for me. I look at the sparkle in their eyes and it's as bright as daylight. One of them I hired away from another company. She was their top cash manager, but her talents were not being recognized by that firm. I thought she had everything going for her, but when I offered her a job, she refused on the grounds that she felt too much loyalty toward her employer. I said, "Well, if you don't have any more ambition than that, I guess I was mistaken about you." I think her boyfriend finally convinced her to take the job, although she still seemed intimidated when she began working here. Now she knows everything I know. She finished her undergraduate degree and is now working on her M.B.A. There is no doubt in my mind that she is waiting for me to move up so she can assume my job and there is no more exciting thought for me.

Variations on the Mentoring Theme

There is no guarantee that there will be a mentor in the future of every woman (or man) who wants one, but rather than suffer a case of mentor envy, we suggest a wider view of what constitutes a developmental experience. Our interviewees provided some insights on variations to the traditional mentoring theme.

"The mentor in reverse" was a concept reiterated by two women who defined this effect as "having someone teach you what you need to know by listening to their lopsided criticisms or ill-conceived advice." If a mentor's job is to teach a protégée the ropes, then a mentor in reverse accomplishes the same task, only backward. While these two women said it would have been more pleasant to receive information on a friendlier basis, both were intuitive enough to find a kernel of wisdom for themselves amid negative verbiage.

A second variation was labeled "the institutional mentor," someone who gives you a key break but does not develop a personal teaching relationship to go with the job. A rereading of the examples of male mentoring experiences seems to indicate that many of them practice institutional mentor methods with the women in their companies.

"Vertical loading," a technique which one woman said she benefited from, involved a tacit act of mentoring. Her boss, while not a man of words, gradually increased her workload and responsibilities to stretch her skills. While no deep friendship was formed between them, he succeeded in guiding her career through setting a pace for achievement and rewarding success with rank and pay increases.

But without a doubt the most overlooked of all mentors is the corporation itself. The management philosophy and company policy of any given corporation can serve, as one woman tagged it, "a mentorial function." Several other women echoed this belief, describing their firms as "run by a generation of visionaries," or "operated under a growth and development system." Finding such a firm requires a little investigative work on the part of a woman, but this chore should be made easier by consultations with network members and allies who work in other firms. While having a mentor may be a dream come true for some, taking control of the environment while you wait certainly can't hurt the ascent of a career.

> The reputation of power, *is* power.
>
> THOMAS HOBBES

5

The Autocratic
Woman

In his classic novel *The Scarlet Letter*, Nathaniel Hawthorne recounts a tragedy set in colonial New England. Hester Prynne, who violated the puritan mores of that culture, was pilloried and then required to wear the scarlet letter *A* emblazoned on her clothing for the rest of her life. The label was intended not only to identify Hester as an adulteress, but also to frighten other women who might be tempted into similar behavior. Two hundred years later, women who are challenging the mores set down for them by contemporary society have been similarly stigmatized. They too have been branded with the scarlet *A*, for Autocratic, Aggressive, Authoritarian, Arrogant. It is interesting that today's scarlet-letter women, just like Hester Prynne, are deplored by women as well as men. Women fear loss of the qualities for which the male power structure has rewarded them. Men fear that their own freedom will be limited by acknowledging the potential of women. Both men and women need to isolate and humiliate the Hester Prynnes lest others be tempted to imitate them. Thus it is that this relatively small number of women who have challenged the existing

division of the pie walk the corridors of corporate skyscrapers
wearing the twentieth-century equivalent of the scarlet *A*.

> I think I come across as too cocky. I've heard that remark a lot from my
> boss, who is a male, and the feedback that he gets when I meet with
> either brokers or customers, where, even if I'm right and they are
> wrong, they do not like my attitude. They said I'd walk into a room
> and basically kind of push my weight around. That always surprised
> me because I always believed that I was always open and smiling and I
> had to make no special efforts to be "nice," and then I get this feedback
> and I'm wondering, Well, why is there a difference between my per-
> ception of me and other people's perception of myself. I don't really
> understand that, but I have heard that a couple of times and my boss
> has said: "I'm not telling you to change, just be aware of it, and try to
> be sensitive to what people may think about you." Consequently, I
> guess I have had to tone myself down.

Since Abigail Adams asked husband John why women were not
mentioned in the Declaration of Independence, women have asked
themselves and society at large why their personal freedom has
been more limited than that of men. By Webster's definition, an
autocrat is "a monarch who rules by (his) own absolute right . . .
in excess, a despot." An autocracy is defined as a state ruled by
uncontrolled power. Yet the root of the word finds its origins in
the Greek word for "self." If autocratic means "ruling by oneself,"
it also means governing oneself. Personal autonomy has both prac-
tical and moral components. It involves the experience and ability
to choose a course of action and the courage to follow that choice.
People who have mastered control of themselves, who are self-
governed, are uniquely equipped to provide directions to other
people, to organizations, and to projects. They are able to meet the
challenges of the complex business world in far more effective
fashion than those who are influenced and shaped by the
pressures, personalities, and priorities of the executive role.

The ability to govern oneself is not gender-related. But rewards
for exerting personal choice and personal autonomy are markedly
different for men and women. Not only are the rewards different,
but the arenas in which self-governing men operate encourage
their personal autonomy while women generally operate in restrictive arenas where autonomy is seen as dysfunctional. The same
adjectives—autocratic, arrogant, aggressive—are applauded when
displayed by men and berated when manifested by women.

Semantic Skirmishes

A subtle, but definite etymological event has occurred. In the English language, where syntax assigns no gender to words, a select list has acquired recognizable gender indeed. Warm, sensitive, dependent, passive, emotional, cooperative, supportive, subjective, are all feminine words, while aggressive, active, cold, competitive, objective, rational, independent, and ambitious are all masculine words. So completely has vocabulary come to reflect society, that a verbal shorthand has evolved. One need merely say to a little boy, for example, "You don't want to act like a girl, do you?" for him to realize that he'd better stop crying.

Two words, in particular, have been locked in this gender battle on the executive front—assertive and aggressive. Through a process of accommodation and trade-off, men and women seem to have reached a negotiated definition of territorial rights over these concepts. It is permissible for a woman to be assertive, but men are aggressive. Aggressive women are, therefore, unfeminine. An entire industry, with seminar, book, and self-help group components, has blossomed on the premise that women are conditioned to be nonassertive and that assertiveness is a skill which can be taught. Moreover, this rationale continues, assertiveness is appropriate for women, while aggressiveness is inappropriate. A measure of this view of appropriateness is the willingness of many companies to pay for their female employees' attendance at assertiveness-training seminars. One brochure for such a seminar carried, as a sales pitch, the ultimate corporate kudos for the program: "I was afraid my secretary would come back from the seminar and act bossy, but she returned a far better team member than ever before."

In a June 1979 *Working Woman* magazine editorial, Kate Rand Lloyd wrote:

> Aggressive women welcome! For a couple of years now I have read books about consciousness-raising in working women that include tips on becoming more "assertive" (not aggressive). In fact, those last three words and two parentheses have gone together the way love and marriage did for Cahn and Van Heusen: "You can't have one without the other." Speechmakers, too, breathlessly add "not aggressive" as they exhort women to be more assertive. A pox on all their upraised pinkies, say I. Such dainty disclaimers, possibly for the eyes and ears of skittish men inadvertently caught within the range of the writers and speakers,

won't wash. Assertive and aggressive mean different things—and each has positive and negative overtones. Let's think positive. My handy Webster's New World Dictionary offers, in part, this elucidation: "aggressive implies a bold and energetic pursuit of one's ends . . . assertive emphasizes self-confidence and a persistent determination to express oneself or one's opinions." Bold and energetic pursuit of one's ends— isn't that what we are all about? To be assertive means to stand your ground. It suggests no forward movement. Status quo may be more rewarding than Backward Ho, but it does not get us much further (as a farmer I once knew used to say). Forward movement requires aggression. The dark side of aggression is, says Webster's, "in derogatory usage, a ruthless desire to dominate." I think I'd rather risk a little derogation than give up bold and energetic pursuit.[1]

The following anecdote illustrates a circumstance in which one woman was completely aggressive:

Did I ever tell you how I interviewed the president of a major leasing company? I was interviewing leasing companies around town. I wanted to consider working for this particular leasing company, but I wasn't sure and I didn't know anybody who worked there. I went to the building, to the floor that the leasing company was on, and walked over to the receptionist. She had just received that day a brand-new telephone intercom system that looked like a spaceship, buttons and lights blinking all over the place. I think it was her second day on the job anyway, and it was chaos for her. So I walked up to her and said that I wanted to see Mr. So and So, the president of the firm. And she said: "O.K., what's your name?" I gave her my name. I sat there, saying to myself, What if she asks if I have an appointment? What will I say, then? It will be so embarrassing, I'll have to say no, and she'll say: "I'm sorry, he's busy, get lost, come back another day," and I've completely blown it, because I've given my name already. What would I do if somebody said, "What are you doing here?" I'd have to sort of mumble something. So I thought his secretary would then come out and say: "Do you have an appointment?" It turns out, he showed up himself. I don't know why he didn't send a secretary. We walked back into his office, a deadly quiet walk back, neither one of us saying a word. Now, normally I would expect him to converse while this was going on. And all I could think was that what he was thinking to himself is, This lady is obviously someone's lawyer who's come to serve me a summons. What is she doing? Is my wife divorcing me? Have my children sued me? What's going on? We get into his office; he closes the door, invites me to sit down. I sit down. He said: "I must have slipped up on my calendar because I didn't notice your name." I said: "To be honest with you, I don't have an appointment with you." He said: "Well, who are you, then?" I told him: "I want to work for your company. I am here to interview for a job." He said: "You just walked in, just like that?"

The act resulted in three departmental job offers (none of which was taken) and a friendship for this particular woman.

One interviewee described her prehiring meeting with the company board of directors.

> The board asked some very tough questions, and I gave some tough answers, and I asked them some tough ones, and they were fairly impressed with my candor. They were looking for people who were not yes-men or yes-women, but someone who would stand up to them and say, "I don't agree with what you just said; now, if you make the decision, that is the way we're going to go, I'll implement it, but you need to have the benefit of my knowledge in this specific area before you make the decision." And that is the way I came and that is the way we've played the game.

Power

Contemporary definition has filled the term "power" with demons by emphasizing control and domination over people, and diminishing the concept of ability and capacity to act. Power is seen as static and possessed by a few, who are therefore perpetually powerful. What a confusing state of affairs! Women now have many more choices; that is one of the visible achievements of the women's movement. But to what avail are choices, if the power to implement them does not exist?

There is a myth that women are not interested in power; that, like aggression, power is a male attribute—it comes with the territory. Responses to our interview questions parallel recent research which indicates that women are as interested in power as men. Not only did the women we talked to feel comfortable about the power they had, but they had evolved a philosophy of power as a force for liberation rather than dominance. Among responses to our question, "What does power mean to you?" were:

> Power to me means something positive, not negative. Some people treat power as a dirty word, but it is only a dirty word if you misuse it. If you use it to step on other people. Do I have it? Yes, I do have a certain amount of it. But I think power is something to be respected and constantly examined. I still don't believe that women are comfortable with that word. Society still says they are not supposed to be.

The ability to control your own, not other people's lives. Not having someone say, "Jump," and you jump. Power means being able to control my life, and I believe that I have achieved that to a great extent . . . and I love it. I don't want to control other people.

Increased options. The more power I have, the more I can determine what I am going to do and what happens to me and my family.

I am comfortable with it. I want it. To me power is the ability to get things done your way. Whether it is right, wrong, or indifferent. That there are people who, whether they are willing or not, whether they are compelled or impelled, do what you want them to do.

Power essentially means to me the knowledge of an organization. Knowing everything you can about every department. That gives you an edge on everybody . . . if you know what's been going down the line. And when you talk about game playing, you really have to know where the power lies . . . and corporate politics. It's important to know the strategies, who's who. There is no question in my mind that there is a lot of gamesmanship played. I do it myself and I think I do it instinctively.

Through my broadcast I have power, the power to select women, interview them, I can meet them. I can do it the way I want.

The women we talked to recognized some of the bases on which their power rested.

I think you have to attain a level that has to be a corporate vice-presidency before you really have the power. It's a policy-making position. Either that, or you've got to be controlling bottom-line profits some way and you're probably not really in a responsible position of controlling earnings unless you have that kind of a title. Otherwise, it's just a curtain, I think, or it's a shield. Someone's saying, "Yes, you control it," but you really don't.

They all knew that I had the ear of the president and that I had a good deal of power and his belief and yet could be responsive and sensitive to them on both a personal level as well as a business level. They knew I knew my stuff and they don't doubt me.

I don't care if I am ever president of a company. To me, that is not the goal, but I do want the authority and the power, or whatever you want to call it, to make the kind of good changes I think will be effective wherever I am. I've got some idea of how I can change things now and I really think I could do some great things if I had a little bit more clout.

I serve on a number of boards of charitable institutions and I think
people seek me out because they think that I have some authority
within the areas that I work. I think they also recognize that I can take
a job and do it and that I can command other people to perform for me.
That would be a form of power, I think. But I don't feel the kind of
power that would command people to do things that they didn't want
to do so that there would be any stress involved in my brand of power.

I'm involved in the hiring and firing process, and whether or not that
has actual power, it connotes power and people assume that it has
power. I've struggled with the question of power for some time and
I've had to define for myself what power meant. I look at it in a number
of different ways—financial power or socioeconomic situations that require certain kinds of power to get things done—and I finally decided
that, for me, it is the ability to get things done, whatever those things
may be, whether they involve finances or people, or what have you, to
be able to make changes.

In this particular position, I think that my power is probably perceived
as much more than it really is by the community at large.

The power of a boss over his subordinates is minor when compared with the power of a mother over her small children. The
children, unlike the boss's subordinates, have no choice in the situation. Why don't some women transfer their parental power role
to power roles at work? One reason may be that they truly are unaware of the connection between parental power and corporate
power and have internalized the parental role as nurturing rather
than directing, of responding to needs rather than controlling.
This is the separate-sphere theory. Men are assigned to the public
world, government, business, and so forth, while women have authority in the private sphere. It may be also that those over whom
a woman has power in her private sphere in turn exert power over
her—they limit her personal freedom.

THOUGHTS THAT BREATHE AND WORDS THAT BURN

For most of the women we interviewed, there was a moment of
truth when they became aware of their own power. It was a specific encounter or incident that forever changed their view of
themselves. In *Power and Innocence*, Rollo May discusses this
phenomenon as equal in intensity to the feeling of the loss of innocence. Jill Ruckelshaus, when asked at which point she became a
feminist, replied: "When I went to my first dancing class and real-

ized that I did not want to spend the rest of my life walking backwards."

The corporate counsel of a Fortune 500 company told us she realized her power when a new woman employee she had befriended said she'd have to break off the friendship because people in her department were avoiding her. They were afraid she could influence their careers adversely because of her closeness to the corporate counsel. The vice-president of a major mineral-manufacturing company suddenly realized people outside her company felt she could influence a broad range of corporate decisions because she had been able to affect some department decisions. A newly appointed personnel vice-president is eternally vigilant about what she says since she realized that her new position gives instant credibility to even her most informal comments.

> I guess the one thing I didn't anticipate would happen is the extent of power as seen through the eyes of the employees. It's a very, very powerful position and I have some trouble with people not talking when I get in an elevator because of "My God, there is the director of personnel"—that type of thing. I am not used to it, and so I have some problems with it. They look at not only me personally, but look at the position I hold and interpret certain things about that.

Women, who are still for the most part powerless, have some ambivalence about taking on power roles for fear of appearing to be like the very authority figures who once dominated them. The element missing in their point of view is that power is not a static construct. Those whom one directs, guides, and influences also have power. Just as children have power to limit the freedom of their mother, so does the dependency nature of management create power relationships.

One woman described her feelings in a new job where she clearly wielded a great deal of clout.

> These people [managers with whom she interacted] hang on my every word. They respond to my requests as though they were royal commands. They are scared of me and I am scared of them. After every encounter I get through safely, I breathe a sigh of relief. And then I start worrying about the next one. But underneath it all, I've enjoyed it and believe it will be less fearful after I've had more experience with it.

Women traditionally tend to confuse responsibility with power. A job that carries increased responsibility does not necessarily

bring more power with it. Many jobs with great responsibility—
e.g., supervisor of the typing pool—have little organizational
power. In fact, being responsible has taken on some of the sacred-
ness of motherhood and apple pie. Researchers who recently ad-
ministered a survey to men and women within the same company
questioned the validity of women's responses to a group of questions which probed perceptions of task responsibility. When individual women were interviewed about these questions, it was clear
that the data had indeed been distorted by the use of the word "responsibilities." Women felt that if they were not responsible, they
were irresponsible. It is this sense of responsibility and their long
experience of being powerless that shape how women will handle
power in its liberating form.

Women who are motivated to achieve power in their companies
need to recognize the milestones on the way to their goal; they
need to distinguish between those who really have clout and those
who merely hold empty titles. All too often, women who are senior executives on the organization chart have little real power.
Here are some signposts we were able to identify which delineate
clout from empty titles:

1. To whom does she report? A vice-president reporting to a vice-
   president is probably powerless. A vice-president reporting to an
   executive or senior vice-president is more powerful.
2. What other jobs has she held in the company? If she has had no experience in the critical cost or profit divisions, she probably has little
   power now.
3. Does she put down any reference to the effect on her career of being
   a woman? Defensiveness often indicates awareness of being in a
   token position. Powerful women have little investment in remaining
   the only woman to make it.
4. Does she credit luck and hard work for her success and say little
   about the help and contribution of others along the way? We all
   know you cannot get to the top on your own—male or female. Top
   executives usually are free in acknowledging this.
5. Does she hire and fire her own staff? The ability to hire and fire is
   closely linked to power in an organization. Women are often in positions where they have subordinates, but do not have the power to
   hire and fire them.
6. Does she meet regularly—formally or informally—with the top executives? Access to high places is visible validation of personal
   power. Often men in relatively lower-level positions are viewed as
   powerful because they "have the ear of the president."
7. How is she spoken of by her colleagues? Personal credibility indi-

cates power. If you ask around about someone and the replies always indicate admiration and respect for the person's knowledge,
achievements, capability, you know that person is powerful.

Though many women are still sorting out their feelings about
personal exercise of power, they seem to be quite clear that they
want to work for a powerful boss. There is good reason for this. In
organizations, a critical measure of power is the ability to marshal
resources—people, money, and equipment—to get the job done.
Powerful bosses can do good things for their subordinates. But
women who are moving into management positions carry with
them the historical vestiges of the powerless. Their subordinates
have little if any experience with women as bosses. The critical
question is: What will she be able to do for me? Until proven otherwise, male and female subordinates tend to doubt her ability to
do much. Power, in the sense of being able to influence the environment, determines attitudes toward women as bosses far more
than the currently touted rationale of "Women make poor bosses."
The ability to manage people is probably equally distributed
among men and women. The freedom to influence the work environment is still more limited for women than for men.

Powerful women are still unusual enough that they evoke a variety of rationalizations. Such women, the gossips hold, are inade-
quate as women. They are making up for this by seeking power.
Along with this is the popular explanation of the rising divorce
rate as being due to all those aggressive women out there, who
either symbolically castrate their own husbands or lure away the
husbands of other women. In either case, it would seem that the
problem lies with the men, not the women.

> I think men who fear powerful women either feel inadequate within
> themselves to begin with, way before women entered their adult lives,
> or they feel threatened. Often an internally weak man will attach him-
> self to a very strong woman and then project onto her his own feelings
> of inadequacy.

Shades of Simone de Beauvoir, who said: "No one is more arrogant toward women, more aggressive or scornful, than the man
who is anxious about his virility."[2] Power-motivated men tend to
have wives who stay at home. Whether they choose that kind of
woman or whether they discourage their wives from working, the

result is the same. These men would be threatened by a wife who chose to work.

The attractiveness of success is a recognized phenomenon. Most men have not known powerful women. The experience is a heady one. For many men, there is a vital attraction to this mysterious female personality. It appears that as many women are seen as more attractive as a result of their success as are viewed as losing their femininity because of it!

The Entitlement Dilemma

There is a system of entitlement in this country which exists parallel to our constitutionally classless society. Spend a day in a boys' private elementary school and you will see how the entitled class prepares the young to inherit the world—the world as their fathers experienced it. These boys know from a very early age that they are different in important ways from their peers in public school. They develop a confidence and a level of positive expectation about the world and their place in it.

Power is linked to entitlement. Royalty, symbols of ultimate power, are also symbolic of the attitudes of the entitled. Their perks come to them by divine right. Power in organizations is derived from, and in turn breeds, entitlement. Contemporary events have cloaked this word with some interesting nuances. Minorities and women, as a result of legislation and regulatory procedures, have been accused of acting as though "they are entitled to" a job, a promotion, whatever. The accusers, on their part, are outraged because everyone knows it is they who are, by tradition, *entitled* to those jobs, promotions, and so forth. When the Supreme Court decided in favor of Kaiser in *Kaiser* v. *Weber*, Weber was quoted as saying: "I was all for equal opportunity until *they* starting wanting *our* jobs."

Repeatedly, many of the younger women we talked to in corporations articulated their own sense of entitlement based on who they were and what their achievements had been, rather than by birthright.

Being the oldest, and being a kind of dominant personality anyway, I
assume I have power, I assume I have a right to it. I assume I should be
in power lots of times, because I think I'm right.

When asked whether she would enjoy more power, one woman
answered:

I'd like to be the queen of England, but the job's taken. Those castles
always intrigued me, and those jewels. I think that I'm not ready for
ultimate power. Of course, I don't have the opportunity to have it
either. But I think that in a few years, I would be much more comfortable with and enjoy much more power to effect change than I have
now.

The women we interviewed were all willing to work hard to
achieve and maintain power. Women's motivations for working
have often been characterized as being weaker than men's or
lumped into some such mushy category as "self-fulfillment." What
we found was that women were willing to work as hard as necessary and for the same rewards men seek. They wanted money, independence, achievement, and autonomy. That is what comes
with power. This group displayed none of the affectations around
power as a burden. Those who felt they had power visibly enjoyed
it. They enjoyed the vitality of being actively engaged in what
they were doing and being able to use their ability to effect change.

Hedging the Risks

A woman executive we interviewed is a devoted poker player. She
claims she has two awesome advantages over her male competitors
at the poker table. She is female and she has never played team
sports. Because they think of poker as a "man's game," the male
players dismiss her as a risk player. In fact, they seldom pay attention to her game style until it's time to count the chips and pay up.
Her early sports training was in tennis, swimming, and jump rope.
What she gained from swimming and jump rope was endurance
and healthy lungs, both of which help her to keep a clear head in
smoke-filled rooms. From tennis, she learned to develop game
strategies. She knows how to figure the risk in game moves and

how to adjust her own game plan to take advantage of an oppo-
nent's errors. She has also learned to enjoy being in control of the
game, and most important, she learned how to win and to lose. "In
winning, you are gracious and modest; in losing, you are gracious
and determined; and win or lose, the next game is a new experience
and you try to avoid the trap that caught you before," she told us.

Risk-taking is indirectly related to the power index. Powerful
people can afford to take risks; powerless people can only strive to
survive. When Queen Victoria lowered her backside onto an un-
seen chair, she was confident that she would not end up on the
floor. She knew that was a risk she could take.

Risk-taking, decision-making, and action all require courage and
a bit of daring. This kind of courage is rooted in self-knowledge, an
ability to "read" the situation, and most important, an understanding of what can be controlled. Making a decision always carries some degree of risk. So, we find ourselves caught in that old
equation again: Decision-maker = powerful one = male. Therefore, if a woman is decisive, she is less a woman; often the soubri-
quet is autocratic. Decision maker = powerful one = autocratic
female—ergo, malelike.

There are any number of excellent discussions on decision theory in the management literature, but decision strategy has not
been as frequently dealt with.

Decision strategy is similar to game theory. The value of a particular strategy is the payoff to be expected from the outcome of
that strategy. Not making a decision when one is needed is, in effect, making a decision. It may be an appropriate strategy, but
should be factored in just as the choice of actions are. Critical elements in risk-taking and decision-making are experience and information. You never have all you need of either. The less you
have of each, the greater the uncertainty.

The Decision-making Approaches

Out of our interviews came several principles that can be used to
depersonalize, defuse, and enhance one's decision-making approach.

THE LAW OF SELF-PRESERVATION

It is ingenuous to make assumptions that your co-workers are principally concerned with common or company goals. Everyone is concerned first with his/her own gain or loss in any situation.

THE LAW OF SELF-ENHANCEMENT

Seldom is someone's action directed for or against another person. It is more likely motivated by the need for self-preservation and self-enhancement.

THE LAW OF SELF-ENLIGHTENMENT

The key to effective decision-making is to be able to analyze the possible outcomes dispassionately, to understand the positions of the other players, and to choose strategies that guarantee favorable outcomes.

THE LAW OF SELF-INTEREST

Self-interests will conflict with each other and sometimes with "the good of the company." But there is no unanimous definition of the "good of the company" because each person sees this through his/her own lens. For example, if you are a project manager developing a new product, unforeseen circumstances may make it impossible for you to keep within the budget. But your product will be terrific for the "good of the company," and so you justify your red ink. If you are a manager in the vice-president's finance office of the same company, you must be a watchdog over requests for extra expenditures. Keeping within—possibly below—budgets is essential for the "good of the company." In both cases, the "good of the company" is also what will make that employee look good. Women, whose orientation to organizations has been to "good causes" and to doing "good," often view the "good of the company" as an undifferentiated, undefinable concept. They then are more apt to take on the company "cause" like a Doña Quixote; to view their colleagues as unprofessional or disloyal; to feel personally attacked; and to experience frustration and burnout. Their careers suffer because they in turn are viewed as poor team players, too emotional, lacking the experience and judgment to operate at higher levels, or they are seen as organizationally naive.

Strategies and outcomes are not the same thing. Strategies are very sensitive to the personality factor. What works for one person may not work for another. Adopting someone else's strategies may make one uncomfortable and ineffective. A familiar question these days is: Does a woman have to act like a man to succeed? The answer is No, and she doesn't have to act like any other woman either.

A Dull Ax Never Loves Grindstones

There is great ambivalence in our society over the concept of leadership. On the one hand we create leader-stars, worship them, enrich them, and fawn on their every word or act. At the same time we grind them down, become disillusioned, topple them quickly from their pedestals while still yearning for the one true leader to appear. Many of our contemporary institutions, including business organizations, have dealt with this ambivalence by embracing the ethic of collective leadership—thus distributing power, weakening the influence of the individual, and rewarding conservatism over innovation.

In "The Second American Revolution," John D. Rockefeller describes the conservatism of organizations. "The deck is stacked in favor of the tried and proven way of doing things and against the taking of risks and striking out in new directions."[3]

Most articles and texts on organizations use the terms "leadership" and "management" interchangeably and distinguish between styles rather than attributes. The debate is between participative and authoritarian styles of management or between task and relationship behavior. In a *Harvard Business Review* article, "Managers and Leaders: Are They Different?" Abraham Zaleznik suggests that managers and leaders are basically different types of people and that the conditions favorable to the growth of one may be inimical to the other. Business organizations need managers to maintain the balance of operations and leaders to create new approaches and explore new directions. "A manager is a problem solver: it takes neither genius nor heroism to be a manager, but rather, persistence, tough-mindedness, hard work, intelligence, analytic ability and perhaps most important, tolerance and good will." Leaders bring intuitive and creative capabilities to their roles. They tend to be self-reliant, charismatic, visionary, and can arouse and mobilize other people's expectations. Leaders work from high-risk positions. For managers, the instinct for survival dominates. Managers need to coordinate and balance, negotiate and bargain, calculate staging and timing and reduce tensions. Both managers and leaders need to marshal the energies of other people to achieve their goals. Managers relate to people according to the role they play while leaders relate in more intuitive and empathic ways.[4]

William James identified two basic personality types, "once born" and "twice born." "Once borns" have a sense of belonging to the system of which they are a part. "Twice-borns" have a feeling of separation. Managers are "once-born"; they are conservators and regulators of an existing structure with which they personally identify and which rewards them. Leaders tend to be "twice born"; they may work in organizations, but they never belong to them. Because they are not a part of the social order of an organization, they are more motivated to seek opportunities to change it. "Once borns" take a stance directly over the keel. "Twice borns" lean to one side or the other, or more aggressively yet, head for the rudder.[5]

Women who are not seen and do not yet see themselves as "belonging" to the formal structure of organizations would by this definition be among the "twice born," the leaders. As Zalenzik says:

> In considering the development of leadership, we have to examine two different courses of life history: (1) development through socialization, which prepares the individual to guide institutions and to maintain the existing balance of social relations, and (2) development through personal mastery, which impels an individual to struggle for psychological and social change. Society produces its managerial talent through the first line of development, while through the second, leaders emerge.

It is this stress on personal mastery and personal struggle that results in self-reliance and inner-directed expectations for high performance and achievement.

Emerson, in his famous essay on self-reliance, said: "To believe your own thoughts, to believe what is true for you in your private heart is true for all men, that is genius." James' notion of "twice born" and Emerson's view of "genius" give some clues to the roots

of the scarlet-letter syndrome. Women who are challenging the
existing balance of power in corporations are doubly frightening.
Not only are they introducing disorder and change into a business
system heavy with the weight of tradition and inertia, but they are
creating havoc with the social system which has ascribed roles
they are now forsaking. The antagonism between leaders and managers, change agents and maintainers, is ever present. The tension
it creates intensifies during periods of change. The labeling of
women's emerging leadership behavior as aggressive, autocratic,
authoritarian, is a response to the threat of change. It is a tactic
similar to one we all used as children: name-calling.

Prima Inter Pares (First Among Equals)

Women have been among the most vocal critics of strong, independent women. The women's movement itself has been characterized by great ambivalence about leadership. From it there
emerged a strong antileadership attitude and a "democratic" or
collective approach which stressed sharing power and responsibility to develop every woman's potential. There was an aversion to
hierarchical organizations stemming from women's experience of
oppression in male-dominated hierarchies and their desire to create alternative leadership styles. This lack of structure created as
many problems as the system it was replacing. It allowed the
media to define the leaders; it encouraged hidden manipulation by
frustrated leaders; it created antagonisms and divisions; and it
hampered the growth of the women it sought to develop. Perhaps
most critically of all, it alienated the independent, autonomous,
self-reliant women whose energies were devoted to their own
career aspirations and who were never incorporated into the
women's rights efforts.
   Several women we interviewed described their frustration with
early activist groups. There was almost a religious abstention from
leadership roles, which resulted in frustration and fragmentation
of efforts. The groups were at the mercy of external judges who
concluded that lack of designated leaders indicated a lack of
leadership ability. This inclination among women to distort the

democratic model continues to plague even some of the more recently formed women's organizations.

The following comment illustrates how women often combine the desire to lead with the ability to follow and the inability to sometimes distinguish which they should do:

> I'm a very good follower, in some ways that's very surprising. I feel that I can recognize superior people, and I'm perfectly willing to follow them if I think they are right. I think I'd be much better as first lieutenant than as the leader of a movement. At the same time, I've often had the occasion to put myself in the position of having to be a leader simply because I couldn't stand not doing it. I'm very comfortable with power. I'm the oldest child, and that's a lot like leading the troops. My brother and sister used to call me the "vigilante." That was their quiet nickname for me, because I used to keep an eye on them and make sure they were on the straight and narrow.

The Entrepreneur as Autocrat

The woman entrepreneur illustrates James' "twice-born" leader. She is a risk-taker—the woman on the trapeze, flying without benefit of the corporate net to cushion her fall. She has a personal and active attitude toward her business goals. She wants to influence her environment and determine the direction her business will take. Few corporations have the capacity to tolerate this kind of aggressiveness and inherent challenge to the tried and traditional when it surfaces in male personnel. It is doubly deleterious when exhibited by a woman. Increasingly, women with these leadership qualities are opting for starting and running their own business. The woman entrepreneur and Henry Ford share at least one philosophic principle: "You'll never get rich working for someone else."

In the great debate over when we will have our first woman CEO, the ranks of the entrepreneurial women in this country get short shrift. One Fortune 500 company, which hired a consulting firm to prepare a list of potential board members (female), told the project director, "Please, no entrepreneurs. After all, anyone can have a card printed up that says president. How can you tell what she's done from that?" The proper response would have been to

direct that gentleman to any one of several dozen women who have
created and/or managed multimillion-dollar companies. The age
of the self-made woman millionaire business owner has only just
begun.

There has been a lack of support of women entrepreneurs from
corporate women as well. Professional organizations which attempted to attract members from both corporate and entrepreneurial worlds found programming virtually impossible. The
needs were too diverse. Entrepreneurial women feel that they are
closer to the guts of the economic system than their salaried peers.
Corporate women feel the entrepreneurs have copped out of the
struggle to master the system. There is some truth in both views,
but clearly the greater struggle is between two different styles and
personalities.

While corporate women worry over getting recognition in a
meeting, entrepreneurial women worry about asking a banker for a
$300,000 loan. It takes a strong belief in your own power to even
consider that kind of responsibility, and it takes a particular kind
of autocratic vision. One woman commented on the personal cost
of being on your own:

> I find myself changing in that I've just gone through a real 360-de-
> gree experience, and I found I wasn't even aware of it. I was getting
> colder, harder, more and more invulnerable, and inflexible. I had some
> kind of, I don't know what it was, some kind of big change, and a lot of
> it had to do with business, and there's a kind of paranoia that develops
> when you're on your own, that you're very vulnerable; you have dev-
> astating experiences that everyone has; it's nothing to do with you; it's
> just the way the cards fall or something; and I noticed this happening. I
> noticed that it was affecting me professionally because I was sometimes
> starting to question my judgment about things. I had to do a real reor-
> ganization of my personality. This was about six months ago, and I
> made a real conscious effort to be vulnerable and to be open. You can
> still get kicked in the teeth, but at the same time I think it is much
> worse not to do that, because you become far less than you have the ca-
> pacity to be if you don't keep that quality.

Another woman described her experience as an independent
consultant:

> They expect you to be original, to come up with original ideas, that's
> the way you make your living as a consultant. The competition is so
> fierce that you'd better have those personality traits. I come across as
> arrogant to a lot of people, and really it's a curtain. I do mental leaps,

and I assume that people are tracking the same way I am, and lots of times I have to stop and go back and fill in gaps and do transitions that I just jump over.

Another woman entrepreneur commented:

> I asked a group of women about buying a foundry and they all said, "But what do we know about running a business like that?" I told them that they don't have to know anything about the foundry business. You can hire a qualified manager for that. Besides, business skills are interchangeable. If you can run a boutique, you can run a foundry. But they just don't see it.

Women who can see themselves running a worldwide business have little time for those who falter on the lower corporate rungs. This blessing of self-assurance is necessary to their view of life. Leaders bring the spirit of entrepreneurship to the corporate environment. This evokes the spirit of the early twentieth century, when individual company ownership was dominant. The entrepreneurial attitude has been displaced by the management of issues approach, but it is alive and well in the newer industries, such as electronics, communications, medical engineering. As these pioneers move from garage to corporate country-club complexes, to public ownership, there sadly occurs a replaying of corporate evolution. The maintainers take charge and the change agents go back to the garages to start again.

Isak Dinesen tells a story in her collection, *Seven Gothic Tales*, of the young woman who saves a ship under mutiny by sitting on the powder barrel with a lighted torch ... all the time knowing that the barrel was empty. Give that young woman a scarlet *A*. She was audacious, aggressive, autocratic, and authoritarian. And she was resourceful and courageous too. The risk was great, even though the powder keg was empty. In a way, this is symbolic of women's position in organizations today. There is a veil of mystery around the power that controls corporations; the secret rites of corporate management are closely guarded; only bona fide club members can be trusted with the sacraments. But women have been, as Dinesen says, "Keeping the world in order by sitting on the mystery and knowing themselves that there was no mystery."

Indeed, I would venture to guess that ANON, who wrote so many poems without signing them, was often a woman.

VIRGINIA WOOLF

I asked a Burmese why women, after centuries of following their men, now walk ahead. He said there were many unexploded land mines since the war.

ROBERT MUELLER

6

The Anonymous Woman

Unless they fail miserably or succeed awesomely, men are doomed to a lifetime of proving themselves. Not so for women. Until recently, most women were reassured that they didn't need to worry about being something, or even somebody. The net result has been, as Virginia Woolf suggested, a reluctance among women to seek credit for their contributions. When women departed adventurously into the work force, the years of invisibility were hard to shake, and women's history of hidden achievement, their style of anonymity, did not automatically dissolve once they sat behind a desk. Even in the work environment, some women found themselves returning to the comfortable, supportive, behind-the-scenes roles, where their achievements were measured, not by their own success, but by the success of boss or colleague or the company itself. The anonymous woman has many masks, each of which plays some part in reinforcing sex-role differentiation, especially in the work place. In terms of women's liberation, the shedding of anonymity and the transition of women from invisible to visible is no less than a metaphor for the entire spectrum of cultural change challenging men, women, and their roles in society.

Home Runs and Noble Causes

Individuals develop characteristic styles for achieving whatever it is they set out to do. According to a Stanford University study by Jean Lippman-Blumen, the more their patterns or styles of achievement are rewarded, the more likely it is that these behaviors will be continued. Most men have adopted a direct style of achievement. Like the batter who comes to the plate, each man knows that any hit he makes will be added, by the statisticians, to his lifetime record, and that, in the excitement of the moment, the crowds will cheer him. From their earliest days, this direct achievement style is fostered in men by their life experiences. Women, on the other hand, are rewarded from childhood on for their ability to establish personal relationships. Thus, relationships become goals in themselves. The result is a pattern of achievement through others, of being the behind-the-scenes player. Successes and failures are not recorded on an individual basis, but are experienced vicariously. Either direct achievement or vicarious achievement may be more appropriate in a given situation. Either can become a trap if it represents an individual's only behavior option. Literature on the fundamentals of leadership consistently identifies two essential qualities for managers to have: task and people orientation. The manager's work, these studies point out, is primarily one of dependency. The manager must count on people inside and outside the organization to accomplish his or her job. Direct achievers often have difficulty adjusting to the supportive and dependent characteristics of the management role. Having been rewarded for direct action, it is a struggle to switch styles or even to introduce aspects of another style. If, as has been said a lot recently, the future productivity of the economy demands that managers be more skilled at personal relations, then perhaps the female achievement style may eventually gain value in a kind of de facto cultural realignment. A less utopian, but more plausible, scenario is that relationship skills will grow in importance, with little change in the opportunity balance for women according to the appreciation in value in the area in which they are said to excel.

Remaining anonymous, a "no-thing," is self-destructive. The woman who succeeds or fails only as a reflection of someone else has never put herself to the test. The problem persists because anonymity, by definition and reward structure, is a very seductive trap. It requires no personal action. Breaking through the anonymity barrier takes both energy and the courage to risk.

The ultimate enticement exercised by anonymity is that it masks failure. Anonymous women can console themselves with the knowledge that no one can pass judgment on whether they could have made it. As long as women remain behind the scenes where no one watches, no failure can be recorded. On the other hand, no crowds will cheer.

The relationship achievement style has been shown, by study after study, to reinforce occupational choices for women which result in career ghettoization. In fact, the movement of women into new occupational groups has not begun to keep pace with their increased presence in the work place. In colleges and universities, women continue to enroll in teaching, nursing, and social-work degree programs in large numbers. These occupational groups share a relationship-dependent nature. However, even women who are preparing for male-dominated professions may fall into the "relationship style."

One case in point is our recent conversation with two women entering graduate school—one in business, the other in law. In discussing their postgraduate career plans, both mentioned the non-profit arena. The law-school student spoke of legal aid to senior citizens; the business student of doing strategic planning for a non-profit organization. When asked what had influenced their decisions, each responded it was her desire to "do good for people." The implication was that it would be more fitting and even noble for them, as women, to work in the social arena. Conversely, the private sector, with its emphasis on a dollar bottom line, was rather alien and, to some degree, evil.

These women are also unconsciously acting on what many women have learned: that the new woman is less threatening if, once on the work scene, she continues to do what she is expected to do according to traditional role definitions. Women find more acceptance in the work place when they state their purpose as working for the good of others or for "the cause." But the choices about to be made by our two grad students, no matter how noble, will only help frustrate achievement for all women. Despite their competitive educational backgrounds and credentials for top-paying management jobs, they will choose to remain at the lowest end of their profession's salary scale. Moreover, their premises are shaky. The realities of organizational life are similar whether the organization is a social or a corporate entity. Choices such as these keep the pay gaps wide and the number of women in corporate management at a minimum.

We do not mean to denigrate the value of the kind of work our two women are choosing, but their *choice*, multiplied many times by the growing numbers of women in professional schools, diffuses our potential power in numbers. When women make career choices which keep them outside the mainstream of an industry, or at several arms' lengths from policy-making areas, they diminish both their own effectiveness and the impact which could be made into new career territories. Simply put, to stay outside the mainstream continues women's role as the handmaidens of the powerful and perhaps subverts *one* social good: wide female representation in the top levels of the nation's business organizations.

The Invisible Woman from 9 to 5

The power structure clearly rewards the male brand of direct and visible achievement. Companies find it far simpler to identify the best salesperson than to identify the best personnel specialist. Even though supervisory and managerial roles actually involve considerable attention to relationships, the organization's reward structure does not factor heavily the level of achievement in this arena. For example, there is a great deal of lip service given to the importance of developing subordinates, but there is little direct reward, and no penalty for failure, in doing so. The rewards are in-

direct, ranging from personal satisfaction to developing a cadre of
allies and advocates.

In one respect, women are highly visible. One can hardly avoid
noticing the single woman in a department or at a meeting. But
visibility through recognition of contribution is still elusive. This
is a result, in part, of women's patterns of acting anonymously.
The staff person who researches, writes, and produces the department report remains invisible unless her name is on the document.

A woman we interviewed said she paid great attention to how
men she worked with regarded secretaries. She felt that was the
clearest clue she had to how they regarded her. Since secretaries
are the only women most male managers have known in the work
setting, they become men's model for women in any role on the
job.

In many ways, the secretary is the office wife. She may not only
perform wifely functions such as serving coffee or running personal errands, but she also rises and falls in the organization according to the fate of her boss. Her power, if any, is joined to that
of her boss and even the size of her office and the model of her
typewriter are determined to some degree by his corporate stature.
The very nature of her role is to be "the invisible presence."

The secretarial role, like the housewife role, has fallen on hard
times. Secretaries are now as often reluctant to admit what they do
as a traditional homemaker who cringes to say, "I'm just a housewife." The qualifier is "just," for it has come to be synonymous
with "not valued."

The connections between the secretarial and housewife roles are
their relationship-dependent structures and the similarity of needs
they serve. Within the corporate bureaucracies, the only haven for
personal feelings usually is in the boss-secretary relationship. The
boss, who may or may not be powerful, can find surcease from the
brutal buffeting of his environment in the cove of his office and the
secretarial relationship. The secretary, in turn, has a structured
and approved interaction with her boss, who values, if not depends
on, her personal-relationship skills. The problem of credibility
arises when a man transfers the vicarious achievement styles of his
wives and secretaries to all women, when he generalizes that all
women are dependent and genetically programmed to live in
someone else's shadow. To the woman looking for recognition in
management, the discomfort with this kind of presumed depen-

dency accounts for some overreactions to such seemingly petty events as having men hold doors open for them or having to struggle with egos and etiquette to pay for a business lunch. A woman executive who lodged a complaint against a restaurant for giving her a menu with no prices on it quipped: "I for one *do* want to bother my pretty little head with what the dinner costs." But these small victories combine more for symbolism than progress when the anonymity barrier is not attacked internally at the same time and with the same intensity.

The staff jobs which represent the majority of positions women hold were aptly labeled by Betty Harragan as "ornamental" to the line department pyramid. Just like the wife at home, or the secretary in the office, women in staff jobs perform a needed but supportive management task. Staff jobs seldom lead very far up the ladder. They exist to boost the efforts of the real company movers and shakers. When one reads the impressive figures which purport to show the increased number of women in management, the reality of ornamental positioning lies just beneath the statistics.

Women, as well as men, are caught up in the traditional view of gender-appropriate work roles. The first women sent out by Sears and Montgomery Ward to repair household appliances were met with great resistance from other women. These stores reported receiving phone calls and letters of complaint, not on the basis of poor repairwork, but simply that a woman was sent to do the job. Studies and surveys on gender preferences for professional services—doctors, lawyers, and the like—indicate that women still have a strong disposition to select male practitioners. This demonstrates women's own uneasiness in accepting the new roles of their "sisters." The same woman who leaves her young child every day with a female elementary-school teacher may be unwilling to hire a woman to fix her refrigerator.

A psychologist who conducts personnel assessments for executive positions within major U.S. companies discussed with us a development he found very puzzling. He said that more and more often during interviews with women candidates, a distressing pattern of responses had emerged. When asked about where they were in their lives, what their personal goals were, and how far along they had come in achieving these goals, these women gave distinctly different answers from those of men. At the core of the distinction, the psychologist believed, was the issue of self-identity. One woman responded to these questions by saying, "I'm beginning to like myself now." Another woman, being considered for a top-level international position, replied, "I'm just beginning to find out who I really am." What these women hint at is the struggle with anonymity. They reflect their own movement toward incorporating the model of direct achievement.

A consultant described one of her assignments which highlighted for her the price women pay, in the currency of anonymity, for coming so late to the direct achievement style:

> In a training session with women managers of a research organization, I was surprised to have each of them list poor writing skills as a weakness they planned to remedy. They were nearly all Ph.D.s. When I pressed them on this issue, they explained that the level above them in the company was entirely male. Every report they had written and turned in was reviewed by men and invariably the writing was criticized. Most of these women were convinced that their reports had to be rewritten by their male superiors, and that this meant the names of those men went on the reports. Since promotion in the company depended on a person's success in getting grants, and since no grant proposals were submitted with the names of the women who did the writing, none of these women was going anywhere. Small wonder they all thought they were deficient in writing skills. They were receiving no recognition and were giving their ideas away like so much worn-out clothing.

This vicarious or relational achievement style has been the fuel of the old adage, "Behind every great man . . ." But whose name enters the history books? Who becomes president of the company? A woman in banking told us of her quick reaction to the specter of anonymity:

> When I first came here, I wrote speeches for the president, and for that you don't get credit. He gets to do the final draft and it goes out under his name. You are anonymous. Now I am involved in futures work, which I like better anyway. I am getting credit. On all these special projects, I write the reports and put my name on each one. I have no way of knowing whether my name will go to the management committee, but it is very clear within my part of the company that I did the work.

Several women we talked to had, in a variety of ways, consciously incorporated anonymity into their operating strategies. A personnel director told us:

Actually, I would prefer not to get very much credit. But I make the choice deliberately. The one time I actively supported a woman for a job, she ended up a failure.

A woman whose job requires some political tightrope walking said:

There are some people who really like to be out front. I don't. I like to work behind the scenes—to match up information with problems and needs—to plan for the next steps. I feel powerful in the company and get what I need from them, including their commitment to help me.

And a management consultant talked about her most recent work project:

Going public with your credits probably is more successful a technique if you can select the public. I have difficulty buying the proposition that hiding from everyone can gain you power, but I do think that anonymity can offer some strategic safety. It can be a viable strategy for dealing with some situations. For instance, right now I am serving as the external staff consultant to a high-ranking executive who is reorganizing his company. Only he knows that I am working with him and probably no one else ever will be told. But I am being well-paid for it and it is an extraordinarily heady experience for me.

For women who are still invisible to much of the working world, to assert that they have the ability to choose anonymity as a strategy is a dangerous gambit. Because women remain invisible as individuals and are regarded, still, as indistinguishable members of a group, they cannot, without jeopardy, play hide-and-seek power games. Women at entry or even midmanagement levels are rarely observed as individuals, and continuing skepticism about the abilities and intentions of women is not levied on an individual basis, but is directed at all women.

The inability of male corporate management to distinguish individuals among their women personnel, especially in lower-level positions, resulted in disastrous promotion decisions under Title VII compliance efforts. Since one woman employee was just like every other, there were few realistic criteria developed for the evaluation of individual performance. Anonymous women were plucked from nonexempt jobs and moved just over the borderline to exempt; but the new jobs were scarcely different from the old ones. Hence, the movement to exempt positions was treated as a single, isolated action, unaccompanied by the usual support systems or future career planning. Often, these new placements predictably were, given the circumstances, dismal failures for both the women and the companies involved. Many of these women fled back to the security of invisibility at their earliest opportunity, reinforcing negative stereotypes about all women's ambitions and performance abilities.

A Case of Mistaken Identity

A five-year veteran in a major West Coast leasing company was required to have her annual physical for the company records. At the end of the examination, the doctor noticed that Terry had arthritis in three fingers on her right hand. With a sincere expression of concern, the doctor asked, "Is it difficult to type in your condition?" She responded, "I am the boss. I have people to do my typing for me." The doctor seemed not only embarrassed, but mystified at the angry retort.

The inability to distinguish one woman from another in the work place, along with the predictability of female job assignments, reinforce stereotypical assumptions. A woman consultant told us of an incident in a hotel elevator during a business trip with a black woman colleague. A gentleman entered the elevator, turned to the black woman, and said, "Seventh floor, please." "She was wearing a blue pantsuit," the consultant said, "and she was black, so I guess he assumed she was a service employee." Our interviews were filled with examples of this kind of mistaken identity, and in all cases the incidents left the women with a sense of rage.

A woman newly promoted to senior vice-president of a mining company told us:

> I have been experiencing a rather startling phenomenon. Every meeting I attend is all-male. It is important that I learn the names of all these players and that I be able to identify them. But when I first walk in the room, they all look alike to me. They're about the same age, they wear the same clothes, they appear interchangeable. As the meeting progresses, however, they become individuals. They make it happen by their active participation and by openly promoting themselves and their particular area.

Plateaus of Invisibility—Grades by Gender

At the elementary-school level, most of the classroom teachers are women. Move on to the secondary and college levels, and men become more numerous than women in the classroom. Once one leaves the trenches of teaching and rises to the administrative ranks, the territory becomes overwhelmingly male-dominated. This is an example of a plateau of invisibility—a level at which the progress of women is stalled and beyond which few if any women can be seen. Another example can be found in the world's kitchens. While women are seen as the chief food-preparation specialists in the home, the famous chefs are invariably men. Beneath the disparity between statistical dominance of women in an occupational group and their lack of representation in the management of prestige ranks within those groups are several cultural value judgments at work. The strongest message is that the value of a job and, therefore, the pay are lower if it is one held by many women. Therefore, as the responsibilities of a position increase—and the grade, salary and perks along with them—the gender of that position changes to male. Look at patterns of employment in department stores. Women sell thread; men sell sewing machines. While women are the primary users of this nation's washing machines, it is rare to find a woman selling them. Washing machines and sewing machines are big-ticket items, which are felt naturally should be handled by men, who, as breadwinners, "deserve" the higher commission.

A more complex example of an invisibility plateau can be found in the industrial history of World War II. When manpower was needed on the front lines, the cultural bias against women's employment in heavy manufacturing was erased overnight. The film *Rosie the Riveter* documents women's World War II work history. In one sequence, the narrator of a government movie is heard to exclaim: "They are taking to welding as though the welding rod were a needle. A lathe holds no more terrors for a woman in a factory than an electric washing machine." The radical transformation of women from dainty homemakers to assembly-line workers, from purveyors of brooms to builders of bombs, happened with the mystical swiftness of a New Testament miracle. But the invisibility plateau returned women to their home duties when the war was won. Like Cinderella at midnight, America's Rosies were back at their brooms. The rationale was that the boys were home and the jobs belonged to them.

This is the rule of our culture: women serve; men do. As long as most women remain locked into patterns of anonymity, little will change in the system.

In *Signs*, Sharon Sutherland, writing on women's professional aspirations, commented:

> Until young women can be convinced to aspire and risk for themselves, they will not be in charge of their own destiny and certainly not of the ship of state. Like the ship's figurehead, women will continue to move toward a destination chosen by someone else, masochistically noble, and ultimately ornamental.[1]

White-collar Robots—Women and the Machine Age

All the major revolutions in technology have been owned by men. Women's roles have been limited to workers on the assembly lines and consumers of the products. The homemaking machinery, sold to women beginning in the 1920s, was not created by their demands. They did not cry out for steam irons and sewing machines. The technology which turned out these products was operating under a life of its own. The machines arrived because the technology had arrived, and all that was left for women was to be the end consumers. At a time in history when the technological revolution in the business world now moves with a life of its own, it is imperative that women not repeat this history. For a few more moments in the twentieth century, women and men stand as equals in the window of opportunity technology has opened in the work place. The ability of women to seize the moment is inexorably tied to the issues and patterns of anonymity. For the swiftly evolving information technology has the potential to reduce its servants to white-collar robots at the same time as it eliminates the traditional jobs of the anonymous work force. The Pink Ghetto is no longer a haven for women.

As the educational consultant, when asked about women's issues in the work force during our interviews, responded:

> When you look at women in the work force today, some thirty-five million are engaged in clerical work. Automation and related technology breakthroughs, which are just around the pike, have very serious consequences in terms of the employment of that great segment of workingwomen.

This woman and many others fear that women are about to get lost in the throes of a technological revolution. Technology will both expand and contract job classifications and opportunities, and to the extent that much of the lower strata of work is routine, it seems safe to predict that women will be found there. Men will be controlling the input and making decisions with the data produced. The experiences of women in the educational community and in sales will be repeated. As white-collar robots, women will fulfill industry's need for interchangeable, disposable people, whose only skill requirement will be speed in pushing buttons. These are the jobs which come complete with built-in invisibility.

There is already disturbing evidence that the buttons are being pushed, the keys punched, by ever-growing legions of women at low-level input jobs. Automated check processing within the banking industry is well-established as a plateau of invisibility for women.

In the typical EDP situation in a company, the entire department—hardware, software, operators, and managers—may be housed far distant from the central operations of the organization. The functions performed and the people performing them are thus physically as well as philosophically isolated from the core of the enterprise. The people processing the information know little about the purpose of their work. The people using the information have little contact with those who developed it for them.

The reality is that many middle- and upper-level male executives are unfamiliar and uncomfortable with the new technology. The director of a business-research company cited many examples of male executives who cannot use the computer terminals already placed in their offices. Senior-level drafting designers in the firm of one interviewee have resisted all efforts to learn computer graphics.

But we are on the verge of seeing a generation of executives retire, and as succeeding generations of managers move up the hierarchy, they will bring more technological familiarity, skill, and utilization.

A Silicon Chip in Her Future

Women must pay the machine age its due. The movement away from the physical determinants of labor and toward jobs which call for intellectual abilities was, and is, a major factor in the influx of women to the work force. The high-tech invasion of business offers women today a realm of exciting opportunities and one unique advantage. Much of technology is new; it carries with it a certain mystique and many old-line managers are wary of it. This situation gives women the power to gain visibility through mastery of new tools. Since these skills will be increasingly valuable to the corporate world, there is hope that the old gender barriers can more easily be broken.

The paradox in all of this for women is that they have had an ambivalent association with machinery. Having been told that a vacuum cleaner would liberate them, women are far less swayed by the wonder of gadgetry than are men. However, there is also the inculcated folklore which casts women in the role of incompetent mechanics and scientific ingenues. Machines, as implements of power, carry the image of responding best to male direction and control. The male identification with machinery was experienced by the woman editor of a student publication at Yale. She attended a technology trade show to view new phototypesetting equipment in the company of two male assistants. At booth after booth when the three arrived, the salespeople inevitably began pitching only to the two men, assuming that she was along as an ornament.

A woman entrepreneur we interviewed built her successful business on marketing a memory board. She hired the engineer types she needed for the manufacturing operation and used her talents and experience to manage the company and to market the product. "I was not prone to tinkering because that's not my orientation. But I knew how to sell to the 'tinkerer.' I simply translated what I knew into their language."

Women should not be seduced into believing they are more or less comfortable with technological change than men. All reports indicate that this is a shared problem. The number of seminars now being offered in the field and not subtitled, "for women managers," lends credence to this.

Jane Forester, a professor at MIT's Alfred Sloan School of Management, has said that the computer will change the nature of a manager's work. It will alleviate some of the more routine and mundane duties and free the manager's time for more creative work.[2] In a similar vein, one Silicon Valley inventor predicted to us that women would soon be running the entire gamut of administrative functions in businesses. "Because women are inherently better at information manipulation tasks," he explained, "they will excel in the high-tech managerial environment. Men," he concluded, "would then be free to go out and make deals and blue sky, according to their natural abilities." Whether these predictions are so much vacuum-cleaner liberation redux or a new brand of technologically inspired sexism is difficult to say. What is clear is that changes are certain to arrive and so are the problems they will bring along with them.

Paul Shay, a vice-president at Stanford Research Institute International, anticipated one probable behavioral tendency currently exhibited by today's high-tech manager. He said:

> What's wrong with U.S. management is that it is too fat, especially at midmanagement levels. In U.S. industry a great premium is placed upon information. If a manager knows something which a colleague or competitor doesn't, the manager has a hedge. The practical effect of this is to hoard information.

Workingwomen must take this particular diagnosis to heart, for it is at the very root of their future in management. The ability to manage information systems can only continue to emerge as a powerful career tool and may ultimately become a more valuable ticket to upper-management box seats than even the vaunted M.B.A. degree.

The most important idea for the ambitious woman to grasp is that technology will change both the nature of management and the skills required to make the corporate climb. Her acquisition of these skills and, hence, her visibility at the highest reaches of technology will spell the difference between a powerful and powerless position in tomorrow's work place.

In the Crystal Ball

At a cocktail party a midmanagement career woman overheard a remark that, within five years, all the functions of a board of directors will be placed on a silicon chip. "Oh, my God," she exclaimed, "you mean just when I expected to be sitting on a corporate board, I'm going to face being replaced by a computer?" "Perhaps so," was the reply.

There is a haunting aura about the coming together of events in the seventies and eighties. The timing of women's movement into corporate management coincides with the evolution of new computer technologies. The machine, in effect, arrived to nudge, not so gently, the anonymous cadre of women who have been the drones of the corporate economy. Given the choice of a person or a machine, the corporations must opt for the machine. This could spell economic disaster for the many women who need the jobs to survive. The script is reminiscent of the *Rosie the Riveter* experience. Only this time, women are being replaced by machines in the name of corporate efficiency instead of by returning G.I.s in the name of patriotism.

On the other hand, the new technology creates opportunities. To seize these, however, requires the willingness to step out and up. If you can do the job now, you can surely manage the machines that may do parts of it.

Booting the System

In computer lingo, inserting the disc which feeds the intelligence to a computer terminal is called "booting the system." The phrase is a derivative of "pulling yourself up by your bootstraps."

Women who find themselves on the frontier of the latter-day technological revolution must similarly boot their systems in order to avoid being stuck at another invisibility plateau—as the drones of the information age. Anonymity has never carried the economic dangers for women that it does now. Women must make technology work for them as irons and vacuum cleaners never could. They must become the managers of this new technology, for the future, as Daniel Bell predicts in his book *The Postindustrial Age*, belongs to those who control the information society.

> Sometimes I feel as though I am a nutcracker being pushed from both sides. I vacillate between an enormous paranoia as a woman and a great sense of being blessed and lucky.
>
> ERICA JONG

7

The Alienated Woman

Betty Friedan's psychological profile of the alienation felt by women in traditional roles made her the feminist Freud. This social alienation felt by women in their traditional roles was only compounded as new options became available. Those who were unable to maintain a firm sense of identity, in the face of an onslaught of dicta, prescriptions, and external expectations, became estranged from their inner selves. Friedan and her followers had truly opened a Pandora's box. The natural order of things had been challenged. Women no longer had to behave as they were expected to behave or do what they were expected to do, but many were aware of some undefined discomfort in their lives. Friedan called it "the problem that has no name."

The American "right" to happiness is based in the Declaration of Independence. Perhaps the greatest disservice done by our founding fathers was to promise, in such a sweeping literary generality, the pursuit of happiness, for we seem to have forgotten the realities of the pursuit. Americans now expect happiness as an entitlement and speak about finding fulfillment as though it were a tangible possession. They monitor their levels of pleasure more frequently than their blood pressure and eagerly follow happiness cults as if one person's triumphal search for joy could be duplicated by everyone else. This utopian vision has survived, despite the rigors of twentieth-century history, but lately the pursuit of happiness has left many a workingwoman feeling defensive, depleted, and depressed. To understand the changing psychological climates which created the psyche of today's workingwoman, we offer the following short profile:

Psychological Drives of American Women in the Twentieth Century

1900: Most women at home. The patriarchal system reigns. Suffragettes begin to threaten.

1910: Women toil in factories to fuel the industrial revolution. War brings wives and mothers into a conflict of state versus self-interest. In recognition of their war efforts, women are given the right to vote.

1920: Women go wild. The flapper is an outrage. Women become targets of the burgeoning advertising industry.

1930: Women become the family bulwarks during the Depression. Hard times try everyone's soul.

1940: Women become part of the war machine again and pay the usual price of patriotism—husbands and sons. For a reward this time out, women give back their jobs to men.

1950: The two-car garage, suburbia. Mom returns home to the traditional family life. A few more of their children and loved ones depart for Korea, but all in all, it's happy days!

1960: Women activists branch out into new frontiers. Protest becomes a way of life, as does national sorrow. Friedan identifies the problem with no name and women discover Southeast Asian geography and more grief.

1970: Women surge into the work force. Liberation becomes a catch phrase. Managerial women challenge corporate America while the rest of the national ego licks its wounds.

1980: Disillusionment blossoms in the aftermath of unkept promises, failed solutions, and in the knowledge of mediocrity. Internal polarization occurs among women on a philosophical plane. The media hypes every first woman achiever, but proclaims women's role models are falling down.

Strangers in a Strange Land

Like the heroines in the stories they had heard as little girls, many latter-day workingwomen hold wistful and dreamy expectations about living happily ever after—not in fairy-tale palaces, but in offices and boardrooms. Once the job, like the handsome prince, has been wooed and won, these romantics believe, the future is royally set. We call this the Lady Di Syndrome.

The belief in the fulfilling magic of a career is one of the most significant errors of logic to be exercised by women in the last twenty years. When women set sail into corporate waters, they ignored or denied the warnings sent out by the men already in the hierarchy. They didn't think about the possibilities of disillusionment, let alone serious health or emotional problems. Women thought it simply wouldn't happen to them. As one male manager we interviewed said: "Women come looking for fulfillment in an imperfect system." But having it all became the new religion for women because it embodied the promise of salvation from the psychological lows of housewifery and motherhood. Like zealots, women embraced this creed, frequently refusing to acknowledge the toll of breaking down barriers or the conflicts of choice which having it all would require them to face.

The result of all this has been an intensification of alienation for the workingwoman. The emptiness of traditional roles was increased twofold when women moved into an environment where they were "the outsiders." And the entrenched groups within corporate America, both the powerful and powerless, dealt with these alien invaders by attempting to diminish their ability to contribute, to garner rank and clout. The more romantic her vision of fulfillment going in, the less prepared a woman was to withstand the ego buffeting of organizational life.

A second error, this one of omission, was made by women when they ignored or denied the confluence of industrial events and managerial theories which had both created alienation and superficially acted to abate it. More than a hundred years ago, Karl Marx saw the alienation of man from his work as a central problem within industrial society. Since Marx's time, attention to and concern about alienation in the work place has been expressed in a variety of ways. Each new focus has been followed by an organizational response, but for the most part management's embrace of ideas has been fairly temporal. Fundamental philosophy has remained unchanged.

When women entered the corporate world, their prevailing attitude was that time could be made to stand still to allow them to gain their footing. In truth, the historical dialectic of alienation was already rushing ahead at high velocity while management was busy steeling itself against change. Women simply stepped in front of that speeding theoretical vehicle and were met with formidable resistance by corporate America. As a guide for workingwomen who want to understand where they entered the ongoing study of alienation, we have constructed a skeletal outline of the major concerns and significant trends which have been used to evaluate and often control individuals within complex organizations.

The Genealogy of Corporate Psychology

1910: Scientific Management arrives. The birth of the efficiency expert is heralded. Frederick Winslow Taylor founds the school of scientific management based on the theory that there is "one best method of doing each piece of work." Taylor asserts that the success of inventors and engineers in developing machines and designing factories can be duplicated by designing a worker and his/her workload. Through machines and engineered jobs, Taylor concludes, the unreliable elements in the production process—people —can be controlled. Technology, he says, is the industrial savior.

1920: The Difficult Human Factor. Even with scientific management, companies experience inefficiencies, labor unrest, and employee dissatisfaction. Since technology is assumed to be infallible, workers remain the scapegoats of production problems. Reached almost forty years before women began their assault on business organizations, this conclusion of organizational righteousness is at the root of barriers set against the acceptance of women. If the structure of an organization is hallowed territory, those who cannot make it in the system must look to themselves for the cause of failure. And for those who have doubts about management's lingering adherence to the premise that workers cause the system's problems, we offer the declaration of a Ford executive who was involved with the ill-fated Edsel: "We were right. The problem was in the quality of the workmanship on the production line."

1924:   The Hawthorne Effect. In search of remedies to the people
        problems of production, management turns to an examination
        of factors in the physical environment of workers. The most fa-
        mous of these studies is conducted at the Hawthorne Works of
        the Western Electric Company. Investigators change illumina-
        tion levels to see if light alters productivity. Serendipitous con-
        clusions are formed when results show that output increased,
        not only when lights were turned higher, but also when they
        were dimmed, and even when they were returned to prestudy
        levels. These contradictory findings prompt investigations on
        rest periods, pay schemes, free meals, and workday length.
        With every change, output and morale improve, and when all
        the changes are removed, the output is the highest ever re-
        corded at the plant. The conclusion is that the feeling of in-
        volvement workers experienced during all of these tests and the
        attention paid them by the experimenters were responsible for
        the increases in productivity. The Human Relations Movement
        of business is born.

1940:   Hail Bureaucracy! The German sociologist Max Weber is
        credited with providing the framework around which today's
        organizations are built. According to Weber, there are six
        bureaucratic characteristics: division of labor, hierarchical
        structure, a formal system of rules, exclusion of personal con-
        siderations, employment based on technical qualifications and
        protected against arbitrary dismissals, and a technically effi-
        cient operating policy used to attain maximum efficiency.
        Weber's concepts, taken in sum, call for a complete depersonal-
        ization of relationships and the elimination of nonrational
        considerations. Essentially, persons should be impersonal func-
        tionaries conforming to patterned job responsibilities. Com-
        bined with some of Taylor's proscriptions, the worker's role as
        an executing automaton, in a process from which he/she is sep-
        arated, is set. The boundaries of alienation move farther out
        than ever before.

1950:   The Rise of the Organizational Man. The social alienation
        which occurred in the 1940s continues as people reject the op-
        pressive work systems created by management and its theorists.
        But the 1950s employee, rather than rejecting systems and rela-
        tionships which are at odds with his/her personal position, be-
        comes, instead, "other-directed," not only seeking to please
        others, but deriving self-definition from them. Here is Whyte's
        The Organization Man and Riesman's *Lonely Crowd.* Not
        only does the nature of alienation change, but also its focus.
        Taylor's efficiency experts concentrate solely on manual la-
        borers, but by the 1950s alienation is piercing the heart of the
        white-collar management cadre.

Mid 1970s to date:
        Me-ism and Human Growth Management meet Monster Infla-

tion and Foreign Importers. A continuing influence by theorists like Peter Drucker is rained on by the sociological fallout of the Me Decade. Employees retaliate against the specter of alienation by creating alternative life-styles with multiple frills. These altered values add a bevy of bennies and perks to the sphere of employee compensation and open up whole new job classifications in personnel departments. But corporate swimming pools and tennis courts only increase production of muscles and tans. Productivity and the U.S. share of world markets sag and grow pale. Japanese car imports bring Detroit to its knees, but not one automaker leaves town. Inbreeding continues as do corporate bailouts for crippled industrial entities. The system is made to seem hospitable, but its stripes remain unchanged.

In 1955 Erich Fromm wrote, in *The Sane Society*, that alienation had "become the fate of the vast majority of people . . . pervades the relationship of man to his work, to the things he consumes, to his fellow man, to himself."[1] The price of man's freedom from the constraints of small-group societies and fixed economic and political orders, according to Fromm, was a loss of fixed identity within a stable (if not restrictive) social order. To this we would add the price of woman's freedom as well. The social shifts and alienation which had long affected the people and organizations of our industrial democracy struck workingwomen with great intensity and over a very concentrated time frame.

Hence, women found themselves placed in a doubly precarious position in the last few years. In the same historical instant, women decided both to forsake their traditional identity and to challenge the existing social order. Like flyers on a high trapeze— with no net below—women leaped from one bar to the next, experiencing an acute sensation of total detachment from anything secure. And in that moment, women wondered if they could grasp the next bar firmly enough and in time to prevent a fall.

The Big Drop—The Dimensions of Alienation

As one woman described her situation, it became clear that she personified the fear-of-falling symptoms:

I was already standing on a small island in a sea of personal troubles. And suddenly I felt myself backed up to the edge of quicksand. Then my boss came along and hit me behind the knees professionally. I don't know if I have enough solid ground left to stand on, nor enough balance to stay upright. I have the sense that I'll either go backward and sink slowly or fall forward into the water and go under.

In 1959, Seeman delineated the five dimensions of alienation as powerlessness, meaninglessness, normlessness, isolation, and self-estrangement.[2] To make these distinctions more relevant, we have defined each with examples of their effects as taken from the interviews we conducted.

Powerlessness refers to the individual's perceived ability to control or to influence his/her own destiny. Powerlessness accounts for the degree of alienation women found in their roles as homemakers. The trade-off of autonomy for security placed women in the position of depending on others for their happiness and/or success. In the work place, Rosabeth Kanter observes, women feel most powerless when they begin to believe that their troubles emanate, not from situations or themselves, but from "the trouble with women."[3]

This woman's description of her company's recent reorganization reflects the alienation of finding oneself in a totally powerless situation:

I arrived at my desk one morning to find someone else sitting there. As part of the reorganization, I had been moved into a new department, with a new boss. It made me feel like I was interchangeable. I had learned a great deal about the department I was in, but that was not valued at all. No one asked me if I wanted to change or gave me alternatives. I was no different, in the end, than the furniture they moved from office to office.

Meaninglessness is experienced when a person cannot perceive the reason for his/her activities, nor understand the functioning of the organization of which he/she is a part. For the workingwoman this has meant an inability to predict the consequences of her own actions and a lack of understanding about the actions of others. For women who entered the work place to find a more meaningful life, the experience of meaninglessness is very painful. To leave the traditional role she had held as wife and/or mother—work which society chronically undervalued—only to find that "women's work" in the corporate world is similarly less respected and less compensated, is a brutal and deeply alienating blow.

> I began to feel like a laboratory animal. I had a number of tasks to perform. My boss checked to see if I did them, but I never found out what happened to my work after I had turned it in. When I asked questions about what we were doing and why or what my boss's boss had said about any given project we had completed, I would get a figurative pat on the head. When I persisted, my boss got angry and implied that my attitude would affect his comments on my next performance evaluation.

Normlessness is the loss of benchmarks and guideposts. It is the feeling experienced when someone is unable to reach desired goals through those channels accepted by society. Normlessness is a double bind for women who feel undefinable anxiety about leaving their traditional role and who find so few women to serve as models in the corporate world. The crux of the women's liberation movement was the expansion of what society considered appropriate goals and choices for women, but in breaking with established norms before new ones had been defined, let alone accepted, the whole of society experienced a transitional period of normlessness. Here is one woman's story of transition:

> I came back to work because I could not find a place for myself among the nonworking segment of women. I tried for a year to live as a homemaker, but felt like a fish out of water. But when I got a new job, I didn't feel as though I belonged in that world either. As the only woman in this department, I am treated like a pariah—and that's on a good day. If someone ever writes a story of my life they could call it "The Woman Without a Country." That's me.

Isolation is what a person feels when he/she senses little or no membership in a community, no sense of belonging in the work place. The term "token" is frequently used to designate the lone woman in a particular department, and in many ways the words "token" and "alien" are synonymous labels for the corporate woman in this position. She has few, if any, guides. She makes the natives uncomfortable. She has no definite norms on which to base her behavior. She is overscrutinized and usually overcriticized, owing to her high visibility. And while she might wish for female peers, often her survival in a job will depend on her ability to separate herself from all other women. The isolated woman is truly a stranger in a strange land. And she experiences a loneliness that includes all aspects of and yet goes beyond that of "the man at the top." Like a turtle, she must carry everything needed for her own survival within the shell of herself.

> I really hit a low point when I first took this job. I didn't know anything about the position. The boss I had at the time wasn't sure what my duties should have been either. There had just been a big reordering of power before my arrival. But nobody clued me in on that. I had no mentor and was surrounded by a whole lot of people who had wanted my job. Naturally they weren't going to take kindly to a person that they didn't think belonged here in the first place. And because of this power trip, I later found out that there were people working behind the scenes to make me look bad as quickly as possible. It took a while before I even suspected what was happening. In short, my first few months on this job were miserable. My boss, who has since left the company, never did bother to explain the politics of this situation or say as much as a fare-thee-well or good luck. I found myself having to fight battles and fires on both a personal and professional level, while I taught myself the ropes single-handedly.

Self-estrangement results from a loss of feeling about one's work or even one's life. It is characterized by suddenly or slowly realizing that you are only going through the motions with little or no satisfaction to be had. This component of alienation has its own anesthetic quality. It implies detachment and depersonalization of motivation—a way of life for many women who fell along the sidelines of the fast track. This component may also occur among those women who have made it through the struggle, only to find the achieved goals far less exciting or satisfying than their expectations. It is at this point that a woman finds herself either running in place or at a total standstill. There were two undeniable examples of women coping with self-estrangement among our interviews; the first a Harvard M.B.A. who planned to leave the business world to open a holistic-health practice of some kind, and the second a vice-president of personnel who was heading up to an artists' community to take up pottery. And while the directions of change they were taking seemed abrupt, both seemed confident that they were about to regain control of their lives. Both also used the phrase, "I've done my time," which suggested to us that the self-estranged person views herself akin to a prisoner.

The Alienation of the Outsider—
The Priscilla Principle

Beyond the psychological derivations of alienation, women in corporations experience themselves as outsiders in a more tangible, physical way. The structure, philosophy, power, culture, and literature of business are male. The few women who have moved beyond the entry level and into the nuts-and-bolts parts of business are true aliens. The situation is stressful, not only for these women, but also for the men, who often have no idea of how to act or talk to their new associates.

Rosabeth Kanter discussed the problems that result from the rarity and scarcity of women in a male-dominated environment:

> The life of women in the corporation was influenced by the proportions in which they found themselves. Those women . . . among male peers . . . often had "only woman" status . . . became tokens, symbols of how women can do; stand-ins for all women. Their turnover and failure rate were known to be much higher than those of men in entry and early grade positions.[4]

Kanter goes on to describe the personal consequences of token status. Women are very visible as departmental oddities on one hand, but have to work extremely hard to gain visibility for their achievements. Their mistakes are easily seen and readily commented upon, and their margin of error is very restrictive, since they are assumed to be representatives of all women. If one woman is late for a meeting, the word gets out that all women are late for meetings. And because she is so frequently called upon to represent her company's "enlightened" policies toward women, a token may have to adopt a survival strategy which includes the masking of her inner feelings and true self behind a veneer of public compliance.

One woman we spoke with referred to this situation as the Priscilla Principle. She went on to explain that this derivation of the Peter Principle—the reaching of one's level of incompetence—had occurred to her as she observed women thrust into impossible positions where they were presumed incompetent and simultaneously thwarted by the system in finding what their true levels of incompetence might be. The widespread existence of the Priscilla Principle, she concluded, was responsible for the popular idea

among women that equality would be won when men and women
could be equally incompetent in their work.

Sirens and Alarms—Noise in the Channel

When women departed from the known environment of traditional roles and set out to redefine themselves in the work place, a
number of internal and external elements, all of a psychological
nature, were set on a collision course. Having it all meant trying to
maintain membership in two separate worlds, and as we have said,
this was a complex balancing act to be sure. The net effect often
left women suffering from a double dose of anxiety and stress,
usually in direct proportion to their expectations about fulfillment.
In the past few years, women have closed the ulcer gap between
the sexes . . . from a 10:1 ratio to a more equal 2:1 spread. And in
recognition of the stress workingwomen experience, a predictable
number of books and seminars have sprung up to teach and en-
lighten and calm.

Stress signals and feelings of anxiety are the radar systems of the
psyche, with anxiety most frequently triggered by some threat to
the inner self. When the balance of the inner self and its environment is threatened, anxiety serves to marshal mechanisms designed to counteract the situation. In the extreme, when there are
multiple and severe threats, the mechanisms will take over and the
individual's perception of reality and ability to act will be distorted. On the whole, however, most of us fall into the category of
"normal neurotics" and apply defense mechanisms judiciously.
From our interviews we were able to identify the key triggers of
anxiety and examples of how some women used their defense
mechanisms in the work place.

An Abbreviated Guide to Anxiety

Repression. "If I can't take it, I forget it," said one woman manager. Her problems were so painful that she chose to repress and

refuse to acknowledge them. Denial is also a frequent form of repression. Older women, for instance, who have spent a lifetime working their way up the corporate ladder often claim that they were never treated differently because they were women. Any incidents along the way which might be clearly discriminatory were deep-sixed in the psyche. For such women, repression and denial have become such automatic responses that in all probability they no longer even recognize the stimulus.

Rationalization. From time to time, each person uses rationalizations to validate behavior—whether to justify something that was done or to excuse something that was not done. But we discovered the use of one rationale unique to women which centered on a discomfort with risk and responsibility. One woman entrepreneur was very candid on this point.

> It was easy for me to watch the company I owned with my husband go down the tubes. I told myself that he was really running it, so the failure was not mine. I knew I was a partner and a shareholder and that I had responsibilities to own up to, but as a woman I told myself, The bankers won't bother me, they'll go after my husband. Until I made the decision that I was indeed responsible for what happened to our company, I was a moral coward. Sad to say, but I suspect that this kind of gender loophole thinking is common in women.

Projection. When one is uncomfortable with his/her feelings, the easy way out is to project those feelings onto someone else. The ego can be soothed when the problem is suddenly made to belong to another. An up-and-coming woman manager described her inclination to use the projection mechanism and its effect upon her:

> The issue of dealing with and relating to subordinates is the problem of the day. When a situation arose, with either a male or a female subordinate, I used to begin by assuming that the problem started with them and not with me. And this is an assumption that I'm learning to check. I think that it comes out of my feeling that my subordinates are jealous of my power and position. My boss suggested, in the most careful of terms, that I might be a bit more aware and understanding of what the people around are really feeling, what their needs might be. Whatever the cause, I hope I can work through this reaction because it makes my work life very unpleasant and my personality a tinge too paranoid.

Idealization. This is the process of putting a halo over someone's head, of not allowing a person/idol to have faults. Token women often find themselves the victims of idealization by their male co-workers. Said one woman, "My male peers handled the discomfort of working with a woman who was as good at her work as they were by making me out a superwoman with the most ingratiating sincerity." And women themselves often apply, to certain role models, the trap of idealization, as we note in "The Assimilated Woman."

Opposite reaction. When one does exactly the opposite thing from one's true impulse, fear and guilt often surface. Some women, for example, are so fearful of appearing aggressive that they adopt a meek, subservient style. Anger and hostility are submerged and these women live constantly with feelings of duality. When such a woman is criticized, she is likely to agree with her critics. And the most alienating expression of the opposite reaction is to be found among those women who are pursuing careers and goals on the basis of their fashionable status. Depression follows prolonged application of this mechanism.

Substitution. This is a benign defense which is used to fill some of life's little gaps and to minimize stress. In the work place, many women substitute long hours on the job for the absence of a personal life. Several of the women we interviewed said that they had substituted for not having children by focusing their attentions on the children of their friends. But the most recurring pattern of substitution we found among women was that of placing the nobility of their work, or the importance of the greater corporate good, above their own professional needs.

Compensation. The compensation process is one of balancing talents and skills to make up for deficiencies. Women tend to overcompensate, however, because they have yet to define their worth in the marketplace or are overly sensitive to external judgments about their competence and qualifications. A male training executive said:

> I think that women are reacting too stridently to every incident within the company. They fail to see that a male executive might say something off the cuff, and that he might not take it very seriously. Women—and I see this universally—tend to place more weight on their shoulders than they really should. I think this occurs because women come to a company thinking about sheer survival.

Many of the defenses women adopt to protect their egos adversely affect their job performance. They become more self-conscious about how they look and act. They worry more about their decisions—not only about the substantive context, but also in relation to their often-ambiguous positions. They become more task-focused and detail-oriented.

The self-fulfillment women talk so much about has to do with their need to find an effective balance for their lives, to control the amount of anxiety taken in at any one time. When the environments at home and at work have successfully been managed to minimize anxiety, the defense mechanisms we've described no longer need to be maintained so intensely. But when the environment goes critical, the result is most likely to be a system collapse.

Breakups—The Polyjeopardy of Burnout for Women

In one of those classic *New Yorker* cartoons, two middle-aged executives, with furrowed brows, sit sipping cocktails over lunch. "Did you hear about poor Walston?" one somberly asks the other. "He was consumed by ambition." Walston was obviously a casualty of high ambition, for those with many commitments and heavy psychological investments in their careers are always vulnerable to disappointment, failure, or burnout. Ambitions, after all, do not come free. If the price is too high or if conflicting commitments drain down the energy stores, burnout is very likely to occur. Burned-out women, unfortunately, leave a sad legacy for the women coming up behind them. The corporate world is looking for proof that women will fail under pressure. One woman's burnout is used to imply that all women will follow her lead. In legal parlance, double jeopardy means that one cannot be tried twice for the same crime. The practice of trying all women for the actions of a single woman, we call polyjeopardy. A passage from one of our interviews sums the case up:

> There's been a lot of talk lately about women who are starting to get near the top. They are recognizing that sacrifices have to be made to get there and some portion of them are starting to drop out. Now, I'm not saying that this is bad, but the business population looks at these women and tries to extrapolate their behavior to the whole population of women. "Look," they say, "we've promoted this woman. We've

groomed her for the top. But when she got close to the top, she decided to have a child" or "she decided that her relationship was more important," or "she decided she wanted a job with less pressure." But what these people fail to see is that the only reason men have not made the same choices is because they never had the option to do so. They have traditionally been the breadwinners. Women continue to have somewhat of a choice in this regard, although the economy has limited the viability of the one-paycheck family. The problem for women has been their failure to realize the number and scope of sacrifices involved in getting to the top. I say, "Don't go into a job thinking that you're not going to make sacrifices along the way—because you will!"

A 1980 *Savvy* magazine article labeled "Topping Out" the latest development in the battle of the sexes being played out in the work place. Being able to prove that women don't really want the jobs at the top, the article asserts, leaves the serious business of success to men. The problem is that not all women want the brass ring, the author writes:

> I know a number of men as well as women who'd just as soon ride around the carousel clinging securely to their wooden horses, never leaning out to reach for the ring. And why not? The rings are actually made of brass, and besides, there's only one per carousel. It would be sheer mayhem if everybody on board were frantically grabbing for it.[5]

The merry-go-round imagery is very appropriate, but we caution women not to believe too readily that the ring is brass and not gold. The devaluation of the prize idea—which has made some disciples among women of late—is often the result of a deceptive sales pitch by corporate men who want to keep the prize for themselves. In speaking to women, or in articles written for women's magazines, or in working relationships, men are tending more and more to describe the prize in somewhat gruesome terms. "You'd be crazy to want such a job," they say, and with that piece of advice given, they rest assured women will be content to stay on the lower rungs of the corporate ladder.

The reality is that within the total population, male and female, only a few will have the ambition, persistence, ability, and timing necessary to make it to the top. Most men, as well as most women, will not get there. Part of the process of defending one's own ambitions entails deciding which prizes one truly wants. A strategic planner for a major clothing manufacturer offered this perspective.

> Part of motivation comes from commitment. I am very committed to me, to what I want to attain, to the goals I've set. I am also committed

to the company I work for and its objectives, in the sense that I want to be professional and get the job done. But I feel very strongly that you cannot work for an organization unless you have a commitment to yourself first. This means that if the company which employs you does not do what you think is right, it is up to the individual to go against the grain, to maintain the self above all else.

We found a woman who might have benefited from this advice. She had experienced a different kind of mayhem on the corporate merry-go-round and allowed herself to be burned out despite her motivation to succeed.

Five years ago I was promoted into a position that was described as a dream job in a beautifully functioning department. I found it to be just the opposite. I identified the problems, charted the direction I thought things should be going in, recommended actions to reach the new goals, and gained executive approval to implement the plan. I turned that department around. As a result, I gained the reputation of "Miss Fix-It" and was put into four different jobs in the next five years. Each time it was in a troubled situation. Each time I worked for sixteen hours a day for the first six months to learn everything I needed to learn, then sixteen hours a day for the next six months to turn everything around. Then I'd be moved to a new setting doing the same thing all over again. I never got to see the fruits of my efforts. I never got to enjoy all the particular business of each department. And suddenly I realized that the pieces of my own life needed to be put back together as much as any of the departments I'd cleaned up. So I left and broke the cycle. I just threw up my hands one day and called "time-out."

What these two comments make clear is the distinction between external challenges and internal ambitions. The situation in which our self-proclaimed topped-out woman found herself is by no means unique. Many people respond to an escalating series of job offers with the feeling that they couldn't possibly turn the offer down, and in doing so, set themselves up for a possible case of burnout. But from the sum of our interviews, there was evidence that this pressure to take on every offer was on the decline among women, who have put some distance between themselves and the idea that they must represent all women. Some women said that they had learned that not all offers were good, nor as promised, and that the mere existence of the offer could be used to leverage up in their current job or pay. All of which simply means that women are not as alien to the ways of the system as they once

were, however persistent the climate of alienation in corporate
America.

Breakdowns—The Corporate Cost of Alienation

There has been increased attention to the cost of stress. Corporations are ever more concerned with preserving the health and
well-being (and therefore the contributions) of their top executives. Accident rates have been conclusively linked to the psychological health of workers. Alcoholism and drug abuse have become
major bottom-line costs in terms of missed deadlines, absenteeism,
and loss of the employee to rehabilitation programs. Many of the
Fortune 500 have already instituted programs to deal with alcohol
and drug abuse, and some offer courses dealing with anxiety, family problems, and stress. Many firms now employ company psychologists or have counselors available to employees. Implicit in
these moves is the recognition within the companies of their responsibility to create an atmosphere conducive to good employee
mental health.

But contemporary corporations, holding on to the legacies of
Taylor and Weber, continue to build up alienation despite humanistic frills. And like their managerial progenitors from the
1920s, today's executives still seek ways of molding workers into
ever more productive units, while resisting systemic change. New
strategies for combating alienation *are* put into practice, but the
greater number only seem to repeat the costly nonperformance
patterns of the past. The addition of psychologists to personnel
staffs and the building of extensive, expensive recreational facilities
are nice touches, but are Band-Aid approaches to the problem.

It is here that the push for the advancement of women in corporations has performed a valuable service to the human-resource
utilization dilemma. Prior to the appearance of women in the managerial ranks, the issue of alienation surfaced only when a person-
versus-system conflict created bottom-line effects—such as high
turnover or grievances leading to strikes or other legislative actions. But when women came along, because they were so incon-

gruent with the traditional work force, critical deficiencies in human-resource management could no longer be whitewashed. The system had to respond as it never did when only male employees were fomenting conflict. The ongoing cost of alienation, coupled with the demands on companies made by Title VII and other social pressures to integrate women and minorities into the management hierarchy, forced some real systemic changes.

The organizational shock of these changes is, in part, responsible for the much-touted theory that women will humanize the corporate world, but this bit of nonsense needs to be laid to rest. The influence of women has been indirect and incorrectly credited. What women did was to raise the male consciousness about their own painful existences, to raise for them the specters of neglected families, of superficial relationships, and of the brutal work environment. Some of the backlash against Affirmative Action and equal opportunity have been articulated through comments like: "What are they complaining about?" or "I've put up with that all the years I have worked here."

Another pressure which weighs heavily on women comes from the residue of their "other life." Bound together like sticks of dynamite are concerns about lost femininity, failed marriages, and the decisions of career that precluded having children. The target of this bomb is the self-image ... and the fuse is guilt. Few women have given themselves permission to choose among roles. Rather they have interpreted their new freedom of choice as being the freedom to add new roles while retaining the old. The spark which sets off the charge is usually fatigue, for the energy needed to maintain equilibrium under these circumstances is awesome, indeed.

One woman explained:

> The thing that almost destroyed me was that I decided to get a divorce at the same time I took a new job. I wanted the job, and my husband wouldn't relocate, so we split up. Besides, the marriage was weak anyway. I got to town not knowing anyone, having to deal long distance with a divorce, and faced with learning my job in a very demanding company. I felt no stability at all in my life, and to some degree my ability to handle my work was impaired.

Among many of our interviews with seasoned women executives, the ability to be less an alien on both the personal and the

professional level had clearly begun to emerge. Here are three observations on what women should be on the lookout for to minimize alienation:

> I think one of the key issues for women is coming to understand their
> career decisions and selections in the corporate world. So many are
> coming in now who have a very narrow area of specialty. They have
> not been trained to think in terms of developing useful talents, only
> desirable talents. Many women enter corporations having foreseen
> only one career path—and only one. If that plan falls through—and the
> odds are against a dream come true—these women fall apart or drop
> out. What I would like women to think about is stepping out of those
> lines which so narrowly restrict them. Of course, the reason that many
> women have developed such a controlled view are the bad experiences
> they have had with the system. So, to minimize future risks, they have
> become focused on credentials and have planned to excess as a defen-
> sive maneuver. But all that this has accomplished is the collapsing of
> access to a wider range of opportunity in favor of what are usually
> short-term goals.

> I think it is very sad that women are getting so focused on their desks.
> They are losing sight of reality. They begin to think, How can I be so
> perfect here that God will reward me? They have the feeling that if
> they just shuffle enough paper, some fairy godmother will come and
> tap them on the head and make them a success.

> The corporate world is filled with people who are good technicians, but
> they have lost out on a lot. They've spent all their lives learning to be
> good at a specific thing that they have lost what my mother used to call
> horse sense. One of the things that has most surprised me about cor-
> porations is how little brilliance there is behind the oak doors. There
> are just people who by fate, luck, networking, or knowing someone
> happened to get a paneled office.

Breaking Even

The women we interviewed agreed unanimously on one thing:
surviving alienation depends on finding havens—whether spaces
between changes where adjustments and recuperation can occur,
or geographical places where the climate is conducive to restoring
the inner spirit. Then there are those people in one's life who are
havens of support. They are a precious gift.

The home is no longer a haven for women in the sense that it once was regarded. In truth, the home was not ever women's haven; it was their life. Women made, or were supposed to make, the home a haven for other people. Oddly, the possibility of exercising life choices may finally make the home a real port in the storm for women, but in a figurative sense they cannot go home again. The tides of social change have moved women, and those changes are in some ways irrevocable and irreversible. Women's lives and their relationship to the historic concept of the home and hearth have been transformed and this is so even for those women who continue to live out the traditional roles of wife and mother.

Individual struggles with this sense of loss may be at the root of the current state of alienation of women from each other. The threat which is made to a woman's self-worth may also account for the polarization of women around such issues as equal rights and abortion. Change is, after all, the enemy of the status quo and it can be frightening even to those who welcome it.

The pressures which shift a person's course are operating continuously, and in the swirling turbulence of our modern environment, many pressures are beyond the individual's control. There are many techniques for relieving the physical symptoms of imbalance which will temporarily reduce discomfort or dysfunction. There are dangers, however, in treating the symptoms alone. This is what corporations have done and why alienation continues to creep up in the work place as inflation does in the economy. The beginnings of control will only come when the root causes of a problem are confronted and each workingwoman will have to face her inner self to divine the origins of any stress, anxiety, or alienation she is experiencing.

And the reason that these individual problems must be acknowledged and redressed is that the pressures of corporate life are not going to go away. Choices will continue to confuse or overwhelm, deadlines be set; work relationships will tax; satisfaction and recognition may never come, may not come in time, or in the amount needed.

This leaves only one alternative—whether one works in a corporation or takes a different track in life—to be authentic about one's individual ambitions, realistically setting goals.

For the workingwoman in corporate America, the words of a

young strategic planner (who since our interview has become an entrepreneur) serve well:

Each woman has to define success for herself. You can't always define it in terms of a corporate title or position. Sometimes that isn't a true measure. I don't define success as going up the ladder. Upper management is no guarantee for happiness. Just look at some of the people who are there. That's something for women to understand. There are so many women out taking M.B.A. courses and defining their futures solely in terms of corporate success and I think that is very wrong. Individuals need to define what is important to them, not a company, and then they need to go out and build a system which enables them to move in the direction of their own interests.

> The recesses of the feminine soul have become
> ransom for the gross national product.
>
> JULES HENRY
> *Culture Against Man*

8

The Affluent Woman

Advertising executives have long been aware that a picture is worth any number of words and dollars when it comes to selling their client's products. The more the buyer sees him- or herself in the image of the ad, the more likely he/she will be to shell out for the merchandise or service. In marketing parlance this technique is known as "triggering the defined ego." But the defined ego of the American workingwoman remains somewhat of a mystery on Madison Avenue. The advertising executives, like Freud, don't seem to know what women want.

In the past few years, feminists have raised a considerable clamor over the persistent use of sexual stereotyping in advertising. Since its premiere in 1971, *Ms.* magazine has published a rogues' gallery of such offensive ads in its "No Comment" section. But beyond sexual misrepresentation is the failure of advertising to portray the statistical reality of the American work force. Rosemary Scott in *The Female Consumer*[1] and Lucy Komisar in "The Image of Women in Advertising"[2] observed that print advertising does not reflect the fact that over 50 percent of American women work, and a significant number of ads continue to suggest that a woman's primary purpose in life is to make herself alluring to men.

In a 1978 poll, 53 percent of those surveyed across the nation said they felt advertising was believable. This is why Komisar labeled print advertising "the most invidious mirror of all," for it is accepted as reality in the minds of the majority of the American public. To the extent that the American workingwoman's world is misrepresented in advertising's mirror by mixed messages and imagery, her recognition as a competent worker is delayed and denied.

Stuart Ewen asserts in *Captains of Consciousness* that the two most important aspects of American industrial culture in the twentieth century are the idea of mass consumption and the development of modern advertising. He dates the beginnings of these two cultural events around the birth of the assembly line at Ford Motor Company. At about that time, Ewen says, advertising began to solidify its "ideology of consumption" with women emerging as both puppet and icon.[3]

In 1928, Carl Naether, an early advocate for women-targeted advertising, proposed that exposure was the key to establishing new thoughts, new desires, and new actions. In other words, Naether wanted to make women aware that they had the power to purchase, not only those items essential for survival, but those extras made necessities through the instillment of a concept he labeled "fancied need."[4]

Naether had the numbers to back up his theory and bolstered his case with statistics which proved women bought between 80 and 90 percent of all things in use in daily life. These were the kind of numbers that no advertiser could afford to ignore. Naether also established the idea that one could create beauty-product ads which would make men irrelevant. Playing on women's images of themselves as sex objects, he contended the victory of illusion won by application of powders and perfumes was, *itself*, a sufficient motivator for cosmetic sales, and guaranteed mighty profits to manufacturers. The beauty-product advertisements of today bear testimony to Naether's insight.

Another leading copywriter of the 1920s, Helen Woodward, forged the link between advertising's contribution to the perceived quality of life and the sale of products. Woodward maintained that consumer purchases often served as socially acceptable releases of frustration. If one couldn't have exactly what one wanted, her theory held, one could purchase something that served as the placebo of desire. "To those who cannot change their whole lives," she wrote, "even a new line in a dress is often a relief."[5]

Consumer economist Elizabeth Ellis Hoyt pioneered her own brand of socioeconomic advertising theory which rested on the concept of marginal utility. It was her notion that it was not so much how a commodity was used, but what image of value could be attached to it. What Hoyt was referring to was the status which the purchase of an item could bring to a buyer. "Marginal utility" soon translated into the imperative of "keeping up with the Joneses."[6]

Many of these early theories depended on changes in social mores. In 1929, the American Tobacco Company felt that public opinion could accept ads which pictured a woman smoking. To help reverse the long-held belief that women smokers were "hussies," American Tobacco hired a psychologist to help organize an Easter parade of cigarette-smoking women, who lit up and puffed all the way down Fifth Avenue in New York.

The assembly-line production of unprecedented numbers of home labor-saving devices was a secondary source of new theories on advertising to women. In *The Selling of Mrs. Consumer*, published in 1929, Christine Frederick hailed the industrially inspired "household revolution," and advised advertisers to join the images of production workers and women so that the natural flow of goods could be assured. Toaster ads of the day proclaimed "465,-000 homes *freed* from burning toast." The gross national product and patriotism merged, and the success of this line of advertising was undeniable. By the end of the 1920s two-thirds of the national income was being used to buy manufactured goods; the consumer society had arrived.

Later theoretical developments incorporated Naether's educational precepts, Woodward's desire placebos, and Hoyt's theory of marginal utility. Women were told their new role was that of mentor of social mobility. Children were taught that they could buy their way into a better life. Ewen observed this process and said of woman: "As her homemaking skills had been reconstituted into a process of accumulating mass-produced possessions, her socio-economic capacities were reinforced on a commercial plane."[7]

By the 1950s conspicuous consumption had become a national pastime, and Madison Avenue exulted in their ability to control the income distribution of millions of Americans. In *The Glory and the Dream,* William Manchester captures both the megalomania of advertising executives and the prevailing attitudes they held about women:

> They boasted, and they had polls and sales figures to confirm them, buyers from Oregon to Cape Cod switched to Marlboros, discarded their undershorts for jockey shorts by Fruit of the Loom, or made pilgrimages to the Loan companies so their wives and daughters could answer affirmatively the famous question which, Phillip Wylie had said, was inherent in all ads beamed at American women: "Madam, are you a good lay?" ... A *New York Times* advertisement for a child's dress said: She too can join the Man Trap set.... Being a successful mantrap entailed being desirable—a good lay—in Wylie's phrase, ideally a great lay. Some social scientists and aging suffragettes worried about women's reckless haste to abandon their hard-won independence, but their voices were muffled. The truth, Carl N. Degler wrote, was that American society in general, which includes women, shuns like a disease any feminist ideology.[8]

In Betty Friedan's literary landmark, *The Feminine Mystique,* Friedan was out to shatter forever the image of "the happy housewife." The "problem that has no name," Friedan said, was a restless longing among the women in suburbia to find identities outside their mass-produced possessions of marginal utility.

But even before the publication of Friedan's book in 1962, there were changes in the American work force which suggested that the price of the consumer society was too high to be financed by a single paycheck per family. Between 1950 and 1960, the number of workingwomen in America rose from 18 to 20 million. Forty-three percent of American women had jobs and accounted for nearly 40 percent of the entire U.S. work force by the time that Friedan's book made the best-seller list. These figures suggest that "the happy housewife" was a myth based upon society's denial of women's real contribution to labor and that it was not so much happiness which was at issue as the economic success of consumerism as a way of life. An interesting statistic appears in the October 1981 issue of *Harper's* magazine. In an article describing the goals of women graduating from Smith we are told that in 1960, 61 percent of all graduates wanted to be homemakers, in 1970, 15 percent of the graduates desired that role, and that in 1980 not even 1 percent chose domesticity.[9]

Statistical searching for the profile of the new woman has been a

virtual one-woman campaign, led by Rena Bartos, vice-president
and director of communications for J. Walter Thompson. She is
the undisputed guru of facts and marketing philosophy surrounding today's consumer feminist. In 1978, speaking before the New
York chapter of the American Marketing Association, Bartos
called the attention of her peers to their lack of modernity. Using
an analogy provided by a duck-hunting friend, Bartos entitled her
address "Women as a Moving Target." She told her audience that
they were living in the past by trying to sell to "any housewife,
18–49 years old." Bartos cited the Labor Department's data and
other related statistics, indicating that not since 1972 had 50 percent of all women stayed at home. The nuclear family had dis-
solved, Bartos said, to less than a third of the nation's population.

By adding questions to their surveys, designed to sharpen and
update their target-group index of women, Bartos stated, the staff
at J. Walter Thompson had created something they called "The
New Demographics," heralded as the first profile of the buying
habits of the career woman. But Bartos made the distinction between women who held "just a job" and those who were strongly
motivated career professionals. She submitted as a differential de-
terminant a statistic which alleged that only three in every ten
workingwomen in America were serious about their careers. With
two-thirds of all women working out of economic necessity and 80
percent stuck in dead-end jobs, this three-in-ten figure seems
mathematically correct, but sociologically deceptive.

Two additional observations made in the Thompson profile
were that "career-oriented women were the heaviest users and
readers of both newspapers and magazines." What Bartos was trying to teach her colleagues was that to ignore the reality of her
working life was to alienate the workingwoman from those products which, by virtue of increasing levels of affluence and sophistication, she had the power and prerogative to buy.

Advertising executives were not convinced that they should
tinker with proven theories and formulas. Even though women
were nearly 50 percent of the U.S. work force, they still spent
enough money annually on cosmetics to fund the Apollo Project.
And the traditional women's magazines (*Women's Day, Family
Circle*, et al.) had circulation figures which ran into the millions,
while publications for the new woman could boast perhaps half a
million readers at best in 1978. Madison Avenue reasoned that the

purchase of attaché cases by women did not preclude the continued sales of convenience foods, textiles, and cleaning substances through ads that showed women in their traditional roles and settings. More money in the pockets of American women meant only that the old standby concepts of fancied need, marginal utility, and placebo fulfillment could be escalated.

What is the advertising industry's approach to the new woman? To gain an understanding of the situation, we conducted two short surveys of the workingwoman's image in print advertising.

You Oughta Be in Pictures

For our first survey, we selected six issues (alternating months for 1980) each of *Savvy, Working Woman, Fortune,* and *Forbes,* and compared the number of ads that depicted women in both traditional and work settings. In defense of all of these publications, it must be noted that the economics of magazine publishing require a heavy dependence on paid advertising, and there is little direct control a magazine may exert over ads sent to them. The market segment and philosophy of a publication may translate into some tailoring of advertisements to meet the defined ego, as is evident in the absence of panty-hose ads in *Field and Stream.* What we were looking for was an indication that Scott and Komisar's pleas for a realistic representation of women's role in the American work force had been heeded. The following chart shows all too clearly that the dominant image of women in advertising remains traditional, with her dual roles as homemaker and man-trapper prevailing over her role as worker.

Magazine Surveyed	Total Full Page Ads in 6 Issues (with women)	Ads with Women in Traditional Settings		Ads with Women in Work Settings	
		Number	Percent	Number	Percent
Savvy	58	40	69	18	31
Working Woman	130	106	82	24	18
Fortune	40	21	54	19	46
Forbes	41	22	54	19	46

What is alarming in these percentages is the lopsided portrayal of women in traditional settings within those publications ostensibly designed for the career-oriented woman. Far from reinforcing the image of women in their working roles, the advertisements in *Savvy* and *Working Woman* continually draw on the marketing models of man-trapping and allure. Among the cosmetic ads, the majority employed beautiful, flawless women. None was of women in work settings, nor did any show women applying makeup at home before catching the bus to the office. Several ads for beauty aids prominently displayed bare-breasted women caressing their skins with some emollient or other. Advertisements for underwear were another allure-dependent group. One Maidenform ad in particular featured a woman in lavender panties and bra, long gloves, high heels, and a floor-length mink coat, standing amid the action on the floor of a business exchange. She is astride a ticker-tape machine and the copy mentions something about her "trading in hot commodities." Such an ad seems to lampoon career women on their own ground. It is not an isolated case.

A secondary issue, when assessing the damage done to the image of workingwomen, is the placement of ads of this sort next to those articles which purport to teach women about business. We found several examples of devastating mismatches of word and image. Take, for example, an ad for "overworked and tired hair," which appears next to an article on life insurance for workingwomen. Or a support-hose ad next to an article on bank-loan eligibility. Or a lady's razor ad which asks, "Are you getting a close shave?" next to a piece titled "Should You Trust Your Lawyer?" Our favorite, however, was a full-page ad for an in-home pregnancy-testing kit juxtaposed with an article "How to Get a Raise Out of Your Boss."

The question must be asked: How will women combat mixed messages and stereotypes when such ads are carried in the very magazines which purport to represent and help them? There is no proof that the subliminal messages contained in them, especially those which depend on the man-trap psychology, are diminished by their proximity to articles on business-related topics. And what images of the new woman do these ads leave with a man who thumbs through one of these magazines in hopes of understanding the concerns of his working spouse or the women in his office?

Scenes of Power

The second part of our survey of the advertising industry's portrayal of workingwomen was interpretive rather than statistical. If the majority of Americans believed what they saw and read in advertisements, just what did they believe about the woman who works? Given Madison Avenue's predilection for manipulating consumer behavior, were there new themes within ads targeted to workingwomen? If so, would they be as influential as "fancied need" or "marginal utility?"

Among the nontraditional ads in *Savvy* and *Working Woman*, which rely on the achieving-woman imagery, were a *Wall Street Journal* ad featuring Redken Labs chairperson Paula Kent Meehan, and a Department of Commerce ad that identified a black woman trade specialist by name. A Merrill Lynch ad also identified a woman securities analyst by name and added a bit of overcompensating copy which read: "I have no problem being a woman in the securities industry. I know my job and people accept me." These ads reinforce the idea that there are so few successful women in certain positions that they can be identified individually. They are not faces in the crowd. They are isolated cases, oddities, purporting to demonstrate commendable corporate responsiveness to women.

In contrast to these ads in career-oriented magazines for women are those to be found in the male-establishment publications *Fortune* and *Forbes*. While few in number (ads which pictured workingwomen in the issues we surveyed accounted for only 5 to 6 percent of all full-page ads), most tend to depict women as secretaries, general clerical types, or data-entry personnel. Exceptions to this rule were the ads for Sperry Univac, Morgan Bank, Citicorp, and U.S. Life. U.S. Life's ad was a full-page color picture of a two-career family at home. Mom was smartly dressed and had an attaché case. Dad was in a three-piece suit. Both appear to have just arrived home from work. They are met by a son displaying his painting of a cat, and by a daughter showing off a lopsided cake. The headline of the ad asks the question: "Will the Working Mother Cause the Demise of the American Family?" The copy gives statistics on working mothers and addresses the current issues of family financial planning when both parents are employed.

A mixed-message series of ads were those of the Henkel Chemical Company. In two of these ads women were featured in testimonial roles relating their lives as the wives of Henkel men who had been transferred abroad. One of the women is identified as a schoolteacher, the other a psychologist, but they appear in these ads with their children or out shopping. The exception in this series featured a stately gentleman relating the story of his sister's work at Henkel. She had, he stated proudly, entered this traditionally man's world very successfully and held the position of division director of edible oils. He goes on to allude again to the gender of the work by describing his sister as "the strongest man at Henkel."

There was one key observation about the business ads we surveyed which summed up the status of women in corporate America. Men are seen behind desks, on the telephone, at meetings, driving earth movers, walking down Wall Street, making deals, and standing near the big computers whose information feeds the decision-making machinery of business. Men are in scenes of power, women are not.

The decisions of consumers continue to be ruled by powerful emotions and anxieties. Both of these factors also describe the aura which many women brought to their lives in the work place. The need for fulfillment, independence, and acceptance expressed by women as their career goals are powerful emotional concepts. The self-repair books and seminars, which fared so well in sales, attest to the amount of money women are willing to spend to put their anxieties at rest. Workingwomen did become a fad, a cultural movement, especially during the 1970s. Women's entrance into the corporate world was invested with an emotional importance that sometimes exceeded common sense. What other motives could be responsible for the disparity between women's dollar disbursements for cosmetics and their contributions to women seeking political office? Why else would women so freely spend up to a quarter of their salaries on dressing for success yet so little in support of the ERA and other women's issues? Madison Avenue executives believed that women were more concerned with striving to look as if they belonged in the gray-flannel environment than with using their incomes to achieve equality through financial clout.

The community of workingwomen, particularly through the network vehicle, created what William Whyte labeled in *The Orga-*

nization Man a peer group of consumption values. Items of marginal utility, Whyte said, or the tokens of status, were acquired on the basis of peer-group pressure and ultimately it was the group, not the individual, which determined when a luxury became a necessity. He concluded:

> Soon the non-possession of an item becomes an almost unsocial act—an unspoken aspersion of the other's judgment or taste. At this point only the most resolute individualist can hold out, for just as the group punishes its members for buying prematurely, so it punishes them for not buying.

This kind of peer-group value system forms the philosophy behind the regular feature in *Savvy* called "Consuming Passions." The column serves as a display case for those items which an upwardly mobile corporate woman may safely acquire to maintain her peer-group status. In the end, women who wanted to hold the same jobs as men took up the same consumer habits as male executives.

One clue to understanding the marketing industry's approach to workingwomen is the "Psychology of Affluence," a theory professionals use to develop their sales strategies. The tenets of this philosophy emerged from the findings of a study by Yankelovich, Skelly, and White of major American values, one of which is identified in the text as the changing role of women. We have listed the seven tenets of the psychology of affluence and applied them to the ads in the 1980 issues of *Savvy*.

"The Psychology of Affluence"

Ads by Product Type Which Appear in *Savvy* Magazine.	The marketing strategies outlined in the development of the psychology of affluence.
Contact lens, beauty institute, perfume, nylons, cosmetics, designer clothes, hair-care products.	Trend toward physical self-enhancement. Spending more time and effort and money on improving one's physical appearance. Things people do to enhance their looks.

Smith Corona type balls for personal letters, direct buys from manufacturers, collector's items.	Trend toward personalization. Expressing one's individuality through products and possessions. New lifestyles, the need to be "a little bit different" from ordinary people.
Jogging shoes, Perrier, pregnancy-testing kits, insurance.	Trend toward physical health and well-being, level of concern with health, diet, and what people do to take control of health self-care.
Cars, gold watches, pens, minks, stereos, credit cards, china, calculators.	Trend toward new forms of materialism. The new status symbols.
Items from "consuming passions" column, T-shirts, books, seminars, services for working women. Social causes.	Trend toward social and cultural self-expression, the cultural explosion and what it means in terms of goods and services, and what they mean to various segments of the population.
Book clubs, sailing clubs, luxury soap, alcohol, movies, sensuous sheets, designer undies, vibrators, travel.	Trend toward personal creativity; growing conviction that being creative is not confined to artists. Each can be creative as expressed through a wide variety of activities including hobbies and new uses of leisure time.
Executive women in Affirmative Action ads, time planners, degrees from schools, recruiting ads.	Trend toward meaningful work; the spread of demand for meaning and challenge on the job, often over and above the amount of money paid.

The importance of this finding for workingwomen is that the extent to which they continue to be conventionally portrayed in their consuming roles and poorly portrayed in their working roles is an expression of their susceptibility to conventional marketing strategies and the evolving societal definition of affluence. The status tokens which women purchase to exhibit their membership in the peer group of upward mobility have been seized upon by Madison Avenue and turned into subtle persuaders and image parodies. Writing in *The Wall Street Journal,* Suzanne Weaver noted that the *Journal* itself had become one such persuader-parody. Over a period of several months, Weaver collected advertisements aimed at workingwomen in which the *Journal* was used as set dressing. Among her collection were ads for quilts, perfumes, and underwear, all typical women's items. Weaver concluded that the *Journal* had become such a status indicator within the business

women's community that advertisers were able to make it a staple
of marginal-utility motivation almost overnight. The statistical
profiles and "New Demographics" were lost in the translation of
the career woman's defined ego.[11]

Hence, women still find they are omitted from scenes of power
in print advertising and confined within the concepts of Naether,
Woodward, and Hoyt and the psychology of affluence. Their dollars are successfully wooed with marketing strategies which pay
only lip service to the emergence of women in the work force; and
their moments of consuming madness, vested with the emotional
importance of a cultural movement, have left them vulnerable to
the established powers of advertising theory.

So women find that they are both captains and captives of culture shock. In the minds of America's image-makers they hover
between the man-trap set and the peer group who wants to have it
all—amorphous entities within the consumer society. Only when
women come to understand their power as consumers will they be
able to use their new affluence to buy the image that they want the
world to see.

Getting a Handle on Capital

In American society money is the measure of achievement. The
more money received, the greater the status of the achiever. This is
true not only for corporate salaries, but for many artistic endeav-
ors, professional services, and the like. It is a very simple equation
which often supersedes any other success measures, especially the
humanistic, internal ones.

The attitudes of women toward money and society's skewed reward system for women's work are subjects for a volume in themselves. Resistance to accepting changing roles among women is
rooted in the economic consequences of such changes.

As an American cultural myth, women have been pictured
holding the family purse strings. Daddy earned the money; Mom
spent it. Business finances, however, were the man's responsibility. Women are seen as handlers of money, not its creators or
executors.

The newspaper caption which accompanied the picture of Reagan's appointee to the post of Treasurer of the United States indicated that this job is traditionally given to a woman. This is the most recent and highest-ranking example of women's image in relation to money which we could find. The Treasurer only signs the bills. She does not participate in deciding where the money goes.

The jobs held by women have been clustered into a limited number of functions within most corporations. The vast majority of women in the managerial ranks are in the personnel and financial areas. But of those in finance, relatively few are making important financial decisions for their organization. A classic example of gender separation in the financial area is that of female trust officers in banking, an area with an increasing number of women at the officer level. In many banks, the duties of trust officers are generally divided between servicing the accounts and investing the funds. Women are more regularly assigned to the service functions, which include a large measure of handholding with clients and little decision-making. Figures, after all, are only a representation of the real thing—money.

Traditionally women's only contact with money was through marriage to wealthy men or inheriting fortunes through one's family. The predominant number of wealthy women today are still wealthy through marriage or other family ties. Exceptions are to be found in the performing arts, and among a small but growing number of women entrepreneurs. Though most women have not made it to the executive suite, many are on the way. Futurist Herman Kahn predicted that by the year 2000 women will hold at least 50 CEO positions within the top five hundred industrial corporations.

Women, as the primary agents of socialization, retain one other holdover image, that of the conscience of capitalism. While fathers, husbands, or brothers were exploiting women (and men) in the work force, their daughters, sisters, or wives were out delivering baskets of food to the needy. Women of wealth were expected to endow society's civilizing or moral causes. This role of the "conscience" has led to the current view that women will humanize the corporation. In this scenario, today's executive woman will become the counterpart of yesterday's executive wives and social dowagers. It is presumed that they will fill the role of the corporation's emissaries to the community, carrying baskets of largess wherever they go.

The women we interviewed all spoke in various ways about money—wanting it, enjoying it, learning about it, using it—but their more progressive attitudes are still tinged by the traditional hang-ups.

The Mystery of Motive

Why do women want to work? What is their motive?

The answer is simple. They need the money. In 1975, 42 percent of women workers were single, widowed, divorced, or separated. By March 1976, the figure had risen to 43 percent and has been climbing steadily ever since. An additional 28 percent in 1976 were married to men who made less than $10,000 a year. Inflation's impact on the prices of housing, food, health care, education, and other necessities has made a second income, or even a single livable wage, a necessity. But in spite of this undeniable economic reality, the national perception of women is that they have a choice in the decision to work. The persistence of this idea is, in part, abetted by statements women make about their employment motives.

Women, except when they are living at the survival level, are reluctant to perceive money as their motive for working. Even when they admit to it themselves, they hesitate to admit it to others. The farther up the economic scale a woman is, the more likely she is to give intrinsic motives for working—the most familiar being the search for fulfillment. This search for meaningful work, which so many women speak of, belies the most insidious of attitudinal traps. When women confuse nobility of purpose with economic reality, when they go on record for fulfillment versus financial potential, the snare is set.

A *Fortune* magazine survey of corporate women managers probed their attitudes about money. The question was asked of all of them: Why do you work? Typically, the last thing they mentioned was money. This response pattern emerged in several of our interviews. Women, it seems, cannot get away from the romance of work, and by their words, separate themselves from the motivations of status and salary so frequently expressed by men. Here are a few examples:

I feel used to being comfortable, but money was never that big a motivator to me. I have always been career-oriented.

I don't have a fantasy salary. I hope that doesn't sound stupid. I have a fantasy job and that is whatever I enjoy. Money is important and significant, but job satisfaction to me goes far beyond money in so many ways. If I enjoy getting up to come to work, if I can look forward to the day, that's the kind of job I want, but that does not mean I do not care about how much I am compensated. Of course, I would have to make a judgment on how fairly I was being compensated for my work. But the job has to be meaningful to me or the money doesn't mean anything.

The only thing I feel about money is that I had to learn how to equate, translate skills and ability into money, and that was hard for me. I have a hard time remembering about money because I like my work so much. There is a great reward in doing what I do. I've had a sort of spotty record in terms of salary. My income has gone way up and down and up again, because I do what I like to do first and am not determining things on the basis of economic feasibility. I am the sole income support for my child and myself. I have a kind of religious conviction that my needs will be looked after, which I have found to be true from my experience, but I wouldn't recommend it as a way of life.

I like money but I would have to admit that I don't really care about it. For instance, if I didn't have a husband who knew when my payday was, my salary check would sit in my purse for a week. I have become a sort of absentminded professor where money is concerned. When someone asks me how much I make, I have to sit and total it all up.[12]

This trend instills the idea among men that women don't *need* to make as much money as they do. As one woman told us: "I think men believe we don't need the money because we talk so much about getting compensated in other areas, in other ways." But not all women are so wistfully romantic. The greater number of women we interviewed had taken off their rose-colored glasses and were looking for the green.

I'm very motivated by money. I definitely want to be financially independent.

If I stay in consulting for the next five years, I should be a partner in the firm by then. My salary should be well over $100,000 a year. If I return to corporate America, I am sure that my salary would not rise quite that quickly. Titles are meaningless because being the president of a very small company can be as much of an achievement as being a vice-president in a huge corporation.

I like money just like everybody else, but the reason it is most important to me is that it gauges how successful I am. You can talk about titles, but these days they don't mean very much. You can't always tell, especially with someone from another company, how much responsibility they really have by title alone. But anyone who wants to understand my job and its relationship to this company can tell how successful and responsible I am by my salary.

I don't have a fantasy salary because I take everything in progressive steps. I never take a job without knowing, long range, where I am going next. For me, I would say between $60,000 and $75,000 is the next step.

I feel friendly toward money. It is very important. I have never believed in the intrinsic value of poverty.

The more of it the better.

There is, of course, a historic precedent for women's confusion over compensation and nobility. The occupations which women traditionally entered, primarily teaching and nursing, were low-paid because the work was supposed to be inherently noble and offer its own rewards. Or as Archie Bunker once said to the dear departed Edith, "Why should anyone pay you for the work God gave you to do?"

The Compensation-Aspiration Gap

Ruth Halcombe, in a June 1980 *Savvy* article, "How to Get a Raise—Quick Tips to Make Money," wrote:

Money is not the only reason why people work. A sense of achievement or satisfaction is important too, but overlooking the money side of working can be a costly error, one that can impede career progress. The woman who continues to ignore money goals weakens her credibility among the male players in the career game. Not caring about money reinforces the stereotype of females as passive people, who are in the game only temporarily, not taking it seriously, not playing to win. Being career oriented means being money oriented.

While we hardly want to be put into the position of advocating greed, it would seem obvious that women need to develop a more materialistic streak when discussing financial compensation. Part of gaining equality will require that we learn to discuss money, and the motivations about making it, in the language understood by most men. Women's devaluation of their own worth is often perpetuated when it comes time to discuss salary. One female executive lamented that "women used to go to their salary-review sessions and sit there with their hands folded, nodding complacently." Indeed, there does seem to be a troubling imbalance between women's rising levels of aspiration, expectation, and achievement and their attitudes about money.

A few of the women we interviewed provided clear examples of how socialization and complacency can get in the way of salary negotiations.

The man I work for now has helped me so much. A year and a half ago I felt I had to talk to him about a raise. I was so nervous I thought I was going to faint. I hated having to talk to him about the fact that I was underpaid. I rehearsed what I was going to say and then suggested we have lunch. We met at noon and I talked about everything but money until five minutes before two. He said he was going to leave to go to another meeting at two and in those five minutes I said everything I had rehearsed. He said he understood and I got the raise within two months, made a big presentation, and got a raise again. Now it is easy for me to give him little hints about raises and promotions.

I have always thought it was worth it to fight for raises and I have always attained what I asked for. But I've seen many women, and men for that matter, who don't ask for what they want. They sit around waiting for someone to come around and tap them on the shoulder and say, "O.K., you're the next one to be anointed here. You've done a very good job. We're going to give you a ten-thousand-dollar salary increase." I have never expected anyone to just give me a handout like that, or to recognize my abilities without me having to raise my hand and say, "Let's do something about me now. I've produced for you. How are you going to adjust my salary accordingly?"

Expectations about salary were compared in a classic study conduted in 1975 by Myra Stroeber and Francine Gordon at the Stanford Business School. Overall, male M.B.A. candidates said that they expected to earn a high of $76,000 at their career peak whereas women's expectations hovered at $45,000. Even when the question was couched in terms of a fantasy salary, this gap of expectation remained: $135,000 for men, $81,500 for women. In concluding his study of the 1980 graduating class from Stanford, researcher Larry Perros found that women, on the average, are less concerned about obtaining personal wealth than were their male counterparts. They assigned less importance to the goal of obtaining wealth and expected lesser salaries. Women were also more concerned with security and were less likely to express a desire for a top-management position.

Perros goes on to say that Gordon and Stroeber concluded their study, of the class of 1974, by claiming that the women in that class were pioneers, who would gradually change the world for the women who followed them. Perros asserts that he found no evidence to suggest that the world has changed much in the last six years. But, he muses, six years is not very much time to change a world. We would differ from Perros' comments only in that the last six years have been notable for the amount of media attention to and cultural propaganda about how things really *have* changed for women in corporations.

On the plus side, many of the women we interviewed had overcome their individual attitude imbalances and were very direct and precise about their expectations and goals.

I am now looking forward to being accepted in this firm as a partner. A partnership is a group of people who agree to work together for their own economic gain. They must also enjoy working with each other. Women who are coming up must understand and meet both of these criteria. The economic-gain part of a partnership is relatively straightforward. I either have profitable clients or I don't. I am able to sell work that keeps me and my staff busy, or I'm not. That is the base-line performance requirement in this business.

I see myself being a wealthy and financially successful woman. I spend little time thinking about what the actual dollar and cents will be. Certainly, within the next five years, I would expect to be making about $100,000 annually.

It's funny you should ask about a fantasy salary because I just got the salary that I have been working on getting for a long time—$50,000 a year. As soon as I got it, someone asked me, "All right, what's your next goal?" My response was that this was a blasted materialistic question. To think in higher numbers, for me, means more responsibility, like being on a board of directors. And since taxes are taking so much of what I earn, I feel more strapped now than when I was making $30,000 a year—I tend to think of my next goal more in terms of position than numerically.

My fantasy salary—$150,000 within the next five years.

Sixty thousand dollars sounds good.

Women are becoming more aware that performance is rewarded in the corporate system through increase in rank *and salary.* And the traditional female attitudes about money and power have changed as they have been addressed by a greater number of sophisticated businesswomen. In the bargain, capitalism has lost a bit of its male identification. As one woman said: "Getting more money is always worth the trouble. Hell, it's the American way of life!"

According to Columbia Business School's Center for Research in Career Development the mean salary for female M.B.A.s in 1980 at the entry level was $9,334 less than males' salaries. Also, the value of the M.B.A. certificate has varied with supply and demand. In 1971, there were 758 women among 21,417 persons graduating with the M.B.A. degree. Women represented only 3.5 percent of this number. In 1981, however, there were 25.9 percent women enrolled in the M.B.A. programs. Out of 56,000 M.B.A.s awarded, 14,500 were held by women.

The Affluence/Influence Equation

"Money is the principal measure by which I determine whether or not I am advancing in my career," as one woman told us. "But money is also an important mirror. It reflects power and influence, so in that sense money is also important to me because of what it infers." This is the essence of what we call "The Affluence/Influence Equation," and it is another step women need to take beyond their old attitudes about status and power.

It is improbable that any woman over the age of thirty and under forty escaped being influenced by economic principles and practices of the late 1940s and 1950s. While they may have found themselves in college in the sixties, demonstrating against the evils of materialism, the imprint of those formative years often returns to the forefront once their career climb has begun.

Women forty years and older are products of a far different formative process. They were either Depression or war children who grew up in ages of scarcity or rationing, but they were no less affected by the American Dream machine of the 1950s. Their perception of the dream, however, was that it was the result of sacrifice and diligence and that the acquisition of material things would come as a reward for hard work and sacrifice.

In the sixties, Rennie Davis and Jerry Rubin stormed the ramparts for social change and decried the capitalist state—the government, the bureaucracy, the leadership, and the politics of the country. Now, less than twenty years later, we find Davis trading in his army fatigues for Brooks Brothers suits.

One of his clients commented:

> Rennie's goal is still nothing less than saving the world, but he found that working outside the system was like attacking a mountain with an ice pick.

Jerry Rubin, now sporting gray-flannel suits and finding a niche for himself in the canyons of Wall Street, has been quoted as saying:

> I don't think I can reform the system, but I can do innovative things. I'm idealistic enough to think that I can have an effect. The bottom line, if you will, in this country, is that the person who signs the checks has power. I don't think that making decisions on the basis of money is wrong anymore. For a long time, people in our age group felt that it was immoral to do something only for a monetary return. There's been a major shift here, due to inflation and a more rational approach. The old expression—put your money where your mouth is—fits into a new awareness.

Rubin's realization of the relationship between money and power and the influence money has to effect change has created a whole new life-style for him. He saw this metamorphosis as necessary to adjust to the times in which he was living. He had made a realistic appraisal of how to accomplish the changes he wanted to see. And he added: "I want people to stop looking at me in terms of the past. I like to challenge images."[13]

This takes us back to women's traditional role as the conscience of capitalism and suggests that it is time for them to challenge that image. It will do women very little good to move into affluence if they fail to understand the influence their money can buy. John Kenneth Galbraith, in *The Affluent Society*, went so far as to make the dire observation that "The problems of an affluent world which doesn't understand itself may be serious and they can needlessly threaten the affluence itself."[14]

Suppose that a woman's organization was suddenly endowed with several millions of dollars to purchase, or shall we say orchestrate, the passage of the ERA, or some other legislation or project to benefit women. How many groups would know what to do and how to do it? How many women understand the affluence/influence system of which they are a part? There has been little evidence to date that women do understand. They have not made the leap of Rubin and Davis across the power gap. They have not, in any significant fashion, put their money where their mouths are. Women have given limited financial support to women candidates, or even male candidates for that matter, who represent them on issues of interest and concern. One woman politician told us:

> When I go to a fund-raising meeting with a male audience and pass the hat, it comes back with twenties and fifties. When I speak in a women's group and pass the hat, it comes back with ones, fives, and only an occasional ten.

Granted, women may have far fewer discretionary dollars to pitch in the hat, but by looking at money as an end in itself, or as simply a means of subsistence or acquisition, they have shortchanged their ability to make change in society. Several of the women we interviewed were more vocal on this point.

> I keep going on to some women about money until my dialectics make me sound more like a Marxist than a capitalist. But it makes me sad that women now have discretionary income and are spending it on lipstick, panty hose, and designer clothes, instead of putting the money where it will do some good. So many don't seem to understand.

> I talk to women who are now making $35,000 a year and they say that they no longer need feminism because they are successful. They say that they are tired of being asked to support women's causes. But in my humble opinion, these women have tunnel vision. They are short-

sighted. At what point can anyone make the statement that there is nothing left for them to do?

When the women in this company all received some money from a lawsuit over discrimination, there was one particular woman who at first refused the money, and when she was forced to take it, gave it away to the Red Cross. She said she had a hard time taking advantage of the system like that.

I think that the only really powerful women we'll ever have are those women with access to large sums of money. And this is another thing that most women do not like to hear. I've had women say to me that money is not nice. That there are more important things. And I say to them, I'd like to know just one thing that is more important. They respond by saying, "My family." I tell them that without money their families are going to starve.

Galbraith makes one other observation about wealth which defines its three basic benefits: "the satisfaction in the power with which it endows the individual ... the physical possession of things which money can buy, and ... the distinction or esteem that accrues to the rich man [sic] as the result of his wealth."[15] Whatever the future of American affluence, whether we are moving to a phase of increased prosperity or whether things stay the same or get worse, society will be constantly reckoning with the disparity between its philosophy and goals and the money it takes to make things happen. Galbraith's explanation of wealth's benefits, when applied to women, suggests they have limited themselves to only the second and third functions of affluence. They pursue the acquisition of possessions and are locked into a kind of status-linked accrual of esteem. Benefit number one—the feel for power—still seems to lie somewhere in the future. Strange to say, but perhaps a good model for women to look at is that of Joseph Kennedy, the late patriarch of the Kennedy clan. He used his money to the limits of influence and is credited with being able to buy his son the presidency. Women need to reconcile their social aims with their increasing affluence, for the creation and control of wealth, in the final analysis, may be the most effective means of liberation.

By Status Possessed

Possessions and power are also the key elements which, combined, produce the status symbol. Here again, workingwomen seem guilty of misappropriating their funds.

Status symbols in the business world provide tangible evidence of real power where it really counts. Gold pens, watches, and clothing standards, exhibited by men among their subordinates and contemporaries, are visual and nonverbal messages about rank and position. The ultimate expression of this unspoken code is the club tie, which was designed so that men could identify one of their own even on crowded city streets. And though superficially subtle, the tie communicates the most profound of all male status symbols—membership in the club. Though women spare no expense in collecting the status symbols of corporate achievement, they haven't really understood that the substance of power, the meaning behind the code, has not yet been extended to their gender.

The men who do not attribute real power to women aren't swayed when confronted by a woman in status attire brandishing status accessories. In the eyes of those who control the economic world and its symbols, an executive woman dressed in a tailored suit might just as well be featuring the emperor's new clothes.

But corporations are adept at manipulating the representative symbols of the unspoken code. Corner offices and wooden (instead of metal) desks are but two of the many tokens of prestige which companies dispense to executives. First choice of vacation time is a lesser, but indisputable token of recognition. All of these in-house perks carry their measure of clout. Before the Affirmative Action mandate, though, these symbols were generally awarded on the basis of seniority, but once women began to accept meaningless titles handed out by corporations eager to comply with the letter, if not the spirit, of the law, the value of the symbols decreased along with the titles.

Women who go after these status symbols quickly become aware of the corporation's mastery of the game. One woman told us that her demand for a five-thousand-dollar raise was countered with an offer of one thousand dollars more per year and new office draperies. Time and experience in the system have increased women's sensitivity to this sleight-of-hand, but although the land-office business in gold-plated card cases continues, workingwomen are slowly learning that the price of maintaining success imagery is high and the return on such investments low.

The Key to Affluence Is Tarnishing

For two-career marriages as well as for single workingmen and women, the prizes are not always accessible. Because of long work hours, many household services must be taken care of outside the home. In addition to routine needs such as housecleaning are the rising costs of housing, transportation, food, and entertaining. In the true American spirit, the newly affluent must look the part. This often requires buying designer label clothing, memberships in fancy clubs, fancy cars, and exotic vacations. Rather than being aided by their credit cards, many are overspending and are in debt. The stress of paying the piper takes away a lot of the fun.

One banking executive told us,

> My husband and I make in the six figures between us. After paying the mortgage on the house, the credit cards, payments on the cars, my children's schools and child care, we are left with $200 for the two of us to blow on ourselves. Also, with all of these expenses, we must work very hard to maintain our life-style. I always said that our marriage was number one, now it's meeting our Visa bills.

Another workingwoman commented,

> A catch for workingwomen is that the cost of appearing affluent is higher. Despite the fact that most women managers are earning less than males, everything from a haircut to a business suit has a higher price tag. Self-improvement is also a costly proposition. Evening classes for advanced degrees, seminars, and so on and so on cost a fortune. The ability to do something luxurious for oneself becomes a question of "Where's the time, and more importantly, the money?"

A woman manager who works for a multinational company observed:

> I invest very heavily because I believe that if you consume everything you earn, you can never get ahead of the game. What happens is that

you always owe your soul to the company store. The job becomes an
end in itself rather than a means to an end. I see a lot of men and
women in this situation, caught up feeding an image that they cannot
afford. They are owned and operated by the company only because of
their paycheck. I will never let an organization define who I am. Sure, I
like to spend money, but I always want the freedom to be able to say,
"Take this job and shove it." I feel power in the knowledge that I could
quit this job tomorrow and be unemployed for quite a while before I
starved.

Certainly one of the joys of money is the comfort it can bring.
One successful woman executive, whose family origins were somewhat humble, said that she enjoys being able, at last, to go into the
finest department stores without worrying about price tags. This
is as it should be; women have every right to enjoy the fruits of
their labors. But recent surveys indicate that women continue to
spend a greater proportion of their incomes on clothing than do
men, despite the fact that their immediate male peers make greater
salaries for the same work. Such findings suggest that women's fiscal priorities need reordering. To the extent that workingwomen,
and particularly well-compensated women executives, spend their
money on acquiring possessions and alternative status statements,
they are squandering some of their potential for power.

Equi-nomics

The issue of equal pay for equal work is often greeted with the
same level of enthusiasm as a rich man greets the prospect of radical income redistribution. A number of studies over the past
several years have come up with some conclusions which show,
without a doubt, that the pay gap between men's and women's salaries is inexorably linked to the profit strategies of American business. It is simply counter to the self-interest of American industry,
these studies assert, to move toward equal pay for men and
women.

The most radical explanation of the earnings gap was written
about in a Scott Burns column entitled: "Mixing Sex with Inflation." Sex-inflation, contended Burns, is a rise in the price of goods
and services that can be attributed to the drive for equal pay
among women. His article on this economic principle included the

following equation. Take the number of women concentrated in a given industry, measure that number against the proportion of men within that same industry, to determine the impact of equal pay on corporate payroll costs. Add to this equation the impact of rising payroll costs to total sales, and you will have a good barometer of resistance with which to predict continued pay differentials. Equal pay, asserted Burns, will cause one of two decisions to be made within companies. They can either raise prices to cover their rising payroll costs, or they can reduce their profits. Burns concludes:

> It wouldn't be difficult at all to argue that the earnings of corporate America are almost entirely dependent on the inequality of women's wages. Indeed, withholding of 40 percent of women's salaries may be the single most contributing factor today in the ability of U.S. industry to engage in capital formation. Behind every dividend is a good, but underpaid, woman![16]

If, as figures tell us, two-thirds of all women work out of economic necessity, it is especially moving to look at a government-sponsored study of the pay gap done in 1974 by the Survey Research Center. The study indicated that had workingwomen, from poor families, been paid wages comparable to those of men, over one-half of those poor families would have risen out of the poverty level. This finding applies to both women heads of families and women who work to supplement their husband's income.

There have been many rationalizations made and many opinions given about the differences between male and female pay scales. All of these have sought to support existing inequities and to look for reasons within the women themselves. But women must reject explanations of the pay gap which focus solely on women's lesser work histories or on their job choices (which typically suggest that just moving to another kind of job will solve the problem or imply that women have had a wide range of choices to begin with). Some people are suggesting that the gap is disappearing, but the statistics do not show this to be true. While within certain industries, or certain occupational segments, the male-female pay gap is perhaps only 20 percent, the national statistical average not only continues to hold steady at a 40-percent spread, but has actually widened since the mid 1960s.

Not only have women's efforts supported the industrial sector of the economy, but they have supported the bureaucratic as well. Legislated inequities, such as those found in the Social Security System and the federal tax system, point up how women's earnings have been used, not for their own benefit, but to underwrite the benefits for others. These inequities also expose yet another area where women have failed to exert power. In this case, women's lack of influence has cost them the loss of control over government decisions which affect their economic lives. The basic economic structure, in terms of the bureaucracy, taxes, social security, and industrial profits, if looked at in one light, seems to be saying that the justification for the pay gap is its own historical precedent. No one claims that there is anything right about it, only that it has simply been going on for so long that to change it would subject another trauma on the already reeling status quo. The women we interviewed agreed, almost unanimously, that equal pay was the major women's issue in the work place. It is an intriguing question to ask or ponder, as more and more women find themselves in upper management with responsibility for the corporate profit picture, whether they too willl succumb to the pressures of creating dividends at the expense of closing the earnings gap.

To recognize that women as a group represent the underpinnings of the American economy is pretty heady stuff, but in truth, they do. And therein lies part of their power. To move from first viewing themselves as powerless within the system to a view in which they control money in its most abstract and influential sense, is a most important change of attitude. Women must turn their interests and energies increasingly to the most basic issues affecting this economy—marketing, production, taxation, fiscal policy, and so forth. To continue to absent themselves from those decisions is to condemn all women to a future of financial inequity and social impotence.

The Nouveau Attitudinal Rich

Our interviews and research tell us that women still have a long way to go in developing new images and attitudes about money. A highly successful woman in banking summarized part of the problem:

I love money but I think it raises a problem for many women. They are
not brought up to know very much about it. They ask me questions
like . . . if I have $500 in my savings account, what should I invest it in?
The answer I give them is . . . forget it. The problem is that women
don't know how to seize their assets. It's cultural conditioning. It's like
not knowing about cars. Women are raised in deliberate financial igno-
rance. Some men are too, but they seem to find out about it. I don't
know why women don't.

But beyond financial education is that bugaboo of romance and
women's continuing confusion over their own work motives.
Women will only move into affluence and the power it can bring
them if they move quickly away from their precarious stance on
the pedestal of nobility. Like Rennie Davis and Jerry Rubin,
women must readjust to the realities of the times, and of the society, in which they live and work.

Nobody said it better than the hero of *The Man in the Gray
Flannel Suit*, Tom Rath:

> As he walked across Rockefeller Plaza, he thought wryly of the days
> when he and Betsy had assured each other that money didn't matter.
> They had told each other that when they were married, before the war,
> and during the war they had repeated it in long letters. "The important
> thing is to find a kind of work you really like, and something that is
> useful," Betsy had written him. "The money doesn't matter."
>
> The hell with that, he thought. The real trouble is that up to now
> we've been kidding ourselves. We might as well admit that what we
> want is a big house and a new car and trips to Florida in the winter, and
> plenty of life insurance. When you come right down to it, a man with
> three children has no damn right to say that money doesn't matter.[17]

> "Now that we have seen each other," said the Unicorn. "If you believe in me, I'll believe in you. Is that a bargain?"
>
> LEWIS CARROLL

9

The Ambivalent Man

With all that has been written in the last few years for and about the contemporary American woman, there has been insignificant attention given to the effect the changing roles of women have had on men. Myron Brenton in *The American Male* spoke eloquently to this point:

> But when the plight of women is given such intense scrutiny, a curious distorting effect tends to be created. Suddenly, the world is seen only through the feminist prism. Suddenly the woman stands sharply removed from the society as a whole, as though her difficulties could really be isolated from the rollings and seethings of societal change that affect both sexes. To the extent that the plight of men is ignored, that of women tends to seem less real.[1]

For our purposes, it was apparent from the beginning that we would need to seek the male perspective on workingwomen.

The men we interviewed were single, married, and divorced. Three had wives with demanding management careers. Others had lived through transitions from one- to two-career families. A few of our male subjects had traditionally defined wives and one of them was hopping mad that he had been cast in the role of ultimate producer. These men had titles ranging from the presidential level down to midmanagement. They worked in the retail, oil, and airline industries, food and consumer-products manufacturing and marketing, government, accounting, and higher education. About one-third had left the corporate world to start companies of their own. Several had daughters, a factor which seemed to weigh heavily on their sensitivity to the future roles of women in the home and in the work place. All of the men we approached for this project were eager to be heard, and while we had been warned by one woman to look out for "the fake feminist man, the one who knows everything you've been through," we believe that our male interview subjects were candid in their self-assessments and the representation of their views.

Unicorns and Holy Wars

It was undoubtedly easier for Alice and the Unicorn, from Lewis Carroll's fantasy, to believe in each other than it has been for men and women in our society. For many men, the image of contemporary women is that of a badly organized band of invaders who have come to wrest from them their birthright of corporate success. Male anger at being invaded is blended with some envy over the scope of women's choices and no small amount of confusion about what all this will mean to their own definitions of self.

Psychologist Herb Goldberg, in *The Hazards of Being Male*, describes today's man in our culture as having reached a growth impasse. It is not that they won't move, says Goldberg, but that they can't. They are "cardboard Goliaths" who lack the fluidity of women. But women have been moving on the crest of a wave so powerful that the wake often towed all comers in its path. Men felt themselves being moved involuntarily and in the forward motion, their perceived loss of control served to heighten their sense of ambivalence.[2]

Only one man we interviewed considered himself a feminist, describing his commitment in language which captures the holy-war spirit.

It is a moral issue. My support of women has evolved as I've gained wisdom over time. There are certain things that shouldn't happen to anybody, regardless of the circumstances. I consider myself a feminist and also consider myself supportive of other minorities. I think once someone has seen these problems, the more they understand why these problems exist and the more supportive they become of the oppressed. I was in Detroit during the 1967 riots. I saw, I lived in those neighborhoods where people weren't working, where there was 20 percent unemployment. All of that was attributed to the blacks, but there were a lot of whites in the same situation. Nevertheless, there was an upswell of antagonism toward blacks. But it had nothing to do with the blacks. They were in that spot because whites had put them there. Perhaps when the whites realize that, they will be able to feel sympathy. Women are in the same position. Women have historically, probably for religious reasons, been oppressed, been held back. I think that women are more intelligent than men, and until men realize that there is a great resource that isn't being utilized, women are going to stay right where they are.

Another man placed the issue outside his personal concerns:

I don't identify with strong corporate feminists, either male or female. Why would men be like that? I think it is a function within our society, in fact, I'll call it a societal need peculiar to this day and age, to belong to certain causes. I think that everyone has a different trigger in their backgrounds, in their personalities, that makes them feel very strongly in one area. For instance, one person may be a raving maniac for the People's Workers Party, railing against the inequities of the capitalist system. Another person might be a screaming anti-abortionist. Another a screaming feminist. I just look at those people as lacking something in their personal lives. They need something to identify with. I personally support various causes myself, but I don't feel that I'm a screaming maniac, except maybe during the football season.

The comments of a man who has a highly successful wife reflect a measure of understanding based on what he has seen her contend with, but he also underscored the male sense of having been threatened and his words are a not-so-veiled warning to women:

There seems to be a tendency to react negatively to the word "feminist." There is aggressive take-charge personality associated with the word. You have to keep in mind that male managers get and stay where they are through a tough survival instinct. If a woman fights with me, if she comes at me aggressively in a business situation, I am not going to have any sympathy. I may even be tougher on her. If she is striking at me where I eat, if she is competing with me for a job, I probably won't have any more understanding for her because of my experiences with my wife and her job. On the other hand, intellectually, where I am involved in trying to help bring a woman into management, the role model provided by my wife does help.

In the words of one man from upper management:

My idea of feminism comes down to the ability to accept the notion that women are responsible and independent and capable of functioning alongside men in our society without differentiating that too much.

This was echoed by another man who said:

Women should come to a job with a "can-do" attitude and not try to imply that the *only* reason I should give them a job is that no woman ever held that position before.

As an element of social physics, ambivalence emerges when the intellectual acceptance of change confronts the tendency of the emotional body to remain at rest. Early in the twentieth-century, Mabel Ullrich wrote: "A man, it seems, may be intellectually in complete sympathy with a woman's aims, but only about 10 percent of him is his intellect. The other 90 percent his emotions." Several of our male interviewees echoed this feeling. The comments of these men reflect the internal conflict generated by the rapidly changing mores of our times. Where emotions have not caught up with intellect, the result is usually a high degree of stress. It may be helpful to examine some of the stress points these quotations have surfaced.

There is one theme that runs through all our interviews with men: the sense that women are demanding something from them, something that is men's to give or to withhold; and that they will set the conditions on which any bargains are struck. Overlaid on that theme is the fear that women may not wait to be given the prize, but may snatch it from under the eyes of its caretakers. Here is the essence of the conflict. It is perceived as a tug-of-war where, for one side to advance, the other must retreat. It is this giving-up or losing an integral part of oneself that is so threatening to men.

The appearance of women in corporations, in peer relationships—in terms of work, salaries, and responsibilities, among other things—incites the fear in men that they will lose their vehicle of self-esteem. A relationship of equals at work suggests to a man that he will be required to give up his traditional role as provider and protector in the home. If he does this, he wonders, who will he be?

This is akin to the problem many a woman has in dealing with feminism and even something as benign as the ERA. For such a woman, the threat inherent in equal rights is that she will lose her traditional role of dependent. For her the question is, likewise, Who will I be? The resistance to change in men, which is generated by these self-doubts, is less the conscious fear of losing a job to a woman co-worker and more the horrendous fear of losing a self-view. *Who will this new man be?*

Without a doubt the most startling answer we received to the question, "Why are you a feminist?" came from the manager who told us:

> Within the space of a year, my girlfriend announced her intention to become a lesbian, and a good friend—a forty-five-year-old vice-president in a high-tech firm and father of three teenaged sons—informed me he was having a sex-change operation. At that point, I decided it was time to reevaluate my definition of male and female.

Women who demand to be treated as equals have met with a panoply of male posturing, but have missed the boat by mistakenly assigning the motivation for all that motion as strictly anti-female behavior. The truth is that men have been attempting to conceal the singular irony of their own dissatisfaction with their careers and their lives. Many men wonder when women confront them, Why would anyone want to be like me?

A passage in *The Corporate Eunuch* paints a reasonably accurate portrait of the hollow managerial man.

> To a far greater extent than ever before, he [the American male manager] does not like himself. He questions the meaning of his life and does not care much for what he sees. He is tired of fighting his way upstream. He longs to find a quiet pool in which he can swim in peace. he dreams of dropping out of the rat race with security, honor and his wits about him. But he has obligations, reservations and fears.[3]

These comments from our interviews suggest that women may have a distorted image of the lives of workingmen and thus they risk building their future on a base with the reliability of a mirage. Most corporate men will tell you they too have questions about achievement and success.

A former manager in retail, now an entrepreneur, observed:

> I don't think it was what they thought it would be—working for someone else. The corporate structure, the corporate game that men have

been acclimated to dealing with is a lot more oppressive than women realized. And men are oppressed by it, make no mistake, but I don't think women realize that.

Similar feelings about the oppressive nature of corporations were to be found in these two remarks:

I wasn't born to work for some large organization that is basically impassive when it comes to my individuality and which looks at me as if I were nothing more than a widget. And that's what most organizations do, but I want more out of life.

I think there is a lack of honesty within corporations about the real issues in life. To me, it is much more important to contribute something positive to society than it is to slave away selling steel or paper or quiche. It goes beyond being a manager, an accountant, or a lawyer. In this economy, everything is a glut. We have thousands of products and thousands of services. No one person is going to make a difference. Anyone who thinks that way is on an ego trip, but they will find out.

The sentiments of one man reflect his concern that men are far more trapped by role definitions than are women:

I think in many ways it is up to a woman to make a man feel more comfortable in business situations. He's probably going through a much more severe role change than she is. I really feel that. Men have been raised with images and expectations that are just totally unrealistic and we have been stuck with them. I'm talking about the macho images, the tough guy. To be feeling and human can be much more difficult for him, especially in business. It's much tougher in that sense for a guy to let go. It is much easier for a woman to manipulate the situation in a positive sense and still succeed.

The founder of a computer-services firm looked back on the price of his success and mused:

When my daughter was growing up, I was busy building my company. I missed so much of her life that now we are like strangers. I can't help but wonder how many women understand that kind of sacrifice. I can tell them right now, it hurts.

For those women rushing out to get an M.B.A. or jockeying for top salaries, one man in his midthirties, who appears to have it all, confessed:

I'm not sure I'm successful. I've had the traditional background. I've gone through the traditional paths to try and find something that would fulfill me. Maybe by some people's standards, monetarily, or by title, I'm successful, but I don't feel that way.

Much of the corporate battle of the sexes is apparently connected to skirmishes on the home front. We asked a number of questions about two-career marriages and executive wives. What we identified was a cultural crevice which formed when women jump-stepped from partners in marriage to competitors in business, with no steadying steps in between. Of the men we interviewed, two did not have working wives at present. One of them said he was desperately trying to get his wife to work, the other expressed his excitement over his wife's impending employment. Of the three divorced men, none had full-time working wives during their marriages. Two of these men said that a working wife's career depended on the needs of the couple's children. A third said, in retrospect, he wished he had encouraged his wife to work, since she is much more interesting to him now as a person than she was during their marriage.

It became readily apparent from the responses to our question on the role of the executive wife that corporations take on lives of their own, complete with values, traditions, and bad habits. This distinction was brought home in the care taken by several of our male interview subjects to separate their personal opinions and standards from those of the institutions and industries which employed them. If one were looking for signs of improvement in the status of women, observations made to us on the role of the executive wife would provide only minor encouragement. The consensus was that things were changing slowly, with the rate of change tempered by the corporate practice of placing a social and business value on wives.

One tends to view the business world as traditional or entrepreneurial. It is pretty clear today that decisions within traditional roles are contingent upon a lot of things. I basically see changes in the traditional role of wife as being a major challenge to business.

I am a good person to ask about that because I don't have a wife and I've been in lots of positions where most men did. In government it matters less, but in the corporate world it is still quite important. If you don't have a wife, people wonder what is the matter with you. How are you to be handled socially? There are all kinds of sticky little problems. In the standard corporate setting, wives are still counted upon as the home people, the one who takes care of the kids, takes care of the house.

She may work but her primary responsibility or job is the home front. That tends to be the standard.

My personal impression is that the wife can be very supportive when her husband has to work long hours or has to go out of town a lot. But the wife is not a tool to be used to gain new business. That is beyond the realm of responsibility. However, that is not the impression within this firm. I believe that using the wife of an executive in that way is to end up just using. And I don't think you should do that with anybody.

One executive thought that his industry was making a move toward a fuller integration of executive wives, although the progress seems somewhat superficial:

There are many activities now that encourage the wives' participation much more. Most conventions I go to now in the food business have encouraged women to attend. There are programs for the women at the convention, things for them to do that are separate from the men or they can join the men. There is an effort made at conventions to involve women in topics and subjects for their own general interest or as a partner to her husband. So it is no longer "You have coffee and go on tours while I work," because women are really involved in the conventions and media activities I go to.

A second trend among responses on executive wives stressed how valuable their skills could be in furthering the careers of their husbands. These skills included: proper handling of business-related entertainment, positive influence on a husband through his ability to bring her into situations where issues and problems are shared, her ability (instinctively) as a problem solver, and her expertise in the analysis of human behavior, which allows her to help her mate by explaining feelings and why people act the way that they do. One regretted that men in business were appraised by social values which favored having a wife who is "sober, a good housekeeper and mother." Only one man expressed concern that women executives will have trouble with their careers if their husbands do not match the qualifications generally expected of an executive wife.

Our representative in academia made a significant point: that while corporations may wish for the traditional role among the wives of their executives, the men themselves now consider it trendier to have a working wife.

A great many more executives would like to see their wives, once the children are not so small, do something that isn't just killing time, something that enhances her and makes her feel good and her husband feel proud. At an off-campus commencement I saw a forty-year-old man, a very successful attorney with strong business connections. He and his wife were married when she was a sophomore in college, and then, when the children were out of elementary school, she went back to college. I was sitting next to her at dinner and she was fantastically enthusiastic about majoring in political science. She was already working as a lobbyist and her husband was just as excited about it as she was. I have seen many cases of that. The image of the guy who says, "No, I want you to stay home," is now negative. The ones whose wives have not gotten out of the house are worried. There is an implication among their peers that they have a neurotic wife sitting around the house whimpering. I've heard them saying things like "I wish to hell she would get on the stick." I don't know how representative that is because I tend to gravitate toward men who are not old-fashioned guys. But things are changing in other areas as well. The wife used to be part of the team. If you have an executive job now, nobody gives a damn whether you are married, what kind of wife you've got, or if you're divorced. The question is you. And in a big city, people don't have the social contacts with the people with whom they do business. Small towns may be a little bit different. In academia it used to be important. The wife was part of it, but I haven't invited one person to my house in the ten years since I've had this job. I could have had a wife or no wife. It hasn't made any difference. But it certainly didn't use to be that way.

Two other men, both about twenty years the junior of our academic, were less certain that social mores were indeed changing:

Among the people I know there are an awful lot of traditional wives; in fact, it's been about a fifty-fifty split between the traditional and the new. I can't think of too many couples like my wife and myself where both are working toward career goals. I don't think the traditional has become that unusual yet.

Most of the wives of executives whom I met struck me as being singularly unhappy, like they are an appendage. The only ones who were happy were the ones who had their own careers.

We couldn't find one man among those we interviewed who didn't enjoy having a working wife. Even when we asked what adjustments they had to make in life-style because of the two careers, not a single disparaging word was heard. The men whose wives were starting out seemed genuinely excited. While economic necessity was not far from their minds, the majority of our male subjects expressed their attitudes about working wives in terms of the quality of life. One man told us his somewhat unusual experience:

I feel very concerned. . . . I think it is absolutely critical that a woman be able to function on her own and not get trapped in the event that something happens to her spouse, be it death or divorce. When you are a housewife and mother, it is tough to make the transition to the work place, there's no doubt about it, but it is an imperative for survival. The only time I would feel negative about my wife working was if she were doing something she really didn't want to be doing. There was a transitional period in my life, between my last and current job, when I tried to develop a business at home. I think that was the most important year of my life because I then found out what it was like to be the mother of young children. It's an intolerable job and more men should have this perspective. For just five or six months they should see what it is like to seek space for yourself and not be able to find it. I'm talking about psychological space, someplace where you are not constantly interrupted, so much so that you cannot maintain a train of thought. It really takes stamina.

Contrast this with the opinions of a man in his early sixties whose wife did not work before their marriage ended:

A woman can work, but with children at home, I think it is O.K. as long as she has the capacity to make the situation work. I have observed women in business both working and raising children and keeping a household with their husbands. This is an enormous responsibility and I do admire people who can do it. But I would only be in favor of this as long as it was really doable and if she was not destroying herself by stretching herself so much that she was losing control of the situation. I think it is better for her if she waits until after the children grow up because she will have the time then. If I were still married now, I would encourage my wife to find something in the career world.

Stories

ROB'S STORY

It's been a pretty good working relationship as far as I can see. I met my wife while studying in Italy in 1970, so I've known her for ten years, although we've only been married for three years. Our situation is one where we agree on one thing, and that is that a career for each of us is very important. Personally, my work demands are such and my outside interests are such that I would have a very difficult time dealing with a mate or spouse or wife, whatever you want to call the other person, who is totally dependent on my life to give meaning to her life. It is as plain, as black and white, as that. My wife is entirely the opposite of me in personality traits, but one thing we do have in common is mutual respect for one another in the area of career development. We share equally on the chores. Although we have a house that requires some upkeep, we manage to knock it off in a pretty efficient manner. We also have a fairly active social life, and despite the fact that we often put in fifty- to sixty-hour work weeks, everything seems to come together pretty well. Our number-one concern is making sure that we spend enough time with one another. We have fairly well organized the duties. If something unusual happens, if, for example, a piece of furniture arrives during working hours, we see whose work hours are most flexible. My office is closer to home than hers. If she cannot work at home that day, I take time off. We are both basically autonomous in work operations, so we can usually work things out pretty well. I can't really say we have any problems.

JOE'S STORY

My wife works and I think it is terrific. Not so much from an economic viewpoint but because of basic fulfillment. She has worked and has been on an equal power base with me since I've known her. We just do the household chores that need to be done. We have someone who comes in once a week for four hours. But I'm as good in the kitchen as I am on the tennis court and so is my wife. I see it as shared responsibility, so our roles are fairly flexible. Life for us is a very well-rounded experience.

PETER'S STORY

If anything, I suspect, our relationship was formed because of her career. I was not interested in being with someone that I had to take care of, and she provided a perfect model for that. And I think that this model has had some movement. We both approached this relationship with a very independent attitude, where neither of us wanted to take care of the other; and when we both realized that feeling this way was O.K., we were able to feel easier about taking care of each other. I don't have a whole lot of hang-ups about having her rush home every night to make dinner. In fact, if she wanted me to be home every night at five-thirty, we'd have a problem because I'm not that kind of person. There are, clearly, agreements and then again there are no agreements. We have lived together for a long-enough time to have osmosed into knowing which of us has certain predispositions. It may be that I'm an obsessive-compulsive about picking up things around the house and she's not, even though I've nagged her about it for a long time. Eventually, I stopped complaining and started just picking things up myself. On the other hand, she sees that I hate doing the laundry and will stuff dirty clothes in my closet until it's ready to split, so she looks after that. We have arrived at a standoff over household jobs in this way, so there is a great unspoken definition. What I am interested in is being able to work out a complex relationship between us. We already have a good many things we need and there are other things we want. We're putting together the whole compendium of things that she has said she is interested in having, in terms of her career, along with mine. I think that doing what we're doing is complicated enough without either of us trying to become the president of Standard Oil or something.

There are a few important conclusions to be drawn from the stories of Rob, Joe, and Peter. A key observation is that in each case, both partners entered the relationship on equal footings. This suggests that adjustments come harder for those whose careers force a change in the rules midstream.

Examples of breakups caused by such interpersonal transition came from two of the women we interviewed:

> My work cost me my marriage. My husband was always very support-ive and encouraged me, but he kept trying to keep up with me as well. The harder he pedaled, the farther behind he fell. I tried to say that this was not important to me, that he keep up, but he began developing personality traits that were more and more childish. I could see that underneath his support was his need to be married to someone who could look up to him on his terms.

> I lived with a man for a very long time. The amount of traveling that began to become part of my career rise upset him. But he could never tell me that he was upset. It would come out in different ways. At first I tried to make concessions to assuage what I felt was his fears: that I was going to be more successful than he was; that I was going to make all these leaps and outshine him. At the same time, I went ahead and pursued my career rather than to wholly give in to his insecurities. I still think that at any one time he could go much farther than I can in what he chooses to do, but we had to part company because I didn't want to feel as if I were solely responsible for his lack of success and that's what I saw coming.

These two stories should raise doubts about the view many women have of the supportive male: the belief that support for her career can be unequivocal. The reality is that the achievements of women are often perceived by men as diminishing their own achievements, even—or perhaps especially—when the emotional relationship is close.

A second observation brings us back to the discussion of male liberation. Rob and Peter both mention how important it is to be free from having to give total meaning to the lives of their wives.

These comments, combined with those of the man who finds his ex-wife more interesting now that she works and the frustration of the older man whose wife won't get out of the house, seem to indicate a growing awareness in many men of the positive aspects of liberation. Equality has begun to filter through to men as a means of lessening the heavy emotional burden of being responsible for another person's happiness.

Altered Egos

It seems that every book about the corporate man includes some explanation of the link between his position and salary and his self-image. We asked two questions of our male subjects designed to ferret out their state of ego alteration. The first question dealt with a scenario in which their wives made more money than they did, and the second query involved how our fellows would feel if they found themselves working under a female boss.

The response to our money question underscored just how much impact the economy has had on the male ego. Ninety-nine percent of our interviewees said that with conditions today, the American Dream made the greatest possible joint income a virtual necessity. The one dissenter was the bachelor among our ranks, who said that he could probably handle parity, but not supremacy. But the overwhelming yes count was shaded by nervous laughter and some conditional elements. Over 50 percent of the answers we received tied the issue of a woman's greater salary to her being in an industry outside that of her mate. The general tone of the answers went like this:

I'm not sure how I would feel about that. I think it would be great, especially if she excelled in her own field.

I'd feel fine about it, although it really depends upon the industry and one's posture in it.

At one point in our life she did. Initially it didn't bother me at all, but eventually I felt negatively because I wasn't working then and she was earning and I wasn't. In the future it would depend upon the circumstances. If she were earning a lot of money it would help the overall family situation and in that sense we'd both be freer. If she were doing the same work that I was doing, I might feel differently.

It is one thing to ask men to be supportive of a working wife, but another thing entirely to ask that they bow to a true competitor. One man summed it up this way:

> The question of having a wife who earns more than me is all too easy to answer with "It wouldn't make any difference," but I'm a very competitive personality. I see myself as being willing to suffer and bear more pain in the pursuit of a competitive goal than she is. It would depend on my life-style and goals. If those goals included reaching a reasonably competitive salary within a job that I was really having fun in, and if she were to go on and outearn me or outprestige me in her job, that would be irrelevant. However, if I wasn't satisfied with what I was doing, if I were deadened and blocked for some reason and she was outearning me, I'd get frustrated. There would be no way for me to avoid that feeling, because I am competitive.

But time and again it appears that the economy has done more to liberate women than any other single factor. Among the mid-thirties age group particularly the issue of ego gives way to bottom-line realities.

> Look at most mortgages today, at the value of homes. Everything is incredibly expensive. Then there is the whole energy question and its effect on transportation. I see it as being two people working together on all aspects of life. Thirty years ago people looked toward improving their life-style. We're looking toward hanging on to what we've got.

The ultimate goal of corporate competition is to reach the top rungs of the ladder. One male manager drew this analogy: "Corporations at senior levels are like the Olympics. There are just so many gold medals to go around." Under these conditions, it seems safe to assume that at no time will the male ego be more threatened than when top jobs are at stake. Predictions about when a woman will surface as the CEO of a Fortune 500 company range from twenty to a thousand years. The responses to our question on having a woman as boss reflect far less attitudinal flexibility than did those on having a wife who earns more money. The extent to which such a situation alters the male perception of self was evident when two men equated having a woman superior to having a younger man promoted above them. The sum of all comments made by our male subjects indicates definite cultural gaps which portend difficulties for women who make it to senior-management levels.

The basis of future change lies in the ability of today's generation of senior male managers to lay the groundwork for those who will succeed them. One such executive confided his self-doubts about being up for the task at hand.

Having a woman boss, that's the toughest question of all. I wouldn't reject it out of hand, but I would certainly approach the situation with more concern and care. Men of my generation have not had that kind of experience. Now we find ourselves in the business of promoting women quite rapidly and in the business of telling men that they have to report to these women. Yet it is an experience we have not gone through ourselves. I, for one, am not very comfortable with that. I don't think I have a good view of all the elements involved, so I must observe what is happening all the time and watch for reactions of one kind or another. To some extent, I see what you might expect. I see among young people, under thirty-five, that if there is any difficulty it almost never surfaces. I'm never aware of what they may be thinking or feeling. Their conduct in meetings is such that it wouldn't show. There seems to be an easy give-and-take, a lot of kidding around, sharing the lead on various presentations. But when I deal with a man who is over thirty-five, it is different. When I worked for my previous employer back East, there were a couple of men who were uncomfortable. They made excuses by saying that I'm not doing well here because this woman doesn't understand how valuable I am to the company. Or . . . she doesn't know how best to do things. Their difficulties lie in the state of the art for coping with this problem. I expect that when the occurrence of a female boss is more frequent, more of the problems will be corrected. But I have no question that today, for women put in a supervisory position, where they would have under them a broad range of men with various ages and educational backgrounds, there will be predictable conflicts.

A representative of a younger generation hinted that, while attitudes might be slightly different for those of his age, the tendency to accept a woman boss is fraught with psychological game playing:

Men today react to having a woman promoted above them the same way they react to being passed over by another man. If anything, it is easier today to be passed over by a woman because a man can always rationalize that perhaps the firm needed to comply with equal-opportunity guidelines, so the company needs women to get ahead. I worked with a black woman who had an M.B.A. and it was easy to recognize that she was a token. Her obvious status made it easy for men to rationalize her success away. The best women are those who are open to being professional and not so focused on their role as women. One moderating factor is the economic situation we are in. Men realize that $30,000 a year doesn't take you anywhere, so they understand that all of us thrown together in the trenches are fighting to pay the mortgage.

Another provocative comment suggests that the eventual acceptance of women as senior managers will be concurrent with the creation of new male-female relationship models.

I've not had a woman boss, but I would hope to rise to the occasion. I enjoy women personally. I like interacting with them. They are often different from men and can be more thought-provoking and refreshing. But while I have no qualms about it, I suspect I might try to use my wiles with a woman boss. I would try to communicate on a business level, but I might be guilty of doing some of the same things a woman might do with a male boss. Like kidding them and treating them like human beings. And, you know, bringing them down to a friend level.

Disassociating himself from the sexual significance of our question, one man chose to frame the issue in terms of the potential of a woman boss to further his career.

The exhibition and use of power by an individual within a leadership role is a critical function. Whether it is a woman or a man is rather irrelevant to me. It stems from what I can get from them. I'm sort of a user of bosses. I want to be able to get something from them or I really don't want to be there.

So what is the measure of altered male egos? Certainly from the answers to our questions, there seems cause for hope that change is on the way. The balance of cultural adjustments, however, appear keyed to the ability of each individual man to deal with the progress of the society as a whole and to assuage his personal identity needs into the bargain. The barometer of threatened egos seems to rise or fall depending on the immediate pressure applied by the women in his vicinity. "The eighties do not differ from any other period," observed a successful woman entrepreneur, "only now we are in a situation in which men are, at least, aware of the competence of women, and if not threatened by it, are able to help promote or support them."

The Uneasy Demise of Sir Walter Raleigh

It was interesting to note that every single answer we received from women on the question of the most humorous event in their careers revolved around the seriocomic aspects of male ineptness. For their part, our male subjects responded to the question "Have you ever been put off by a woman's behavior in business?" with a somewhat predictable litany of complaints about overemotionalism and defensiveness. Neither side suggested deliberate ill will or intent to display sexism or inappropriate behavior, but both implied that there was an abysmal lack of awareness. We believe that both sexes would like nothing better than to hit the bull's-eye. It's just that the culture keeps moving the target.

> I was trained to open doors and all those other mannerly things and I'm having a hard time kicking the habit. I'm learning, though, that for some people letting a woman open her own doors or get in or out of a car without a man's help is part of acknowledging her ability to be independent and in charge of her own responsibilities. Part of my new awareness comes from my girlfriend, who will say, "Hey, buddy, you just blew that sky high." By that she means that I'm not sensitive enough about the way I express or do something.

The compelling need for a corporate Emily Post emerged clearly in the following tale of manners related to us by a woman who has three hundred people reporting to her:

> The most amusing things that happen to me are all basically related to how men outside the company interact with me in situations where I obviously have the upper hand. I recall one such situation when a gentleman had flown up from Southern California to see me. He wanted to talk about relocating into this area. When he came into my office, one of the first things he said was, "Well, I've really been excited about meeting the person who would be able to make the decision about our proposition, and when I found out that it was a woman and"—and he stumbled for words—"and a very attractive woman at that, I became even more excited." Now, there were about four men in this meeting in my office. I just sat behind my desk while he continued rambling nervously. Here was a man who was a top executive in his corporation and he was having difficulty holding a conversation with me. Finally he said: "You know, I was in the board meeting the other day and there were about twenty-seven people around the table. They were all men except for one young lady, who also happened to be quite attractive. I waited for a break in this very dull meeting and then I said, 'Well,

it's nice to know that in the midst of all this dullness we have a beautiful young girl . . . lady . . . woman . . . in here with us.' Well, she let me
know immediately that I was out of bounds. It turns out that she was a
lawyer and was quite competent." He just kept rattling on as I sat there
looking at my colleagues, who were obviously wondering how he was
ever going to get his foot out of his mouth. I was wondering how I was
going to make a decision on his proposition after this display, but the
bank did not approve his company's financial request, so he did not get
the lease.

But on reflecting, this woman made her sympathies felt about
the uneasy demise of Sir Walter Raleigh:

Things like this happen all the time. Men just don't know whether to
address you as "lady" or "woman" or "girl." It's almost the same as the
confusion over the terms "black," "Negro," and "colored." Men never
know whether they should open the door or pull out a chair or do any
of the things they were told to do in the days of chivalry. I'm the first to
admit that I enjoy all the little amenities that come with being a
woman, so how can I expect them not to be confused? I watch them
constantly stumbling, putting their feet in their mouths, and have
nothing but sympathy for them. No matter how high up they are in an
organization, there is a primary functioning gap that they have in relating to women that we all have to help each other overcome.

We agree.

Rubbishing the Issues

A peculiar paradox among many executive women is how sensitive
they are to criticism from men about how sensitive they are to criticism. Of all the intercultural battle cries, none so stiffens a
woman's defensive posture as the accusation that she, or her sisters, are simply too emotional on the job. Responses to the repeti-
tion of this stereotypical image vary among women from total
denial to suggestions that if men would allow themselves the prerogative of emotional release, they would have far fewer ulcers.
Physical manifestations of repression aside, there seems no escap-
ing the tearful debate. But one male manager offered a rather
straightforward analysis of source and solution to the emotional
question:

The worst thing a woman can do is "get cramps" over office incidents, but I have observed this pattern time and time again. Women take a very critical approach and sometimes tear everything down if just one thing is amiss and that's just too negative for me. They seem to have very little sense of humor when it comes to company screw-ups. I've thought about where this kind of behavior comes from and have concluded that many women come to business with too many preconceived notions of what it is all about. They can't separate themselves from their jobs. They are looking for too much fulfillment from an imperfect system. In the military, they have the term "snafu," which stands for "situation normal—all fouled up." Well, snafus are like boomerangs, and too many women just don't know how to duck when they see them coming. The worst woman I ever met in business attributed every one of her job difficulties to male domination. She never took personal responsibility for anything and it became impossible to talk to her. When a business problem becomes so contaminated by an individual's emotional position in life, there are no grounds for discussion. I call this technique rubbishing the issues.

Taking this thought a step further, another man suggested that emotionalism needs to be expressed, but in ways which men can identify with:

I worked with a woman at General Mills. She had a very good business-school background, but she had a tendency to cry under pressure, under constructive criticism. That really put me off. I can personally relate to a woman who slams her fist down on the desk or uses a well-placed four-letter word. But this stereotypical sign of weakness, of emotional release through tears, I have problems with. Maybe in the back of my psyche, I relate tears to the amount of maturity a person has gained, the kind of maturity it takes to deal with the day-to-day fears of business. I think when you let your emotions down too far, it shows a lack of maturity. It lowers my esteem of people when I see them lose their composure time and time again.

One of our female interview subjects also commented on emotionalism and shared a private and poignant communication on the subject:

I've seen women getting emotional on the job a number of times and it distresses me because it perpetuates a stereotype that I personally dislike. Men, I know, are as emotionally charged as women, but they discharge behind closed doors. I'm personally not a crier, because I've never seen that crying changes anything. I try not to cry without going back to see what is really disturbing me and what solutions I can create to deal with the problem. One day I realized that my daughter had never seen me cry. I took her aside and explained to her that just be-

cause I didn't cry didn't mean that there was anything wrong in doing
it. I tried to tell her that different people handle things in different
ways.

The daughter in the story above is now ten years old and expresses
her desire for a career in business. It will be interesting to see what
qualities of emotion she will bring to the work place and how they
will compare or contrast to those of the rest of her generation.

Former chair of the Equal Employment Opportunity Commission Eleanor Holmes Norton commented on the issue of emotions
in a *Working Woman* magazine interview.[4] The thrust of her ar-
gument suggested that women are not "more emotional" but simply more aware of the emotional elements in a given situation, due
to their enculturation as females. The conclusion of this line of
reasoning is that this ability to understand a wider range of emotional components makes women inherently superior in understanding situations.

Sacred Cows and Cold Wars

Anthropologists attach the devaluation of women in all societies to
female identification with the natural side of life as opposed to
male identification with the products of human consciousness or
culture itself. Cultural resistance to change often brings about a
rather rigid set of role assignments for men and women. As a
woman who has survived several levels of corporate climbing
told us:

> Just because you are a female, you've been singled out as someone
> who's playing a different role. Maybe they don't know what that role
> is, but they assume that it's not the same as the male's.

Indeed, men may not know exactly what a woman's role in a
company should be, but the underlying assumption is that her
placement has something to do with traditional views of women as
the primary agents of socialization. If the corporate manager must
accede to the entrance of women into his ranks, he can overcome
his uncertainty and rise to the occasion by assigning them job
classifications based on the accepted stereotypes about their natu-

ral or instinctive qualities. Women, themselves, have exacerbated this process by continually calling attention to "people skills." Hence, women are placed in soft positions like human-resources management, personnel, or corporate social responsibility, where their feelings and social graces seem to complement organizational needs.

We asked our male interview subjects, "Will women change the corporate world and if so, how?" Implied in our question was the assumption that most men see female nature as so different from male nature that they would automatically expect female-dominated management to bring about changes in the prevailing climate of the business world.

> The important thing to understand about my company in the early to mid seventies was that women were treated like sacred cows. People were afraid to offend them, or fire them, or whatever, because the company didn't want lawsuits, especially lawsuits concerning whether or not women had been discriminated against. So everybody was gunshy, you might say. But while we were forced to go out of our way to accommodate women throughout the company, the people at the top really didn't want women to succeed. They didn't want any positive role models out there for other women to emulate or fashion their career paths after.

> We've made an attempt to address the problem with affirmative action. We are bringing in our token women and that is where things stand at present. Companies are involved in the image of bringing women in, not as people, not as professionals, but as women.

> I get the impression that in many large organizations, mine included, women who are in top-management positions are being put on display. The ulterior motive is to be able to say, "Look, here is a woman who is vice-president of marketing," and "our chief counsel," or "the secretary of the corporation," and "if other women do well, then they can attain the same thing." It is tokenism, plain and simple.

Introducing a few or token women is, for many organizations, the ideal way to comply minimally with legal and social directives without upsetting the comforting familiarity of the existing culture. From the male perspective, tokenism revolves around the encouragement of complacency. The male rationale of the numbers game states that one *is* enough, and once "she" has been found, sufficient accommodation to all women has been made. Margaret Mead documents how the adolescence of males, in most societies, is built around a series of rituals which provide each man a progression of benchmarks to measure his place within the group. The rituals bring acceptance and the comfort of sameness. The injection of women into the traditionally male corporate society has acted like a series of hammer blows against the unwavering surface of sameness, often shattering all rituals on impact.

There are certain aspects that won't change. The board of directors have historically been real men's clubs. They have a sense of paternity that is quite contagious. There are jokes that belong more in a men's club than in a public organization and sometimes men have lost sight of the fact that a board-of-directors meeting is a forum for protecting the interests of stockholders, male and female. As women have come into this atmosphere, the nature of some meetings has changed altogether. Usually for the best, I might add. The meetings are more businesslike, less subject to tangential trips and proclivities toward the let-me-tell-you-a-story mentality. Now it hasn't lost all of that, but there is a certain screening process going on. Most guys were taught to be gentlemen, so they're not going to rattle the cage with bad language or tell tales about traveling salesmen. So there is a tendency for the whole event to be a little more socially acceptable in terms of manners and to spend a lot more time on business.

I think that women will not change the way that companies do business. That is a function of economics, not sociology. But there is a generation now at the top which will have to leave before this reality is accepted. They may moderate their views over time about women's contributions to the organization, but only the new attitudes of the younger generations will be able to replace the old myths completely. I can't conceive from the workings of my business, the oil industry, that having women in certain roles will change a whole lot, but then we don't happen to have a lot. While the industry is under enormous pressure to look for women to slot in at certain levels where the quotas and hiring responsibilities are rather severe, the contention is that there aren't a lot of women to have. It is a sort of the ultimate Catch-22 situation.

So, as in India, where sacred cows roam the streets while people starve, the management ranks of America bristle with the incongruities of ideology and pragmatism. The old conventions survive despite the obvious need for all human talents to be loosed in the free-enterprise system. A former marketing man turned entrepreneur summed it up this way:

I think in the next ten or twenty years, there will be change. But initially, there will be considerable uneasiness when women enter the

boards of directors meetings. But once we start treating them like individuals, once we get to know them as people, we will be able to judge
them for their achievements and intellect. I would like to think that
men in America are pretty open-minded and that they will not be cas-
trated by having to deal with women as equals. What they should be
interested in is the bottom line. In corporations it is the duty of everyone to increase the net worth of the company, but we lose sight of that
sometimes.

Yet keeping an eye on the bottom line and simultaneously acquiring the vision of women as individuals of intellect and achievement seems a very farsighted proposition in a very nearsighted
world. The second group of answers to our question on how
women will change the corporation focused on some mispercep-
tions about both the nature of women and the nature of the work
place. The comments suggested a susceptibility among some men
to transpose their traditional image of women onto industrial situations. The result sounded dangerously close to a corporate version
of biological determinism.

I would like to think that in the next five years there will be a subtle
revolution within business and industry, particularly within large corporations. We will see more women, and the kind of assets they bring
to business, getting involved in upper-management decisions. It will
make these companies more humanized. I think that it has always been
one of the major complaints of our society that corporations are this
kind of inhuman machine that consumes us all. Yet when one looks at a
balance sheet, one never sees personnel listed, even though the people
involved in a business are the key element. I think that business has always lacked a feminine side to it. It has always been overly male,
overly aggressive, overly competitive. I think those factors comprise
the general mistrust toward business. So women will bring to companies something which they need to be worthwhile places.

On first reading, this passage appears to present a philosophical
position favoring both women's talents and the benefits of cultural
change. But on closer examination, three significant elements surface.
Element one returns us to the nature-versus-products-of-human-
consciousness debate. It views the assets which women will bring
to business in a limited, stereotypical way. Rather than separating
women's traditional roles from their new opportunities, this argu-
ment presumes that traditional roles will simply be transferred to
the corporate setting. Implied is the perception of women as the

primary agents of socialization. This devalues the broad range of contribution individual women can make to the organization. The scenario of countless Executive Janes bringing civilization to the multitudes of Corporate Tarzans belies the inescapable reality that Tarzan had already mastered the jungle environment by developing keen survival instincts.

Element two is built upon the premise that the jungle of business has been made treacherous and untrustworthy through its association with male qualities, and that the environment will benefit from inculcating a feminine side. The fallacy here is in the assignment of gender to such qualities as competitive, aggressive, and human. Both men and women can be any and all of these. Organizations encourage one set of characteristics and reward them. As one man who dissented from the socialization imagery commented:

> Business will not become more compassionate, nicer or less tough because women are in it. The logic of any situation is determined by the context and the purpose. If you have women boxers, the game is not going to be any different because the name of the game is to win by knocking your opponent out of the ring.

The 1970s witnessed the synchronous merging of two societal trends which have blurred cause and effect. Often referred to as the Me Decade, the 1970s springboarded the issue of a personal right to fulfillment into the corporate environment. A generation that seemed assured by a plateau of affluence plunged the tip of Maslow's hierarchy into the corporate conscience. Management was met with unprecedented demands from employees that their need for dignity and self-expression be reckoned with. This drive was spurred by the dual specter of an increasingly automated work place and the consequences of specialization. Enter the massive influx of women lobbying for fulfillment through work and the two trends become a version of the chicken-and-the-egg paradox. A second dissenter to the socialization position said it another way:

> I think that women will not change business. Once an issue comes up, you sit down and address the problem. There is a tactical emphasis. It is nothing more than a bunch of minds and imaginations addressing a problem. Women bring nothing different to this situation. If you are looking at how you are going to market something, you sit down and analyze the markets and figure out how you're going to get to them. Finance, human relations, strategic planning, it's all the same. All you

need to know is what's going on, what's relevant. I see zero difference
here between men and women.

This brings us to element three: the ontological view that the
qualities of women, set loose in the sphere of business, have the capacity to change the nature of bureaucratic institutions. It is here
that an understanding of the dynamics of cultural change must be
applied. Leslie White argues in *The Science of Culture* that we
may be wrong to believe that we can ever understand our social
institutions thoroughly enough to direct or control change within
them.[5] Corporations, as we previously noted, take on lives of their
own, which is why they can be seen as impersonal, unresponsive
entities, completely separate from the philosophies, feelings, and
needs of their employees.

Chocolate-chip Cookies and Chicken Soup

The not infrequent male need for havens from their brutal world
at the office leads many men to ask women within the corporate
world to provide comfort and solace the way Mom used to do.
That solace is sought more than ever is proven in one way by the
proliferation of specialty shops in business districts dispensing
chocolate-chip cookies and hot soup, true symbols of nurturing
and security.

In *Kiss Sleeping Beauty Goodbye*, author Madonna Kolbenschlag wrote an epilogue called "Exit the Frog Prince." It contains
some thoughts about the profound dilemmas faced by many men
today. Hinting that men feel a sense of abandonment, she also observes their resentment at being made the heavies in this century's
cultural upheavals. Men resent being blamed for women's misfortunes and ill-treatment in the corporate world, and resent also that
they have no group to blame for their own misfortunes. They are a
terminal dump site. Women wallow in casting aspersions on men
as the source of their difficulties without seeing how self-destructive the practice of blaming can be. Forward motion on the part of
both sexes requires the review of these kinds of negative emotions.
The pervasiveness of blaming only gets in the way of reconciliation.[6]

If one plays out the present scenario, there are very few choices for women who are ambitious and career-oriented, except to move into jobs now held by men. But the point of this discussion is not that men should become what women are, nor women what men are, but that something new, a model which enlarges the parameters of all human behavior, will lead to the desired changes in the work place.

In the final analysis, it is men who will control the rate of organizational change. This change will not occur before men recognize that their own self-interest lies in altering the status quo. To date, there is little evidence to suggest that they have moved very far in that direction. Rather, the movement of women into new roles has been viewed as an assault, as a process of taking away, as an aberration from the traditional. But just as the frog prince was released from his spell by a kiss from a princess, so men in our culture may find themselves released. It took both the frog and the princess to make change happen; the frog helped the princess develop and she helped him live out his inner self. So cultural change will take interaction between men and women. We need each other.

Social science affirms that a woman's place in society marks the level of civilization.

ELIZABETH CADY STANTON

What goes on in people's minds, and in their hearts, is more important in determining the fateful future than what goes on in laboratories and production centers.

DAVID LILIENTHAL

10

The Answer

The 1970s have been called "The Decade of Women." Indeed, one cannot assess the volumes of literature nor recall the voluminous media coverage focused on women during these years and find grounds to argue with that claim. Yet it is difficult to see and put into perspective an era's major phenomena when one is immersed in it on a daily basis. In our view, the rise of the workingwoman society, occurring as it did among so many rapid social and technological changes, is more aptly labeled, "The Quantum-leap Decade."

The quantum-leap mentality has an unsettling effect on society and its members. It builds a sense of expectation based on mistaken assumptions about how rapidly change can be assimilated, and much of what is written under these conditions confuses short-term trends and fads with movement toward structural social change. One day no one had heard or thought about women in management. Overnight, a quantum leap gives everyone the impression that management ranks are filled with women. Society mistakes its sudden awareness of workingwomen for an in-depth understanding of their actual acceptance and achievements in the work place.

After each leap, individuals, participants in the era of self-consciousness, begin to review their lives against what they think is supposed to be happening, against what people are presumed to be doing, and against the values others are said to be embracing.

Workingwomen, in an attempt to keep pace with the perceived speed of change, often failed to detect the major patterns within their lives and the systemic origins of the situations confronting them in corporate America. When we abandoned the quantum-leap approach in favor of slowing the process down, of looking at the space between the leaps, patterns and perspectives began to emerge. From the signs and symbols we gathered, there seem to be answers to the question, What lies ahead?

The Search for the Missing Link

When they were little girls, most of today's career women played house or school, acting out adult roles they were expected to fill. But by the force of change and by their own choices, these women have grown up to lead lives, to be people, they know very little about. And when they realized the evolutionary chain had been broken, women sensed a certain void.

In "The Achieving Woman" we discussed the challenges faced by pioneer workingwomen. In unexplored territory, buffeted by the elements and adrift in time, these women defined new norms of behavior, rewrote the rules, and made contributions despite their distance from traditional systems of support. In "The Ageist Woman," we introduced Mead's concept of the three stages of cultural development and noted her observation that we had moved to the Prefigurative stage, in which the ties to the past have been broken. "There are no elders who know what those who have been reared within the last twenty years know about the world into which they were born."[1] Each generation, Mead concluded, now had to learn survival from its children.

The high price of pioneering, when combined with the shock of the new, sent women searching for ancestors, for the missing link that could help settle the more troubling aspects of transition. But women soon realized that they could not go home again, nor were there ancestors whose lives could serve as guides for the present. What many women are developing, in place of the quantum-leap philosophy and the quest for having it all, is a feeling for what W. Lloyd Warner called "the emergent process," or what Leslie White called "the flow of culture." Workingwomen have begun to realize that they are their own missing links and to value the importance and scope of their pioneering efforts. They are beginning to realize that any pattern or model of behavior can quickly become constraining when subjected to the whirlwind of social change. As one woman executive observed:

> I think that the most important thing that women have to do is break away from the stereotypes that we have brought upon ourselves. We have allowed people to hypothesize and postulate about us and to put us into a trick bag that says, "This is the way it is for women, therefore, women have to be better, do better, be twice as good." A couple of years ago they used to say that to blacks, and it just isn't true. When women recognize that often it's not having all the information in our heads to do a job, but knowing where to get the information, the doors will begin to open and the pressure will go down.

And this prediction, offered up by a successful entrepreneur and mother, reflects the sense of excitement today's women hold about future generations:

> I think that we are going to have a nation of teenaged executives. When I think of my children and of the children of other working mothers, I see a generation to which it has never been a question—Will I work? And this change portends the nature of relationships and roles in the coming years. My daughter, for instance, has decided that she is going to be a self-made millionaire by the time she is twenty years old. Originally she had said she would do this by sixteen, but with experience she has expanded that figure upward to twenty to be more realistic. The point is, it has never occurred to her that she will not work. In fact, she can't wait to get out there.

Women have been out in the work place long enough to know that there are no reliable answers in the past, nor is there flexibility when one tries to conform to a single model or ideal. Women's quest for their missing link and the alienation experienced by the

pioneers are ebbing as cultural trends. Women no longer doubt
that they can contribute to the work of corporate America, they
only wonder how long it will take for the business world to acknowledge that they are equal to the task. And in the knowledge of
their competence comes a certain freedom. In a speech to a professional women's group in San Francisco, a futurist from SRI said:

> People today, men and women alike, are starting to realize that if you
> are willing to change, if you have the guts to let go of all the stereotypes
> you were taught, you can be free of their constraints. People are start-
> ing to realize that if you have the courage to let go of the models you
> were given—of what you should do because you are a man or a woman,
> or because you were born somewhere, or were your parent's kid or
> anything else—there is an exciting world out there, one where you can
> be more of what you really are.

Truth in Packaging—Task Equality as an Idea Whose Time Has Come

The success of a woman, her admission into important jobs in any
institutional setting, is not predicated on her abilities, but is dependent on her acceptance into the male power structure. And
there are no definite signs to date that the male power structure has
been able to identify its self-interest in giving women admission.
In fact, just the opposite seems to be happening; the male power
structure appears intent on maintaining its position of power. In
reviewing the literature on women in management and the comments made in both our male and female interviews, we must conclude that the fault for a portion of this lack of male flexibility
must be laid at the feet of the women's movement.

At one level, it is easy to accuse the media of distorting or exploiting the image of women and of thereby keeping the lid on
their acceptance in new roles and occupations. On the other hand,
women really haven't done much to take control of marketing a
better or more realistic picture of themselves and their goals. From
its infancy, the women's movement allowed feminism (used here
as a term to connote the drive for a more egalitarian society) to be
"marketed" in extremely strident or ambiguous packaging with
little thought given to the buying psychology of the market seg-

ment they were trying to reach: men! Perhaps part of this problem derives from women's historic position as reactive consumers, perhaps not. Whatever the reasons, women acquiesced in allowing their image and aims to be presented in such a way that they were perceived, not as a pervasive slate of issues, but as single and diverse issues of interest to only a small or select group of women. This allowed men to feel comfortable in ignoring feminism, as it was obviously a product that only the other guy, the one who had the problem or the need, was destined to buy.

Male resistance to change was also heightened by the posturing and presentation of feminism's early pitchwomen, who frequently looked or acted in radical fashion to make their points. And no man wanted his wife, and certainly not his daughter, to look or act that way. He couldn't see a life or a world filled with little Bella Abzugs, and he could use this negative imagery to his own ends. He could ask his wife incredulously, "Is this the way you want to be?" making her reject the product on the basis of its image-makers. France's Simone Veil, president of the European Parliament and former French Minister of Health, took note of this situation and gave credit where it was due, but she also observed changes:

> The feminist movement was useful, even if some of its action were occasionally excessive, because if it had not been, there would not have been change for women. But today's women are more sophisticated about themselves. There is improvement. They are less defensive. They are less likely to feel that they have to be like men.[2]

Ms. Veil is correct. Women are more sophisticated, and as such, they have the ability to take feminism or, at the least, some of the basic tenets of equality and move the product off the shelf. They have been out in the work place with men long enough to have learned where their previous sales campaign went wrong and to take back control of repackaging their aspirations and objectives to appeal to male self-interest. Not to take back that control spells disaster, for there is an important link between the problems women have in selling a philosophy of equality to men and the problems they have selling themselves within corporations. Why? Because it is essentially the same sale to the same audience and in both cases failure to capture the customer's attention can result only in continuing lack of acceptance.

The first step in any new campaign or new image for women
calls for doing away with the monotone clichés of old. Women
must move out of the entry mode—where they focus on the demand for admission and imply that failure to admit them is
wrong—and begin selling themselves based on what they can contribute to the bottom line. In nearly all of our interviews with men,
this observation emerged in some form. While taking a measure of
responsibility for creating barriers and uneasy situations in the
work place, these men felt that women were far too bogged down
in dealing with their position as a corporate woman versus seeing
themselves as a woman with a task to perform within the greater
company purpose. One man went so far as to admit that he, too,
might feel the need to overcompensate for his gender were he the
lone male in a group of twenty female managers.

But all of this takes us back to the conclusions of our chapter
"The Ambivalent Man." Women must find ways of stressing simi-
larities between themselves and men rather than dwelling on, or
even worse, imitating the differences. Among the follow-up interviews on the future, there were several comments on the movement toward reconciliation and its vehicle, women's own growing
sense of confidence:

> I am concerned that too often women have taken an adversary position
> where men are concerned and I don't think that this mentality will
> break what we perceive as the male front. All we may get for our truble
> is more opposition, especially if we keep drawing the battle lines in in-
> delible ink. I, for one, don't want to work against somebody, whether
> in business or the home.

> I think that the question of whether or not there is a future for women
> in the work place has finally been established. Credibility is the key
> issue here. Once women recognize for themselves that they are credible
> workers and begin to ask for credible salaries, many of the other issues
> will be resolved.
>
> Most important is that a woman in business know herself. She must
> recognize her own capabilities and then take steps to achieve what she
> sets out to do. Once she has been able to see herself she will be able,
> secondarily, to come to a place where she no longer sees men as mon-
> sters . . . the wolf . . . the male opponent. She will see that many men
> are, in reality, just like the Wizard of Oz.
>
> I am optimistic because I personally feel that I have torn down one
> web after another. Things are no longer the mystery to me that they
> once were. And I've learned that overcoming male prejudice, which is
> most certainly there, has a lot to do with me. Whether it is as simple a

We also don't have the facility to bring about class action suits, which immediately destroys any legal course that a woman might take. The court deals with each case on a one-to-one basis. It's Jane Doe against XYZ corporations, even if there are several identical complaints. Each woman must bear her court costs individually. Once we get the right to bring class action suits—and we are working to win a decision on this point now—then a lot of things will happen. But for now, who's going to have the financial ability to take on a giant corporation single-handedly.

But any piece of legislation which attempts to control human behavior always creates new imbalances when the old are redressed, and of course, there will be backlash. And efforts at compliance with such legislation always demand a tremendous amount of time, talents, and energies. In the case of Title VII, sadly enough, many of those efforts have been expended in an attitude of cynicism. Worse, the changes which were put into place were without the benefit of future planning.

On the whole, responses to Title VII have been more on paper than in practice, short-term rather than long-range, and devoid of systemic evaluations regarding the human conditions in organizations. In other words, what have been hailed as changes are more appropriately labeled mere rearrangements, and tenuous rearrangements at that. They are ephemeral and as such easily blown away by any prevailing political or economic winds.

Peer's Law states that the solution to a problem changes the nature of the problem, and this is where American management finds itself today. They have discovered that legislating equal opportunity solely by the numbers simply makes women statistics, not productive, contributing employees with viable career opportunities and their by-product, motivation. And here we find ourselves back at the question of critical mass. The problem is no longer getting women into corporations, it is getting them beyond entry-level barriers, beyond jobs with limited responsibility and narrow experience situations, and beyond tokenism. The limits of the power of laws come down to what goes on in people's minds and in their hearts. Discrimination is, therefore, an expression of cultural lag and there is no proof that simply increasing the number of mandates to change can force the culture to move at anything other than its own pace.

But lack of vision is not an affliction peculiar to corporations. Women's fortunes in the business arena are inexorably linked to the institutional health of the corporate entity. Social forces, governmental intervention, and political and economic impacts on the world marketplace are each environmental factors affecting the climate of corporate America. Too often, women have been prone to viewing the importance of their own achievements or the urgency of women's issues to the exclusion of an understanding of the corporate world and its problems. Equal pay and the debate over the bail-out of Chrysler are seldom tied together as issues, yet they are both economic elements competing for the attention and resources of management. Women have the ability to bridge, rather than separate, these issues, and the most important bridge among them may be that which connects the nonutilization of capable employees to the corporate surplus of red ink.

In a recent editorial in *Working Woman* magazine, Kate Lloyd remarked on how much she missed seeing women experts on panels which sit and debate the solutions to the world's most pressing problems. What her comments suggested was that if women could spend their energies and their abilities to solve these larger issues, perhaps the equality which they seek would be brought along in tow. While the issues addressed by Affirmative Action are critical, they are not separate from the whole corporate system, and women need to begin combining their concerns and goals back to the context of that whole.

Making the Best of Having It All

Management guru Peter Drucker has written that the old family unit was the center for production and, therefore, survival. Now, he says, the family's old duties have become institutionalized or fulfilled by specialists, leaving only the function of emotional support. If Drucker is correct, it is easy to see the core of the conflict men are experiencing. When women go to work, they threaten the last traditional outpost of support for men and, in turn, challenge men to provide support functions based on peership rather than paternalism. Demanding that the family unit and male and female roles be instantly recreated in their mirror image is, perhaps, the most radical quantum leap fostered by the rise of the working-woman society.

Because it seems unlikely that economic conditions will change
to allow a return to the traditional working-father, nonworking-
mother family, and because workingwomen are not about to give
up or deny themselves promising and profitable careers, the need
to make the best of having it all is a top priority. Most of the
women we interviewed believed that the best could be made of the
situation, although there was one very dismal prediction:

> We have experienced being a vanguard. Women have gotten together
> and utilized their strength, which is being very open with one another,
> very trusting with each other. I think that the majority of women's
> movements which have sprung up have been very beneficial for women
> in terms of the exchange of information and data. It's brought out the
> best in us. What has not happened to men is this same measure of trust.
> The men's organizations which started out five or six years ago, when
> the women's movement was still burning bras, have not taken off, not
> succeeded. I think the reason for this, the reason for the difference be-
> tween the two groups, is that women have learned that we need each
> other. I am hoping that the future will bring more of an understanding
> between men and women; that men will allow women—and I say
> "allow" because they do have the power—that men will allow women
> into business and be joyous that they are there. And that women, hav-
> ing ventured out into the work place, will appreciate their husbands
> more, will appreciate what their husbands have to offer.
>
> After all this change is observed, I think that we will experience a
> cohesive period, particularly for the nuclear family. Right now the nu-
> clear family is very much is disorder. It is in a state of flux and change.
> And we have seen recently that this has become a concern at the federal
> level. Everyone is anxious to know whether or not the nuclear family
> can or will continue. We have come to a place where the assumption
> can no longer be made that there will always be a man available to sup-
> port his wife or his family. This situation has thrown into the wind a
> lot of theories. But what it all comes down to is resolving our interper-
> sonal relationships. I'm an optimist about all of this. I believe that
> women will begin to say, "I've discovered all the male strengths within
> me," and men will say, "I've discovered all the female strengths within
> me." They will have reached a point where they can respect each other
> and need each other.
>
> The biggest changes I can see will happen in roles. I think women will
> understand much more what the pressures of working are and have
> been on men; and in return, men will understand more about the prob-
> lems which women have faced. Ultimately, I'm hoping for a much bet-
> ter level of relationships between men and women. Of course, as a
> result of all of this, the role of the male will change substantially. There
> is going to be a greater opportunity for sharing in the home. Perhaps it
> will even be that homes themselves will be redesigned. For instance,

my husband has just discovered that he likes to cook and we have discussed the addition of a second work area and range top to our kitchen so that we may prepare our family's meals together. The style of living that we appear to be moving toward may be a dramatic factor in the way our living spaces are designed in years to come.

Household chores, my husband has discovered, can be a source of relaxation. We try to focus in on what needs to be done. In our minds, we can come to say, *"We* are running this family." It's not *"I* have to go home to do the laundry." It is all part of an entire system and I think that, more and more, two-career couples will find ways to derive pleasure from running their homes together.

The support and encouragement of a spouse is invaluable. It can allow for one less area of self-doubt. It can also give each partner a broader ability to take risks in search of success. If two people are earning adequate salaries, either one can take advantage of the financial base to do things in a career which might not otherwise have been possible. It opens the door to a greater expression of all of our talents at a time when the world needs talent very badly.

And speaking for the down-siders:

On the negative side, I can see that we may experience a lot of men and women jumping off buildings, but for very different reasons. Men who have not been able to establish a support system for themselves, and perhaps not been able to resolve the elements of their personal relationships, are prime candidates as jumpers. Among women, I believe that those who have decided not to have children will arrive in their forties with the feeling that they are missing something . . . and that something is going to be children.

Which brings us to the issue of those children who are already here. The need for day care will continue to be one of the most pressing concerns of workingwomen *and* -men, and for their part, women are well aware that their ability to accept ever more responsible positions within corporations is dependent on gaining access to adequate day-care programs. As one woman observed:

As far as the future goes, I think that until we've gotten a really organized system of day care, one which recognizes that the majority of women work and will continue to work, until we have that—whether subsidized by the government or handled privately—women aren't going anywhere.

The mother of four, an entrepreneur in the restaurant business, agreed with this statement, but gave a possible answer to the day-care question which grew out of her personal solution to the problem:

> In terms of child care and the workingwoman, I think that the future holds something wonderful for the older woman. In my own case, I have had a marvelous experience with having an older woman live in with us to take care of the children. The experience she has had, that feeling of really being needed, can come open to those people in our society who have gone so grievously untapped. It gives society an opportunity to strengthen the basic nuclear family and to use and value the contributions of what is, perhaps, the most underutilized segment of our population.

Of course, adequate day care alone will not solve the psychological stress experienced by working mothers. There may be no absolute cure for feelings such as those expressed by the woman who confided:

> I'm terribly guilt-ridden. Every time I see another mother sitting and reading a story to her child, I feel very guilty because I don't get a chance to read a story to my child every night. Sometimes when I tuck him in I'm so bushed that I compromise myself and get through a paragraph and tell him that I will continue tomorrow night. I feel guilty every time the school sends me home a note to tell me that he has acted badly in some way. I always feel that if I were home with him more, that if I spent more time with him, he'd be a more perfect child, rather than the pain in the ass he tends to be. But I'm a single parent. Have been for eight years. What choice do I have?

Among the men we interviewed, the majority of whom were fathers, the issue of day care was repeatedly mentioned as a pressing concern. From all of their comments, we have selected two which are most incisive:

> On the surface and in theory, the idea of corporate day care is a sound one. It might very well create, for corporations, a kind of patron image which they are lacking. The lack of this kind of image in itself could be at the heart of our declining productivity. Employees feel, "If the company doesn't care about me, why should I care about it?" So they hold back, they become demotivated. Unfortunately, I read recently in *Fortune* that statistical studies on productivity among those corporations which do have day care produced a mixed bag of results. This does not speak well for the future of such programs. My belief, however, is that the incredible number of workingwomen in the United States is going to force companies to disregard these statistics and push ahead with day care.

And from a man who had established a day-care program for his staff:

> Day care is not enough. We have got to find other alternatives which lessen a professional woman's feelings of guilt over her children. We have got to find ways of shifting responsibilities so that children do not become an irritant between a workingwoman and her husband. We need to face up to the fact that the traditional family is only one way of raising children. In Israel, they use the kibbutz alternative. But whatever society chooses to do, they must decide quickly. There are too many children wandering around now without enough attention, and in the long run, if society does not come up with solutions, we are all going to pay a terrible price.

To the guilt-ridden mother and others who share her feelings, social scientists offer some consoling research findings. In a nationwide survey of children with working mothers, the majority tested were found to be more self-reliant, risk-taking, and independent than were children of nonworking mothers. This may be little comfort for the feeling that one is failing in one's parental duties or missing important experiences with one's child, but there is also little room for debate over the value of traits such as these in our ever more complex world. As the man who had established the corporate day-care center concluded:

> The character structure of people is more important than the Constitution of their country, than their buildings, than their wealth. If you have a population with self-esteem, it doesn't matter. You could blow up the entire society and they will reorganize and rebuild it. But if a population is full of psychologically fragile people, with low thresholds of frustration and the inability to assume risk, the country becomes less and less competent and eventually collapses.

Window to the Future

What women have brought and will continue to bring to the work place is a break with the past. They have made things visibly different and, in doing so, have called into question the ways that things have been done until now.

The leaders of American industry are increasingly alarmed about declining productivity and diminishing profits. There is talk that Americans have lost faith in the work ethic, a belief which is substantiated in several national surveys. Some respected futurists and theorists, using the Japanese model, have suggested that the problems lie, not with production workers, but with management, especially middle management. But middle managers are only the maintainers of the system. They were hired for their ability to be maintainers. The entrepreneurial types, innovators, and other non-conformists who applied for the same jobs were usually turned away. It is ironic that industry leaders so eagerly subscribe to indictments of middle management, for this organizational genre is its own creation.

What this behavior indicates is that American business has reached a significant level of discomfort. By its actions the admission is made, however begrudgingly, that the status quo can and must be altered. This allows us to confidently predict that there will be changes coming in both the philosophy and practices of corporate America. It may well be just another round of cosmetic changes—surveys, reports, reorganizations, and the like. More likely, however, the changes will result in an actual cutting back of deadwood and a reordering of selection and performance criteria. The important point is that change is coming.

The value in this knowledge for women is that, whatever changes are made, they will open a window of opportunity. In "The Autocratic Woman," we talk about once- and twice-born leaders. If and when this window opens, it will admit the twice-born, those who appear able to move the system, not simply maintain it. Women, who have been on the outside until the last few years, are, by definition, twice-born. They come to the corporations full of fresh ideas and with no investment in the way things were done in the past.

But to make it through the crack in the window, women had better be ready to move "greased to slide through," because the crack will not stay open for long. The sooner a woman begins preparing to take advantage of this opportunity, the better; and this preparation requires the critical skill of being able to read the system. Women must be poised to seize the day.

Equal to the Task

When the gatekeepers of corporate America say, "If only I could find a qualified woman . . ." today's woman answers, "I am equal to the task." Embodied in this response is the measure of how far workingwomen have come in understanding both themselves and the system.

When our society laments its lack of leaders and heroines, perhaps it is because we are looking in the wrong places. If there was one unifying theme in all of the stories we collected, it was the theme of courage. The women we interviewed were deadly serious about their career goals and contributions and most had overcome considerable numbers of internal and external obstacles to get where they are today. These women have reached the point where they are able to deal with the realities of the paths they have chosen. Earlier fantasies which they may have had have been discarded and replaced by confidence. Women have been in the trenches and have not only survived, but often excelled. And what women gained under fire was more than simply a testing of their individual skills. They have learned that the most significant barriers between women and the upper reaches of management are set within the system. Women have seen the reality of corporate male mediocrity. The secrets of running the show have been revealed as not so magical, not so mysterious. Women are no longer vulnerable to the idea that they are missing some credential or managerial trait.

Today, when a woman declares that she is equal to the task, there is a new meaning to the word "equal." She does not mean a parity with men, or a sameness with their life-styles or values. What she does mean is that she is both a peer and a rival. For the women in corporate America understand that there are still new territories to be won, but they have also come to realize that they are pacesetters in their own right . . . and on their own terms . . . equal to the tasks that lie ahead for corporate America and for us all.

Notes

Introduction

[1] Leslie White, *The Science of Culture* (New York: Grove Press, 1949), p. 74.

1. The Assimilated Woman

[1] Michael Korda, *Male Chauvinism* (New York: Ballantine Books, 1973), p. 71.
[2] Kate Millet, *Sexual Politics* (Garden City, New York: Doubleday, 1970), p. 56.

2. The Achieving Woman

[1] William Chafe, *The American Woman* (London: Oxford University Press, 1977), pp. 135–36.
[2] William Whyte, *The Organization Man* (New York: Doubleday Anchor Books, 1956), p. 143.
[3] Vance Packard, *The Status Seekers* (New York: Pocket Books, 1959), p. 268.
[4] Cynthia Fuchs Epstein, "Institutional Barriers: What Keeps Women out of the Executive Suite," *Bringing Women into Management*, eds. Francine E. Gordon and Myra H. Strober (New York: McGraw-Hill, 1975), p. 11.
[5] Joan Kron, "The Almost Perfect Life of Denise Scott Brown," *Savvy* (Vol. I, No. 12, December 1980), p. 28.
[6] Speech given by Mary Cunningham at the Commonwealth Club, Sheraton Palace Hotel, San Francisco, February 27, 1981.
[7] Chris Welles, "Money Manipulating Catches Up with Sandra Brown," *Savvy* (Vol. I, No. 11, November 1980), p. 30.
[8] Eileen Keerdoja, "A Nobel Woman's Hectic Pace," *Newsweek* (October 29, 1979), p. 21.
[9] Amy Orrick, "The Success and Failure of Working Women in Television," *Working Woman* (Vol. 5, No. 2, February 1980), p. 18.
[10] Harry J. Crockett and Jerome L. Schulman, *Achievement Among Minority Americans* (Cambridge, Mass: Schenkman, 1973), p. 86.

3. The Ageist Woman

[1] Margaret Mead, *Culture and Commitment: A Study of the Generation Gap* (New York: Doubleday-Natural History Press, 1970), p. 10.
[2] Speech delivered by Sally Gibson to graduating class, University of Minnesota, October 20, 1959.
[3] Judy Kessler, "What's the Case for Taking a Young Lover? Tony Tucci's Answer at 60 Is Her Own Life," *People* (August 13, 1979), p. 65.
[4] Marilyn Fabe, *Up Against the Clock: Career Women Speak on the Choice to Have Children* (New York: Random House, 1979), p. 92.
[5] Elizabeth Cady Stanton, Speech delivered at International Council of Women, 1888.
[6] John Brooks, "The New Snobbery," *Atlantic Magazine* (Vol. 3, No. 5, 1981), p. 88.

4. The Associated Woman

[1] Lionel Tiger, *Men in Groups* (New York: Random House, 1969), p. 126.
[2] Melinda Beck, "Old Boys' Clubs—Women Keep Out," *Savvy* (Vol. I, No. 3, March 1980), p. 44.
[3] Adele Scheele, *Skills for Success: A Guide to the Top* (New York: Morrow, 1979), p. 83.
[4] James Reston, "The Hazards of Ordinariness," *San Francisco Examiner* (September 23, 1979), p. 18.
[5] Daniel Levinson, *The Seasons of a Man's Life* (New York: Knopf, 1978), pp. 96–101.

5. The Autocratic Woman

[1] Kate Rand Lloyd, "To Our Readers," *Working Woman* (Vol. V, No. 6, June 1979), p. 10.
[2] Jessica Benjamin and Lilly Rivlin, "The de Beauvoir Challenge: a Crisis in Feminist Politics," *Ms.* (January 1980), p. 50.
[3] John D. Rockefeller, "The Second American Revolution: Some Personal Observations," *Harvard Business Review* (Vol. 55, No. 3, May–June 1977), p. 72.
[4] Abraham Zaleznik, "Managers and Leaders: Are They Different?" *Harvard Business Review* (Vol. 55, No. 3, May–June 1977), p. 67.
[5] William James, "The Varieties of Religious Experience," *Harvard Business Review* (Vol. 55, No. 3, May–June 1977), p. 74.

6. The Anonymous Woman

[1] Sharon Sutherland, "The Unambitious Female: Women's Low Professional Aspirations," *Signs* (Vol. 3, No. 4, Summer 1978), p. 774.
[2] Ellen Bentley, "Mastering the Techno-Future," *Savvy* (Vol. II, No. 2, February 1981), p. 39.

7. The Alienated Woman

[1] Erich Fromm, *The Sane Society* (New York: Holt Rinehart and Winston, 1955), p. 87.
[2] Max Seeman, "On the Meaning of Alienation," *American Sociological Review* (Vol. 24, 1959), pp. 783–91.
[3] Rosabeth Moss Kanter, *Men and Women of the Corporation* (New York: Basic Books, 1977), pp. 6–7.
[4] *Ibid.*, p. 14.
[5] Kathleen Fury, "Topping Out," *Savvy* (Vol. I, No. 8, August 1980), p. 24.

8. The Affluent Woman

[1] Rosemary Scott, *The Female Consumer* (New York: Halstead Press Division, 1976).
[2] Lucy Komisar, "The Image of Women in Advertising," *Women in a Sexist Society: Studies in Power and Powerlessness*, eds. Vivian Gornick and Barbara K. Moran (New York: New American Library, 1971), p. 304.
[3] Stuart Ewen, *Captains of Consciousness* (New York: McGraw-Hill, 1976), p. 11.
[4] Carl Albert Naether, *Problems in Business Correspondence* (New York: McGraw-Hill, 1927), p. 48.
[5] Helen Woodward, *Through Many Windows* (New York: Harper and Bros., 1926), pp. 85–86.
[6] Elizabeth Ellis Hoyt, *Consumption in Our Society* (New York: McGraw-Hill, 1938), or *The Consumption of Wealth* (New York: MacMillan Company, 1928).
[7] Ewen, *op. cit.*, p. 106.
[8] William Manchester, *The Glory and the Dream—a Narrative History of America 1932–1972*, Vol. II (Boston/Toronto: Little, Brown, 1973), pp. 946–47.
[9] Barbara Grizzuti Harrison, "What Do Women Want?" *Harper's* (October 1981), p. 39.
[10] William Whyte, *The Organization Man* (New York: Doubleday Anchor Books, 1956), p. 89.

[11] Suzanne Weaver, "Images of Women and *The Journal:* A Status Report," *The Wall Street Journal* (November 16, 1979), p. 22.

[12] Robertson Wyndham, "Women M.B.A.s—Harvard '73—How They're Doing," *Fortune* (Vol. 98, No. 4, August 28, 1978), p. 53.

[13] Joan Chatfield-Taylor, "Nouveau Rubin: A Sexually Candid Capitalist," *San Francisco Chronicle* (January 26, 1981), p. 19.

[14] John Kenneth Galbraith, *The Affluent Society* (New York: New American Library, 3rd paperback ed., 1978), p. 57.

[15] *Ibid.*, p. 60.

[16] Scott Burns, "Mixing Sex with Inflation," *San Francisco Examiner* (November 2, 1980), p. 20.

[17] Sloan Wilson, *The Man in the Gray Flannel Suit* (New York City: Bentley, 3rd ed., 1980), p. 7.

9. The Ambivalent Man

[1] Myron Brenton, *The American Male* (New York: Coward-McCann, 1966), p. 88.

[2] Herb Goldberg, *The Hazards of Being Male* (New York: New American Library, 1976), p. 47.

[3] O. William Battalia and John J. Tarrant, *The Corporate Eunuch* (New York: Crowell, 1973), p. 79.

[4] Ann Corran, "Eleanor Holmes Norton Attacks Job Bias," *Working Woman* (Vol. 5, No. 3, March 1981), pp. 43–44.

[5] Leslie White, *The Science of Culture* (New York: Grove Press, 1949), p. 131.

[6] Madonna Kolbenschlag, *Kiss Sleeping Beauty Goodbye* (New York: Doubleday, 1979), p. 208.

10. The Answer

[1] Margaret Mead, *Culture and Commitment: A Study of the Generation Gap* (Garden City, New York: Natural History Press, 1970), p. 75.

[2] Fred Ferretti, "France's Simone Veil Looks Beyond Feminism," *San Francisco Chronicle* (June 16, 1981), p. 19.

[3] *Ibid.*

Bibliography

Brenton, Myron. *The American Male*. New York: Coward-McCann, 1966.
Chafe, William. *The American Woman*. London: Oxford University Press, 1977.
Cowles, Virginia. *The Astors*. New York: Random House, 1979.
Fabe, Marilyn. *Up Against the Clock*. New York: Random House, 1979.
Friedan, Betty. *The Feminine Mystique*. New York: Norton, 1963.
Galbraith, John Kenneth. *The Affluent Society*. New York: New American Library, 3rd ed., 1978.
Goldberg, Herb. *The Hazards of Being Male*. New York: New American Library, 1976.
————. *The New Male*. New York: Morrow, 1979.
Kanter, Rosabeth Moss. *Men and Women of the Corporation*. New York: Basic Books, 1977.
Kolbenschlag, Madonna. *Kiss Sleeping Beauty Goodbye*. New York: Doubleday, 1979.
Korda, Michael. *Male Chavinism: How It Works*. New York: Ballantine Books, 1973.
Levinson, Daniel. *The Seasons of a Man's Life*. New York: Knopf, 1978.
Manchester, William. *The Glory of the Dream—a Narrative History of America 1932-1972*, Vol. II. Boston/Toronto: Little, Brown, 1973.
Mead, Margaret. *Culture and Commitment: A Study of the Generation Gap*. Garden City, New York: Natural History Press, 1970.
Millet, Kate. *Sexual Politics*. New York: Doubleday, 1970.
Naether, Carl Albert. *Problems in Business Correspondence*. New York: McGraw-Hill, 1927.
Packard, Vance. *The Status Seekers*. New York: Pocket Books, 1959.
Rubin, Lillian. *Women of a Certain Age: The Midlife Search for Self*. New York: Harper and Row, 1979.
Scheele, Adele. *Skills for Success: A Guide to the Top*. New York: Morrow, 1979.
Scott, Rosemary. *The Female Consumer*. New York: Halstead Press, 1976.
Seeman, Max. "On the Meaning of Alienation." *American Sociological Review* 24, 1959.
Tiger, Lionel. *Men in Groups*. New York: Random House, 1969.
White, Leslie. *The Science of Culture*. New York: Grove Press, 1949.
Whyte, William. *The Organization Man*. New York: Doubleday Anchor Books, 1956.
Wilson, Sloan. *The Man in the Gray Flannel Suit*. New York: Bentley, 3rd ed., 1980.
Zaleznik, Abraham. *Managers and Leaders: Are They Different?* New York: Harper and Row, 1979.